Cupid's Wild Arrows

intercultural romance
and its consequences

edited by Dianne Dicks

Bergli Books Ltd.
Weggis, Switzerland

Cupid's Wild Arrows

intercultural romance and its consequences

Edited by Dianne Dicks

Copyright 1993 by Bergli Books Ltd.
Weggis, Switzerland

Bergli Books AG
Eptingerstrasse 5
CH-4052 Basel, Switzerland
Tel: 061 373 27 77 /Fax: 061 373 27 78
e-mail: info@bergli.ch
web: www.bergli.ch

'Daughterly Love' by Rosi Wolf-Almanasreh has been adapted and translated from her story entitled '*Wie es einer Deutschen ergeht, die einen Ausländer heiratet*', in '*Türken raus? oder verteidigt den sozialen Frieden*', Rolf Meinhardt (Ed.), Rororo aktuell 5033, Hamburg 1984, with permission of the publisher and the author.

'Samir Between Two Worlds' by Marlies Knoke has been translated from '*... und ich bin bunt!' Bi-kulturelle Erziehung in der Familie*, 1990, edited by Heidemarie Pandey, IAF, Frankfurt, with permission of the publisher and the author.

'Ode to the Potato' by Susan Tiberghien was first published as 'Cultural Differences Over the Humble Potato' in THE CHRISTIAN SCIENCE MONITOR, 1989. Also her story 'At Home in Two Languages' was published in THE COURIER, 1991, and as 'The Language *Du Jour*' in the CHRISTIAN SCIENCE MONITOR, 1991. Both stories are reprinted with permission of the author.

'Hail Britannia' by Elayne Clift first appeared in 'Telling It Like It Is', Published by KIT, Manchester, CT, 1991, and is reprinted with permission of the publisher and the author.

Cover artwork by Cornelia Ziegler

ISBN 3-9520002-2-1.

Contents

Beyond Frontiers

Warming Up

by Susan Stafford

As the bus rattled along on its way from the airport to the city centre, I felt more and more uneasy. Everything seemed so strange! The bilingual street signs, the man with a horse and cart delivering sacks of coal, two scruffy children on one run-down bicycle, the way people spoke. This was Dublin, more like a provincial market town than a world capital; elegant in parts, decrepit in others, and unpretentious overall. This was John's home town, it was just before Christmas and I was there with him for the first time to meet my prospective in-laws.

I began to ask myself what I was doing there. Was it all a mistake? I had been brought up as an only child in a comfortable, English suburban, middle-class home and now, of all things, was planning to marry an Irishman from a family of ten. Our backgrounds could hardly have been more diverse. My Church of England schooling contrasted sharply with his more rigorous Catholic upbringing in which religion pervaded every aspect of life. In addition, the political tension between our two countries meant that I had grown up with a stereotyped, derogatory image of the Irish. My family had been negative towards John at first. Would his family see me as a villain, a haughty English intruder?

By the time we reached the terraced house in the side street where his family lived, my heart was thumping like that of an actress about to walk on stage for the first time. The front door key stood in the lock. John walked straight in as if he had just returned from a day's work. To my great relief, only his mother, Ma, and the three youngest children were there.

"Ah, John! It's grand t'see yeh!" was Ma's greeting. "Come in, love, sit down by the fire. Yeh must be frozen, child!"

The last remarks were addressed to me and I was promptly installed in an armchair in front of the blazing peat fire with half a tumbler of port "to warm yeh up." A "quick bite to eat" of turkey and ham soon followed, although it was mid-afternoon.

After we had eaten, the older members of the family began to drift in and were fed using a kind of shift system, which seemed rather chaotic compared to the orderly mealtimes we always had in my home. They were never introduced, and each time I had to ask their names. The fact that they were all so surprisingly different in manner and appearance made it easier to remember who was who.

Meanwhile, Ma settled down to telling me, as a newcomer, the family history at great length. I had difficulty in understanding the Dublin accent, and frequently had to ask John for a translation. This made me feel more alienated than ever. It was not just the accent; some words were strange and the sentence construction varied from the curious to the incomprehensible.

"English words grafted onto Gaelic grammar," John explained at one point, but I could not always be sure he was being serious. He himself had lost his accent during his years at a British university.

The speed at which the narrative was delivered in one long waffle, interspersed with many asides such as "wait till I tell yeh," also caused problems. One story about five-year-old John taking his younger brother to confession "for cursing," leaving him in the confession box, where he fell asleep, and then going off and forgetting him, only became clear when John himself repeated it to me later.

Religion and politics were never mentioned, and on one occasion the eldest brother even apologised for some rebel songs being sung on the television.

The older members of the family drifted out again towards evening so that the whole family was never there all at once. Last to arrive was "the Father," as Ma called him, a quiet man who seemed happy to leave all the talking to his wife. I found some comfort in the fact that I was not the only outsider: there was already one daughter-in-law, the eldest brother's wife, and she was not a Dubliner.

It was a relief, finally, to be sent off to bed in a neighbour's house with the words: "See yeh tomorrow, God willin'," and yet, tired as I was, it was hard to get to sleep. A picture of some saint with his golden halo hung over my bed, reminding me where I was. I suspected that the family did not know what to make of me. They were friendly, but cautious, just as my family had been with John. For my part, the difficulty in understanding was creating a barrier. I could not follow the jokes, let alone join in.

The next day gave us a chance to get out and go sightseeing, despite the cold. After we had toured the city, I wanted to see the sea, which was just a short walk from where the family lived. So we walked down to the 'strand', as the beach was called. John had been boasting about the "golden sand where you can walk for miles," but I was disappointed: the tide was in, and the beach reduced to a mere twenty yards of sand with strips of what looked like little pebbles but turned out, on closer inspection, to be tiny shells.

"When will the tide be out?" I asked.

"I suppose, in the evening," John answered.

"We'll have to come back," I said. I was fascinated by the idea of wandering with John across these 'miles of golden sand'.

Christmas Eve arrived. After the evening meal, the house seemed particularly crowded with most of the family present, plus various girl-friends and boy-friends. The conversation was fast and jolly and more incomprehensible than ever. Finally, the feeling of not being a part of it became too much for me and I wanted to get away for a while. I whispered to John that I would like to go for a walk, and he announced our intention to Ma.

"Aa, don't yehs go out again. Yeh must be jaded, child," was her response.

Despite the protests, out we went.

"Where are we going?" asked John.

"Down to the beach," I replied without hesitation. I wondered whether I should tell him about my growing doubts. But how? I couldn't just say 'Listen, we don't really belong together. It's all too different.' He'd probably just laugh.

It was a clear night, although the wind was bitterly cold. We walked through the quiet streets to the deserted sea front. Lo and behold: the sea was nowhere to be seen. We started walking across the sand, out towards where the sea should be. For ten minutes we walked until the city was just a faint glow in the distance, with a string of sulphur beads marking the road along the sea front, but still the waves were no more than a far-off sigh.

"Now do you believe me?" asked John.

"Yes!"

Frozen right through, we clung together. The Pigeon House lighthouse flashed intermittently. Somewhere to our left a curlew called. We were completely alone. This was our world, wherever we might be. It was as if we had found one another again after a long absence. The moon swung briefly from behind a cloud and disappeared again.

Shivering, we decided to walk back. Candles had been lit in the windows of many homes we passed. "To light the Holy Family on their way to Egypt," as John explained. A man, so drunk he could hardly keep upright, staggered past us playing 'Silent Night' on a mouth organ, perfectly in tune.

"They'll never believe us when we tell them where we've been," said John as we reached his family's house.

He was right. None of the family members who were at home that evening could be convinced that the two of us had been down to the beach. They thought John was joking as usual. Finally, it occurred to me to show them the traces of sand still stuck to my boots. Ma was astonished.

"Yeh let him take yeh down the strand?" she said, "Sure, yeh must have been frozen, child."

Jumping to John's defence, I admitted that it was my idea. That did it.

"Oh, Jeese!" exclaimed Ma, "Our John's marryin' a mad girl!"

The whole family dissolved in laughter.

"The pair of them's mad," added the eldest brother, quickly, to soften the last remark.

He need not have worried. By then I was laughing as much as anybody. So the teasing continued: "Ah, I bet they found some way of keeping warm," and "Now, who in their right mind would go strollin' over the sand at night?"

It became a family joke. On Christmas Day, every time another relation or friend of the family arrived, someone would say: "You'll never guess where John took Sue last night."

The story progressed a little, until we were "paddling in the sea at midnight." One of the brothers, leaving to escort his girl-friend home, announced: "We're just going down the strand!"

"You'll never dare come back here again," John told me in mock seriousness. "The whole city will know soon."

As a result of all this good-natured teasing, suddenly, I felt that I had been accepted unconditionally. I was no more a foreigner than the eldest brother's wife, from County Waterford, or even John himself, of whom they commented: "He's more English than Irish since he's been over there."

The accent was also slowly becoming easier to understand, the strange words more familiar; I could begin to appreciate their humour and their easygoing attitude to life. The ice was broken. I, an only child, a loner, had acquired an extended family.

My future mother-in-law knew that it would not be taken amiss if she jokingly sent me off to bed with the remark: "You can get up early tomorrow mornin' and polish the furniture!" ♥

Does Anybody Speak Bimoba?

by Agnes Bieri

When I disclosed to my parents my intention to marry a white man, the first thing that came out of my father's mouth was "Are you getting out of our mind? Do you realise the complications if you want to live with this man in his country? How long have you known him? My daughter, only street girls follow strangers."

When I told my mother I would have to learn another language, she exclaimed with surprise, "You speak English with him. What other language do you have to learn?"

"A Swiss language, for he is Swiss."

"And what is this language?"

"Swiss-German."

"Oh dear, if things don't work well, you are always welcome home. By the way, is he going to learn Bimoba, our language?"

My mother encouraged my father to accept my choice of husband. "She is twenty-seven and mature enough to take care of herself."

My fiance's mother received the news in Switzerland with mixed feelings too. The news of her crazy son with his black girl spread like wild fire among relatives.

Nobody wanted to take any responsibilities in my case. My father never said "Go with this man." My mother said, "I wish you luck when you go."

We left Ghana without bidding my people (my village) a formal goodbye to receive the ritual blessing of the elders.

My boyfriend offered me a return ticket to see his country. We stopped over in London to see my brother. I felt the pangs of the cold already. It was early May — springtime, but I was freezing in my woollen suit which this brother we were visiting had sent me while I was in Ghana. I had no stockings on. I ran to every patch of sun escaping from the buildings and trees to get warmth. The next morning I bought a spring coat, a pair of warm shoes, stockings and gloves. "I look like an army officer," I told my boyfriend.

"Never mind, if only you are warm enough."

In Switzerland I met my parents-in-law-to-be who spoke no word of English. My father-in-law-to-be brought me flowers to welcome me. I did not understand what this meant and only much later learned the meanings of giving flowers: for love, birthdays, appeasement, condolence, etc. His father embraced me, touched both cheeks of mine with his. My mother-in-law-to-be did the same, which was for me an unusual way of greeting.

We had a meal of *Pasteten* with white wine sauce and mushrooms. I had never eaten mushrooms. They seemed so slimy and stinky and I was afraid my stomach would not like them. Neither had I had milky white wine sauce before with little soft balls of what they called meat that were nothing like the chewy meat we have at home. I had to touch my glass of red wine with the glasses of all the others at the table before drinking. I was told it is customary to do this and look into the eyes of the other person and say his or her name as your glasses clink together. It seemed strange. I tried to explain that at home the elders at a meal will spill a drop of a drink on the floor for the departed souls before all others drink.

Two days later we had *Fondue* for supper. In the centre of the dining table was a thick white soup in a special ceramic pot boiling slowly over a special stove with a flame. I was given a special fork to pick a small cube of bread taken from a basket and told to dip the bread in the soup, stir to get the bread coated with the pasty soup before eating it. Cheese was something completely new to me but I ate it, passing the test to live in Switzerland. That night I dreamt I was home and my mother had made a meal of rice balls with peanut butter sauce, okra and chicken.

Once we went out for a walk and my friend bought ice cream. I asked him where we could sit down to eat. To my surprise he said we would eat it while walking. "No! Grown-ups like us don't eat on the streets in my country," I said.

"Here you can do it," he replied.

Nervously, I managed to finish my ice cream.

Another time my friend announced that we would visit his friends in Berne. "Agnes, we are catching the 11.17 train."

"What an odd time," I thought, "why not at a round time of eleven o'clock, eleven-thirty, twelve o'clock?"

After riding in two trams we got to the train station. My friend was in such a rush. He made double steps between running. I remembered he had told me the trains depart hourly so I wondered why we had to run ourselves out-of-breath to catch our train. Before I could complain that grown-ups shouldn't run in the streets he kept exclaiming between breaths, "Run a bit faster or we'll miss the train."

I ran reluctantly after him, aware that others were running in all directions too. In the train, with both of us panting I asked, "Why did we have to run like this? We could wait for another train."

"Our friends are waiting for us at the time this train arrives in Berne."

At that time I did not yet understand that everything is on schedule. The time of arrival, time to stay, talk, eat, a short walk, return to catch the train at 18.25. It seemed our friends would be offended if we didn't act according to the timetable. In Ghana there are more important things than time.

After we got married and during my pregnancy I began to get a bit worried that we couldn't afford to bring my mother here to take care of me after my giving birth just as it is done at home. I also worried that both the baby and I would not get the herbal baths for strength and energy. How could I get my pepper soup with dried smoked meat and dried okra to heal the wounds of the womb? And what of the millet flour water to produce milk for the baby? I was in constant fear that I could get ill if I didn't get all the *matnaa* attention. *Matnaa* means afterbirth. These fears were forgotten very soon. I had to do with a few substitutes or none. The nurses bathed my son with plain water. I had camomile sit-baths to heal my wounds. I drank *Lindenblüten* tea and *Rivella blau* to produce milk for the baby. We left the hospital after one week's care from the nurses and doctors. My son came out of the hospital circumcised as demanded from my home.

When our baby was five-months-old we were transferred by my husband's employer to Tanzania. As an agriculturalist, he had a contract for three years with a Swiss organisation to work on a small-scale dairy development project. On our way to Tanzania, we went back home to Ghana. My husband could experience the ritual presentation of dowry which for Bimobas is 'exchange'. Marriage is an exchange between two families and not just between a man and a woman. Family A seeks the hand of a daughter from family B for their son. Family B has also to get a girl from family A for their son. If this girl from family A is not yet of age to marry, then family B will have to wait until she is of the ripe age.

If family A has no girl for exchange, a daughter born from the marriage of their son and daughter of family B will be given to family B to settle the dowry of exchange. But family B cannot marry this girl who is a relative. She would be given in exchange for a daughter of a family C.

This type of dowry exchange succeeds as long as the tribe with this custom marries within or amongst themselves. But with formal education and as people travel from one region to another and even sometimes outside the country, this tradition is difficult to keep because people keep marrying outside the tribe. Ghana is divided into nine regions and each region has several groups of tribes with each tribe having unique customs.

A second dowry system was adapted to suit the situation. If you don't belong to this tribe of 'exchange', then you are allowed to offer a ram or male sheep, a *calabash* of cola, two barrels of *pito* which is a local drink made of sorghum. Cola is a firm, red or white oval fruit eaten as a stimulant. The cola is chewed and the meat is used to prepare food so that the two families come together to eat and drink and bless the newly-married couple.

At my home in Ghana everybody in the village was pleased to see us. I was a bit plump at that time so they felt I looked well. The child was for them a good sign that the marriage will fare well and for this reason our dowry was accepted. My husband offered a ram, a *calabash* of cola and drinks to the elders of the household. Rituals were performed and we received the ancestral blessings.

In Tanzania, a former British colony, English and Swahili are the official languages. The neighbourhood and the people working with us spoke mainly Swahili so we had to learn that language. We discussed what language we should speak to our children. Should they learn strange languages apart from ours? Yes, we decided they could. My husband and I carried on with English at home and very soon the children learned Swahili from the neighbourhood.

Our second child was born in Tanzania in a small Mission hospital in Igwogwe. All the other women who had just given birth had their mothers around to bathe the baby and help carry it home that day or the next. My mother was not around and the mid-wife only wiped my freshly born baby daughter and handed her to me.

"You mean to tell me the baby did not have a warm, thorough, welcome bath?" my mother stamped angrily when I told her this birth story.

"Yes," I replied very softly, "I was too tired to bathe the baby that day. I only did it the next morning." For one week I nursed and cared for the baby and me. I could have left the hospital the day after she was born but because of minor complications I had to stay a week in hospital and receive injections against a probable infection.

"Poor you and poor baby. I only hope this baby does not develop that strange bodily odour that one gets if he or she never had that the first bath after birth," sighed my mother.

Today my daughter is healthy and does not carry any strange odours on her.

After three years in Tanzania, we were transferred to Rwanda, a former Belgian colony where French and Kinyarwanda are the official languages. I spoke no word of French and Kinyarwanda at that time and neither did our children. We had then three children, the youngest was nine months old. My husband could speak and write in French but he didn't speak Kinyarwanda. The people we worked with spoke French. The neighbourhood spoke Kinyarwanda and sometimes Swahili. I had to work hard to learn both languages all alone to be able to live there. It was really difficult at the beginning, but I managed to get along, sometimes speaking Swahili to communicate with the local community. It was not long before the children started speaking both French and Kyinarwanda even though we still spoke English with them at home within the family.

After three years in Rwanda we returned to live in Switzerland for good. On the way back we stopped to visit my parents and relatives in Ghana. My parents speak English, so it was easy for them to communicate with my husband and children. But some other relatives can't speak English and found it difficult to communicate with our children. My aunt said to me, "My dear niece, Meliga," Meliga is my name at home, "what have you done with the children? They speak no word of Bimoba. For us they are lost!"

"I know what you mean," I said slowly, "but they are not completely lost. They will always know that somewhere their people speak a language different from English, French, German, or whatever, because of me and their skin colour." I tried to explain to her why we couldn't learn Bimoba, that I was the only one who spoke it at that time when we were clouded with so many other languages to learn while the children were growing.

I promised her I would help the children retain some of their cultural background. I have done this, for example, by occasionally cooking a festive dish of '*boot*' – a typical Bimoba dish once every new year to remind them of their roots. At least once every week I prepare a Ghanaian or an African dish. We also try to visit my family in Ghana as often as expenses allow. As I promised my aunt and as testimony of my mother tongue, I sometimes look with my children through the Bimoba bible received from my mother.

Back in Switzerland again, we stayed for the first four months with my helpful parents-in-law while looking for an apartment. The children and I shared the task of learning Swiss-German and the so-called High German. Within six months the children spoke Swiss-German quite well. I couldn't handle it so easily. I took lessons in High German but heard Swiss-German all the time. Having to keep track of all the timetables with three children didn't allow much time for an intensive language course.

Once my husband and I went home to Ghana and left the children with their Swiss grandparents because it was not convenient that time to take them along. We were back after one month and to my surprise the children spoke Swiss-German among themselves and to their father as well. I had to convince them to come back to English for my sake when we were together as a family. To help them keep up with their English, each child has an English lesson with me once a week starting with a dictation and reading.

After five years in Switzerland I am taking a High-German course again and learning Swiss-German from my children. Our son, the eldest, managed to keep up speaking French thanks to his aunt and Godmother with whom he spends two weeks each year in Geneva. Her family speaks only French. Our daughters forgot their French. They were much too young when they stopped speaking it to learn Swiss-German. I think the moment they want to learn it, it will be much easier since they understand quite a lot of words.

I sometimes wonder how long it will take for me to learn to speak Swiss-German well enough to be understood easily. Once a Swiss woman invited me for a cup of tea. She told me to be at her place at "*halb-drei*" but I interpreted it as three thirty. There was some confusion when I appeared an hour late. In such a situation there are many possibilities for misunderstandings to occur.

Sometimes my husband and I have different attitudes because of our upbringing. I have told him that if I go out and have to fight for my life and I happen to lose an arm, I will continue to fight with my other arm until I win or lose. I cannot go home and tell him to help me as he cannot be expected to do this. But my husband should be responsible for my welfare. If I am sick he should take me to see a doctor or medicine man. If I am insulted on the streets, he should defend me. He is not always so sure about when I want his help and when I don't.

We also have different attitudes about cleaning. My husband accuses me of pushing dirt and rubbish from one corner to the other before cleaning it up properly.

Sometimes I defend myself then by telling him, "Yes, what does it matter anyway if cleaning is finally done. What are you people doing all day? Their feet firm on the ground, their hands resting forever firmly on a brush and their minds on how to get rid of some little spot. You scrub and scrub and clean the whole time and end up each day tired and exhausted without having any fun." Sometimes we start out teasing and wind up in serious arguments.

My family loves very much the palmnut soup or palmoil stews I cook for them. It is a very attractive sauce, red orange in colour and rich in vitamin A. But its stains are very pronounced and can only be removed if exposed to sunlight. I get so amused watching my husband if we are eating this sauce. He is on guard every second, checking for and wiping out immediately every trace of a spot. Dirty dishes are shoved back immediately to the kitchen and washed up right away. Sometimes when the children beg me to fix palmnut sauce I tell them "Oh no! I think it's better if we save our nerves." We all laugh about it and I go ahead and cook it anyway.

Sometimes there are questions you have to ask yourself if you are married to a person of a different cultural background or of a different race. Is it love that holds you together? Is it the children? Or the challenge? From my experience I think it's all three and the readiness to learn from each other. Each may feel at times as though there are some strange things to cope with. Sometimes one party has to sacrifice a little bit more than the other for awhile until the situation reverses their roles. ♥

Kaleidoscopes

by Kim Baumann

An exam paper I recently sat for asked for the nationality of the examinee. My brain squirmed. Besides, the space provided was very stingy. I squished into cryptic form:

Nationality: Australian-Swiss-Vietnamese.

And this is where my tale begins. It is a romance involving an intercultural marriage, a thriller that spans the corners of the globe, a detective story involving an identity search and the confessions of a bohemian teenager.

Dad is Swiss. Mum is Vietnamese. So, to cut a long love story short and to save my poor parents from too much media exposure, I will only say that once upon a time they met and, knowing it was true love, they married. However, instead of fading into marital bliss and obscurity, Dad received a position at an Australian university and, with modest aspirations, they immigrated to Australia. Like courageous fools or foolhardy martyrs, they began a family with three daughters in a new country — it was a new beginning.

As a child of this intercultural marriage, I have always enjoyed diversity, variation, many-sidedness and colour. Both my parents had to learn about a totally new culture from each other AND integrate into Australian life. Our household is furnished accordingly. Inside there are lots of Oriental paintings and furniture whereas outside our garden is a parade of geraniums, tulips and gladiolas. Even our humble fridge shows signs of diverse consumption — remains of a Swiss Emmenthaler cheese, packed Aussie pies and frozen spring-rolls for quick snacks. Our literature ranges from HEIDI, SWISS FARM-HOUSES to THE VIETNAM WAR and such authors as Dylan Thomas, Bertolt Brecht and Confucius. On noisy days, my sisters listen to rock and roll from the stereo. On bad days, Dad is patriotic and listens to yodeling. We even have a household language — English for normal communication. However, when we kids are naughty, we receive a scolding in Swiss-Vietnamese linguistics.

When I was younger, I used to feel I was 'different'. I have a mixture of both Asian and European features and am therefore entitled to classifications such as Eurasian, 'mixed' and 'hybrid'. I was a terribly tall, lanky kid in primary school and while other kids had cute names such as Snoozie Suzie or Candy Sandy, I spent my childhood with less flattering nicknames such as 'Chopstick' or 'Kimmy Long Legs'.

I look back good-humouredly to the time when I was teased by some boys about my nose. I spent three sleepless nights wearing a peg on my nose in a desperate attempt to mould it into one befitting a Grecian beauty. My nose, not knowing whether to be Asiatic or European, ended up with a 1:1 ratio — long with flat nostrils. I did not know about facial surgery or genetics then. Nonetheless, I have been mistaken for a Mexican, a Spaniard, a Melanesian and even an Indian, not to mention the millions of times people ask if I'm Chinese or Japanese. The usual stereotype idea is: If an Asian has black hair (s)he is definitely

i) Japanese

ii) Chinese

iii) both the above.

I think it is very slovenly and inconsiderate to see only similarities in hair colour and then assume an Asian is either Japanese or Chinese. There are not only many physical differences between Asians but countless social and religious differences as well. An Englishman would be insulted beyond pardon if you called him a Yank, not because being American is derogatory but because assuming someone's nationality is disregarding someone's unique identity.

My teenage years were spent searching for an identity, an idol, an ideal. Being a teenager is never easy. But modern society attempts to confine humanity to stereotypes. Although humans all have the same basic needs and aspirations, we are all individuals with a once-forevermore-copyright. Being born in a multicultural family simply amplifies one's uniqueness. No wonder I could never relate to the Marilyn Monroe image.

Racism is one of the greatest barriers to any intercultural marriage. Even today, an intercultural marriage is seen as one of the 'seven sins'. It breaks centuries of tradition because it demands that both parties accept each other's culture as part of his or her own identity. What's sinful in that? Overcoming biases and prejudice is not easy because it is human nature to mistrust those that are different. I have learnt from my parents and other family friends that in an intercultural marriage, no matter what difficulties arise, there is no barrier too great for love. Our family reflected the uniqueness of an intercultural marriage but it also provided an intricate portrait of life, in our case with an Australian lifestyle. We are distinct individuals, but like all families, we have general desires and attitudes that are universal. We build bridges that gap barriers, enabling humans from totally different cultures to learn from each other, relate to each other and discover new capabilities within ourselves.

I have been abused for being partly Asian. I have been abused for being partly European. It hurts badly, but I don't feel embittered, only sad that humans never realize how diverse they are. I remember standing up in class and telling a future medicine student, who had just made a very insinuating racist remark, how unique humans are. I told him that no matter how different we look, what gods we beseech, what tastes we have and no matter how abstract or concrete our ideals are, we are all humans, striving for the same basic needs, dreams, hopes. I could not face the stares of my classmates so I walked out of that classroom with my nose . . . yes The Nose . . . in the air at a 90° angle. (Partly to keep snot from dripping and tears from rolling down.)

I am a proud Australian and consider myself a true blue dinkum ozzie. It is my homeland, speaks my language, reflects my childhood and influenced my first friends and school years. Yet never will I deny the other kaleidoscope of nationalities that are part of me. That is why I am now in Switzerland living with my grandparents and hoping to become a decently sober, respectable and diligent citizen and not be corrupted by chocolate, skiing and snow-white horizons. Later, I will visit Vietnam and see the other dimension of me, not only the war-torn country but a land full of grace and dignity.

As a child of a multicultural family, I have many challenges, opportunities and aspirations. I am entitled to a rich, diverse life. Having parents from different cultures has broadened my horizons so that I see life through many perspectives. I do not see myself any longer as different, but as unique. My uniqueness allows me to be part of the human race without total loss of individuality. I try to accept, acknowledge and be three cultures within one person. Having intercultural parents teaches you a lot about love, life . . . the universe?

When a dear friend asked whether I would like to marry an Australian, Swiss or Vietnamese, I simply answered: "All three!" But that, gentle reader, will be another story that will have to come later. ♥

Belly Dancing and Football

by Judy Erkanat

I married into a second culture without a second thought, perhaps because I live in California where the native born are less common than white rhinos. Mustafa, my husband of eight years, is a Turk. But Mustafa and I soon realized that we had not only married each other; we had also established a complicated web of alien alliances. We had each acquired a set of in-laws about whose cultural and personal idiosyncrasies we knew very little. Small stumbling blocks in our path to marital happiness soon loomed as huge brick walls.

Before I could become part of Mustafa's family in Samsun, on Turkey's Black Sea coast, I had to make myself known to them and overcome their initial resentment for keeping their favorite son from returning to his homeland. Ours was not the traditional marriage with prior parental approval. I came as a rather unwelcome surprise. To them I was a stranger from an even stranger land.

Mustafa had his own hurdles to overcome with my family. Though he had the advantage of meeting them before we tied the nuptial knot, it took some time for them to overcome their mistrust of him as a foreigner of mysterious origins and to know him for the individual he is.

Between us, Mustafa and I achieved an early understanding of what we wanted from our married life. Mustafa thought of me almost as someone from his own culture. My Italian-American upbringing had taught me hospitality, good cooking and proper housekeeping; the very skills necessary to keep a Turkish husband content.

For his part, Mustafa was modern in his views toward women and never tried to keep me from working or living life on my own terms. The decision, for example, for me to stay home and care for our children rather than go back to work was a mutual one. It satisfied my maternal urges and it kept Mustafa happy with the stable, reliable homelife that he wanted.

We had met in a friend's Turkish restaurant. Mustafa was a guest. I was the entertainment. Belly dancing had been my evening and weekend avocation for many years. It supplemented the income from my job as a manager for an electronics company and gave me a creative outlet that kept me in good physical condition.

Mustafa had come to America shortly after his mother's untimely death and only months before our first encounter. He was in California to complete his university education at the suggestion of his father. Before Mustafa could pursue his master's degree in engineering, however, he had to master English, something he was still in the process of doing when we first met.

Though he had no intention of staying in America, let alone get married there, it wasn't long before our relationship matured into something that we both wanted to make permanent.

From the first, my family was dubious about Mustafa. They had never approved of my belly dancing and they were having a hard time accepting a man I had met while performing. My parents assumed that Mustafa was just another boyfriend, perhaps a bit more exotic, but hardly to be taken seriously.

I had recently turned thirty-four and my Italian-American mother had given me up as disappointingly childless. I had never told her about my desperate desire to marry and have children. My biological clock was ticking loud enough to keep me awake at night. Finding Mustafa seemed to be the answer to my prayers for a sincere, family-oriented man. Little did I know that our families would turn into the only serious problem in our marriage.

Mom's doubts were founded on my past. She had rarely approved of the men in my life. Was this just another mistake, she wondered. Would I get hurt, taken advantage of? She resigned herself, as she saw it, to be there to pick up the pieces of my life yet again, if and when Mustafa disappointed me.

She put off meeting Mustafa for several weeks, apparently dreading the event. But the day finally arrived. We were taking her out for her birthday. She was alone because my father was out of town on business.

We were sitting in an outdoor cafe in Carmel-by-the-Sea. A cool breeze pulled in the salty scent of the sea. From our table, we could see the pearly sand and gleaming waves. The faint pounding of the ocean echoed across the cobble-stone streets.

Sipping her *cappucino*, my mother began abruptly. "I had a dream about you last night, Mustafa."

OH, OH, I thought. HERE IT COMES. Was this one of those emotionally comforting, prophetic dreams that Mom had at infrequent intervals in her life? If so, they were always uncannily accurate. I could only hope that it was in my favor.

"In it, I saw a man," Mom looked at Mustafa. "And I knew that I didn't have to worry about my daughter any more. I felt that she would find lasting happiness with him." She hesitated. "In my dream, he looked like a young Gregory Peck." She eyed Mustafa's black hair and fair complexion, then frowned. "But the man in my dream had green eyes. Yours are brown, aren't they?"

Mustafa looked at me as I gasped. "No," he said in his slow English, removing his sunglasses. "My eyes ARE green."

This satisfied my mother, who trusted the message of her dream all the more when Mustafa later proved himself hardworking and successful at his job and, eventually, a good father to our two daughters.

Mustafa's mother had also had a dream. When she was pregnant, the revered father of modern Turkey, Mustafa Kemal Ataturk, appeared to her, telling her to name her child after him. She did and Mustafa Kemal, her third child, proved to be much easier to manage than his troublesome older brother, Umit. He became Mustafa the Well-Beloved of his proud, upper-middle-class family.

I, on the other hand, was the oldest child of four and my growing up had caused my parents much consternation. I had always been 'contrary'. Knowing that Mustafa wouldn't be my parents' first choice as a son-in-law made him all the more attractive to me.

I had reached adulthood pretty much by trial and error. The errors stood out in my father's memory. But, when it came to Mustafa, Dad steadfastly kept an open mind. He was determined to keep my problems with men in the past separate from my current beau. He saw my success in his field, the electronics industry, as an indication of my intelligence and believed that someday I would find the right fellow.

As he told Mustafa, "She is a good girl who's had some bad breaks." If he had any doubts about his new son-in-law, Dad kept them to himself. My brother Jim had just married a girl he had only known a few months. At the news of my engagement to Mustafa, Dad quoted his own favorite son. "Like Jim said, it's your life and if you're making another mistake, you'll be the one to pay for it."

Dad had helped a young Turkish engineer at his last job. Fortunately for us, the Turk had left a good impression. At Dad's toast upon our engagement, he paraphrased Will Rogers. "I guess you could say that I've never met a Turk I didn't like." At the time, he knew two.

Mustafa's father, on the other hand, was of the old school. He couldn't lend his approval to a marriage about which he had had no say whatsoever. He voiced concerns that his son had married just to stay in America. His doubts were amplified when, just after we were married, a Turkish friend returned to Samsun. He had a picture of me in a belly dance costume that he showed to Mustafa's uncle. Late one night, our telephone rang.

"Why didn't you tell us that she was a dancer?" Mustafa's father was furious. This was worse than he had expected. Though I had quit dancing after my marriage (I was trying to get pregnant and had lost my need for the stage), I knew the stigma that dancers carried throughout the Middle East. Things looked bleak indeed.

It took twenty minutes of long-distance discussion for Mustafa to convince his father that I really was a manager in an electronics firm. "Belly dancing was just her hobby before we were married. Besides, being a dancer in America isn't like in Turkey. Here people simply enjoy the show and go home." He smiled at me. "Judy was never one of THOSE kinds of women."

But things remained cool for awhile. Letters from Mustafa's father stopped completely. Letters from his older sister, Shadiye, grew very infrequent. When letters did come, they were filled with questions about her brother's health and what he was eating. She doubted if I, as an American, could even boil water.

The tension of the breach with his family soon took its toll on Mustafa. He and I began to have some serious arguments. We began to question our ability to make the marriage work. Unlike me, he had always had the approval of his family. It was killing him inside to know that he no longer had it.

I began to fear that perhaps he couldn't live without it. My respect for my husband suffered during this period. At times he appeared weak for needing his family's approbation so much.

In the midst of this marriage-threatening turmoil, I got pregnant. But, instead of adding to our discord, the coming child served as the bond we needed to pull us together. Mustafa recognized that his primary concerns were now me and our baby. He reset his priorities and we decided that his family would eventually accept our marriage if we were just patient.

Communications with Turkey were at an all-time low when we got a telephone call from Mustafa's father's wealthy younger brother, Dursun. He and his wife, Nuran, were coming to California for a visit. I was finally to get a chance to redeem myself with my in-laws.

Dursun and Nuran expect the best when they travel. Red carpets aren't necessary, but they do like red labels on their scotch. I gave up our bed for them, catered to their slightest whim and schlepped them to every discount shopping establishment between Los Angeles and San Francisco.

My husband treated all this as only what was expected of me as his wife.

After two weeks, without a second off for good behavior, I was exhausted and frustrated at his lack of sympathy.

"I don't understand why you're so upset," Mustafa greeted my silent tears in the back room. "They can't be THAT much extra work." The next week, he took a few days off work and we all went to Los Angeles together. After only two days, he was ready to turn around and go home. Now HE had to do everything for them; order their food, turn on the lights in their hotel rooms, all but tuck them into bed at night. I felt vindicated when my husband at last appreciated my former efforts.

When the seemingly interminable visit finally ended, Shadiye called. "Is Judy still standing?" She asked Mustafa, knowing full well how demanding her aunt and uncle could be. I was comforted by the empathy in her voice.

But my efforts with Dursun paid off. When the wandering couple got back home, they told Mustafa's family that he had married an American gem. A staunch ally, Dursun even tried to convince the family that Mustafa was doing well in his career. I had also taken the blame for his going into hamburgers rather than engineering. Dursun told them that Mustafa was a manager of a chain of restaurants and that he made more money than many engineers. But the family still clung to their dream of the prestige of having an engineer in their number.

In many ways, they were as stubborn as my Italian grandmother. She had first met Mustafa at a family celebration on the Fourth of July. Grandma had immigrated from northern Italy some sixty years before and her heavily accented English was as incomprehensible to Mustafa as his was to her.

At dinner, she turned a critical eye on my handsome Turk. "A friend of mine was married to a Turk. It turned out that he had two other wives back in the old country." Her eyes narrowed suspiciously. "Just how many wives do YOU plan to have?"

"Oh," Mustafa hurried to explain, fearful of grandmotherly censure. "Only one. It has been against the law in Turkey to have four wives since before I was born."

Grandma raised one eyebrow, yanked up her dish and marched over to the buffet table for a second helping of homemade lasagna. Sitting down again, she resumed her interrogation. "So, you're a Muslim, then."

"Yes," Mustafa was having trouble getting his food past the nervous lump in his throat.

Grandma nodded sagely. She knew nothing about Islam, and had no desire to learn. "As long as you bring your children up Catholic," she finished.

Mustafa held his tongue, wisely realizing that he could raise his children as

Muslims, as he and I had agreed, but that he didn't have to burden my grandmother with the details.

Our children were the main reason Mustafa won a place in Grandma's heart. Seeing him in the role of a good provider and an affectionate father made all the difference to her. Sometimes a bit of diplomacy and some time is all it takes to cement a relationship.

My brother, Jim, was also pessimistic about my Turkish husband. "He's probably just after his permanent residency," he warned me, insensitive to my feelings and stubborn in his prejudice about Middle Eastern men.

Tears welled from my eyes as I wondered if I would ever be able to bridge the gap between the two men I loved. They had met several times, but Jim refused to say more than a quick hello. "He wasn't even planning to stay in America until we decided to get married." I tried to explain.

"We'll see," Jim buried his feelings about my husband until the end of the next American football season. Mustafa's love for the game brought them onto common ground. Jim was impressed at how fast his new brother-in-law picked up the rules and seemed to be able to call the plays even before the coaches did.

Soon Jim, who has never been out of North America, realized that Mustafa, even though he was from another country, was just as concerned with my welfare as he was. Rather than a threat to my well-being, Jim learned to view Mustafa as a contributing member of our family ready to do his share at moving time or participate in the holiday traditions of his new country.

But this new understanding didn't prevent Jim's resentment from surfacing again in his opinions on the names we were considering for our first baby. I was hugely pregnant when we told my family our decision. "If it's a girl, we'll name her Giovanna, after Grandma's mother." Everyone smiled and sighed happily. "If it's a boy, we'll call him after Mustafa's favorite uncle, Seyit."

There was complete silence in the room. Jim was the first to speak. "But what if the poor kid wants to play baseball?" he protested.

"He can play basketball with Kareem Abdul Jabar." Mustafa was by now adept at handling my brother.

"What will I call him?" moaned Mom, "I'll never be able to pronounce that. What is it? Say-eet?"

In the delivery room, when the doctor held up our beautiful new baby girl, Mustafa's first reaction was one of relief. "At least now we won't have a problem with your family about her name."

I regularly sent pictures of Giovanna to my in-laws back in Turkey. When our second daughter arrived, we gave her a Turkish name, Shirin. This helped mollify Mustafa's family. Letters came more often and they seemed to be getting used to the idea of an American in the family. Mustafa and I decided that it was finally time for a trip to Turkey.

My excitement was overshadowed by my fears. I was about to face the primary obstacle in my marriage: my in-laws. I had been living with their disapproval for six years.

Mustafa had, with time, entirely won over my family. With frequent contact, they no longer heard his accent or saw him as intrinsically different. He was one of the family with his own favorite foods, sports and television shows like all the rest of us.

I had travelled overseas many times before meeting Mustafa, but this was my first trip to Turkey. I redoubled my efforts to learn Turkish and absorbed Turkish customs from friends and books, determined to succeed in person where I had failed from afar.

Mustafa could only take three weeks off from his job. We decided that we would go over together and that I would stay on longer with the children. We found our plans hampered by heavy summer bookings when we tried to coordinate our visit with Shadiye's July and August hiatus from teaching high school. I would have to stay an additional two months or return home with Mustafa. I decided to take the chance and stay the maximum. I wanted to have plenty of time to achieve my goal and become part of the family. After all, Mustafa had had six years to cement relations with my family. I had as much to accomplish in just three months.

The thirty-six-hour journey, including twenty-four hours in the air from San Francisco to Ankara (via New York, Frankfurt and Istanbul) with our two daughters, aged three-years and nine-months, ended with a sleepless night in Ankara at Dursun's home. (Our girls were still on California time.) The next day was spent on a bus in the pouring spring rain on the last leg of our journey to remote Samsun.

Mustafa's father met us two stops before the main bus terminal, barely greeting me and frightening our oldest daughter with his brusqueness. Later, I learned that this was his typical behavior when nervous. We arrived at his house exhausted, only to find Shadiye livid that she had waited in vain at the bus terminal for our arrival. Things were not starting out well.

After a quick meal, other relatives began arriving, family by family. I perused the crowded room, my eyes bleary with fatigue. In one corner loomed the family patriarch, white bearded Haji Ishak. I went directly over to him, confident in my knowledge of Turkish culture gleaned from all that study and advice.

Swallowing my nervousness, I reached for Haji's hand, meaning to touch it to my mouth and forehead as I had just seen Mustafa do. I remembered my Turkish friend in California, Hilal's, advice. "If you do this, older people will really love you for it," she had explained, demonstrating the unusual obeisance. "It shows respect and a knowledge of tradition."

With these words in my head, I tried to do my duty. Much to my surprise, Haji fiercely resisted my attempt. Shocked into stubbornness, I grasped his gnarled fingers and pulled up. He pulled down, firmly.

Determined to show all those present that I really was part of the family, I decided to risk exposing myself to uncompromising Turkish scrutiny and bent at the waist to lap level to greet the bony back of Haji's hand.

It worked. Still savoring the thrill of my success, I was taken aback when Haji jumped up and threw his arms around me, showering me with blessings. "*Mashallah*! God keep you!" he cried, visibly impressed. "This girl is one of us." I was now an official *yeni gelin*, or newcomer, as Turks call their brides, both recent and established, for the rest of their lives.

My father-in-law was still, however, reluctant to accept me. As it had been between Mustafa and my family, it was time and repeated exposure to me that finally won him over. Near the end of my stay, I began to understand enough Turkish to counter his caustic humor with quips of my own. He laughed when I teased him, right along with the rest of the family, about quirks like his penny pinching. Demonstrating a sense of humor can be difficult in a second language, but it finally gained me entrance into Mustafa's father's heart.

Shadiye had her own misgivings. She wanted to know why her brother wasn't an engineer. Mustafa explained about his career choice and the security and relative prestige of his position. She remained dubious, but her continued questioning opened up the lines of communications between us.

After Mustafa returned to California, I was squeezed into Shadiye's already crowded home. It was a trying experience, adjusting to caring for my two children without many of the modern conveniences that I was used to back home. And the total lack of privacy grated on my already frayed nerves.

But I learned to appreciate the compensations, such as the many willing hands always around to help with my girls, when, at home, I was usually on my own. I tried to be generous with my children. I swallowed my fear and followed family advice on childcare as much as I could rationally do. This warmed up Shadiye considerably.

I also pitched in to help with whatever I could. This kept me from getting bored and normalized my role as sister- and daughter-in-law. I got to know the family and understand their concerns about having an unknown outsider marry Mustafa.

I went so far as to say the Arabic words that made me a Muslim. Since I am religiously ambivalent, it caused me no personal qualms, bringing me increased status within the family and making me seem less of a foreigner.

When things got tiring, or I began to miss home and husband too much, I reminded myself that I would be leaving soon and concentrated on making the memories good ones. I tried to keep a smile on my face, a positive outlook and a relaxed attitude. The reward was watching curious stares turn into welcoming smiles when I came for repeat visits at the homes of various family members.

After a few days back in Turkey, Mustafa had whispered to me, "I could never come back here to live."

I, on the other hand, found that I could probably make the adjustment to life in Turkey if the need arose. The food, the people and the culture were hospitable and accommodating. Apparently not everyone finds it so, however. At one afternoon tea with Shadiye's teacher friends, the ladies began to complain about the foreign brides in their families.

"My brother's Dutch wife is really lazy," one woman said with distaste. "She comes for a visit and just sits there, doing nothing."

"She may be afraid to offend you by doing something wrong," I volunteered in my halting Turkish.

Shadiye pulled herself up proudly. "Well," she began, happy that I was able to follow the conversation. "When I get home from work, Judy has the laundry and ironing done, the house clean, and dinner on the table."

A murmur of appreciation swept over the assembled company. I was poured another glass of tea and urged to try just one more piece of pastry. I could only blush at Shadiye's exaggeration of my accomplishments, realizing that it signified a true acceptance of me as her sister-in-law.

In the time since our visit, the letters from Turkey have become much more frequent and my name is now included in the address. My wrists, neck and ears sparkle with the golden jewelry that I received as befits any new bride in Turkey, another sign that I had been accepted as part of the Erkanat clan.

It hasn't always been an easy road, but what marriage is? Compromise has long been the secret to our marital success. According to Mom, my husband is a better-than-average son-in-law. To me, my intercultural marriage now means that I, too, have an extended family in another country. And I wouldn't change that for all the tea in Turkey. ♥

Three Times an Angel

by Sarah Paris

Dear Cousin,

It's an unusually clear night here in Los Angeles, and I'm drinking 'Black Velvet' with apple cider because that's what my friend Joe and I used to drink, many years ago. We would drive up to Griffith Park, sit on the warm hood of the car and watch the night animals scutter by and the lights of the great city below us, and we would drink 'Black Velvet' with apple cider.

I heard tonight that Joe is dead. There is very little I can do now other than remind myself why his poor and seeming lost life touched mine with such grace.

* * * * *

It was Christmas Eve when I met Joe. I had been in Los Angeles for two months, my first faraway break from the smallness and safety of Switzerland. I still walked the streets with the blind innocence of a country bumpkin, doing things I would not dream of doing nowadays. But I was learning, and that day's lesson had been particularly harsh: My neighbor across the hall had been shot while I was sitting at the typewriter. The shot sounded like a pebble thrown at someone's door, and it barely registered until I heard the scream a few seconds later.

It was Christmas Eve, and after the ambulance and police had come and gone, I just couldn't stay in the place any longer. Lonely, scared and hungry, I walked up and down Hollywood Boulevard. Every place I knew was closed. Finally, I tried this private club I remembered from a visit some weeks before when an acquaintance had taken me there. It was a dingy hole-in-the-wall, full of old hippies and small-time riffraff.

I knocked and was immediately confronted by dark eyes glaring at me through a little window. Clearing my throat, I said with what must have still been quite an accent in those days, "I'm a friend of Joe's," as I vaguely remembered some guy by that name from my previous visit.

When the guy replied, "He's here!" I was taken aback; but it was too late for a retreat, the door opened and the bouncer waved at some tall, skinny, charcoal-black man sitting at the bar. "Hey Joe! Someone here to see you!"

The charcoal-black man, whose face I'd never seen before, turned around, took one good look at me and opened his arms with a smile as wide as the Mississippi: "My Chrism's angel! Hey, come on, sit down! Have a beer! You hungry?"

And so I found myself on that Christmas Eve eating string cheese and drinking beer courtesy of Joe, who made me laugh and called me 'his angel' even though it was already quite clear that it was he who had taken me under his guardian wings.

We communicated through gestures more than words as I barely understood even a third of the things he said in his Southern drawl, but I believed him when he told me he was taking care of all lost children on Hollywood Boulevard.

On roller skates, no less.

Joe went most places wearing his skates, as it was his theory that the world was a much friendlier place when you could just glide in and out of it. He got me a pair too, and I soon found out that he was right.

All these things happened a long time ago. The places we hung out are mostly gone now, and so are the people we've known.

The only one that remains is Dave, the Boulevard's puppeteer, and he was the one I finally tracked down and who told me about Joe's death.

I can't say I was surprised. When I tried to call Joe some time ago, his phone was disconnected. So I stopped by his place the other week. It hadn't changed, the smell in the hallway was still the same, only my nose more sensitive now.

A Mexican family opened the door of apartment number 3. They had never heard of Joe, even though he had lived in that crummy building for over ten years.

Dave told me Joe died five months ago. It seems Joe's brother Tom — a broody and violent alcoholic and always suspicious of the 'white folks' Joe invited into his life — died just before him, suffocating in his sleep.

Joe had been quite sick for a long time. The loss of his brother, of his other, darker self, must have loosened something in his tough, stringy body, and he passed away only days afterwards.

They sent both brothers home down South where their old mother still lives. I talked to her on the phone, once, during those early days with Joe. She was a sweet, soft-spoken lady, always concerned about her "chillun" living in Los Angeles and especially worried about Joe, who was her favorite.

I wished I could at least have sent flowers or something. There never seemed to be anything I could do for Joe; and there was so much he did for me.

He even took care of me long after we stopped seeing each other. After my divorce, the one thing I had to keep me warm and chase the nightmares away was a little plush dog Joe had bought me which I named 'Skate'.

Skate still keeps the nightmares at bay.

* * * * *

I suppose we made a funny couple, the Swiss poet and the tall, middle-aged, jive-talking truck driver from the South.

He was my first black friend, and he and his pal Dave were the only ones from 'my side' at the wedding, after I had come back to the States and ended up getting married. I don't like to look at the old wedding video anymore, but tonight I watched it, just to see Joe's good face again laughing as he danced with me. Despite his poverty and illiteracy, he was never awkward, never out of place. His great heart made him the classiest gentlemen I've ever known.

* * * * *

When I last saw Joe, his son injected his daily dose of insulin into arms that were even skinnier than I had remembered them. Joe was diabetic, had ulcers, a burn-scarred shoulder, and his sight never recovered from the sliver that got stuck in his eye once when he was fixing a car.

I had been around, that day, and drove him to the emergency room of the Hollywood Presbyterian Hospital. It was Saturday night, a full moon, and luckily for Joe, he wasn't in a lot of pain because the doctors had to take care of several stabbing and shooting victims before they had a chance to fix up poor Joe's eye.

He seemed all right, afterwards — even got into a fight to defend a scrawny little street kid. On his skates, of course. In the end, no one actually got hurt, but seeing Joe fight made me more aware of the toughness beneath his gentle eyes, and I realized why I always felt so protected, why people on the Boulevard didn't mess with me. I was Joe's girl.

In reality, we weren't lovers, but that was nobody's business. He wanted to marry me, though. "Marry me, then you can stay here with me forever!" he'd say. But at that time, I had no plans to stay. Los Angeles was a place to write about, then leave behind. I had no idea I would be here ten years after I first arrived.

Switzerland, to Joe, was a place somewhere near the North Pole where people went to work on skis. I never felt the need to tell him otherwise.

During those first months of our friendship, Joe would still answer his phone with "Joe's Bar and Grill" — acknowledging the fact that he always had a bottle of whisky handy for lost souls, as well as some steaks, ready to be thrown on the backyard barbecue for hungry street kids.

Later at night, we would go to 'The Nest', that black hole on Hollywood Boulevard which became such a familiar place to me and where each song in the decrepit juke box turned into a memory.

Jesus, the spaced-out prophet (he really did look amazingly like El Greco's Christ) would walk in and read Joe's future, staring deeply into the black man's pinkish palm. "One day you will be rewarded for carrying other people's pain," Jesus pronounced, then he put his hand on Joe's stomach to take some of that pain away for at least a while. Nowadays, I know people in Malibu who do that kind of thing for $250 an hour.

Later Joe would order another round of Buds, give me a quarter for the juke box and have me play our favorite songs: THREE TIMES A LADY by the Commodores, HOTEL CALIFORNIA and maybe a creaking Billie Holiday blues to top it off. Joe would sing along with complete abandon in his high-pitched falsetto voice, serenading me with a boyish smile.

Sometimes we would dance, he on his skates that made him even taller than he already was. My Funny Valentine, indeed.

And he never had a harsh word for me, not even when I left him one evening to spend the night with his buddy Sonny, the sloe-eyed, smooth-moving hellcat whose name wasn't really Sonny.

I had always pretended not to like Sonny, but Joe was no fool. "If you slept with him you could stop dreaming about it," he said once.

I've got nothing in common with him," I replied defensively.

"Then why do you want him?" said Joe.

For him, life's truths were simple.

He only asked for his car keys back.

* * * * *

When he couldn't hold a job anymore because of his health, Joe took to fixing up old cars and reselling them. One day, we drove to Southeast L.A. to find some old buddy of his, a side-walk mechanic, to help with a brake job. Payment was a half-pint of 'Black Velvet'.

There was quite a gang of skid-row rabble there, watching the procedure. I wore my usual nondescript clothing, yet couldn't manage to empty my face sufficiently, and they started to hassle me, realizing that I didn't belong.

Joe told them I was there to collect material for a book. That was the wrong thing to say. "Books? Books! Never read one! Shi-it, we don' need no books heah!" They started to close in, but Joe calmed them down, and in the end we got out of there okay, mostly because Joe didn't show them how scared he really was.

Myself, I wasn't scared. I was too stupid then.

There were so many things I was not quite aware of in those days. It was Joe who taught me so much about the city, what to do and not to do. Except, he never told me not to get involved with Sonny.

* * * * *

Just because we didn't have sex doesn't mean Joe didn't try at times. He would make those huge I-want-to-eat-you eyes and make a grab. Then he would laugh like a child, and I would forgive him immediately.

After I married my American husband, Joe withdrew very politely, always the gentleman. He was getting pretty sick now, anyway, and he didn't go out much anymore.

He would stay in his stuffy apartment where a million tacky and useless items would keep him sweet company, where a hundred old photographs plastered the walls, an old polaroid of him and me among them. And he still would adopt lost boys and girls who would talk for hours on the phone and eat all his food. But he was always glad to see me, no matter how long I had been away. "My angel," he'd say and smile, a little sadly now.

* * * * *

I had become a screen writer, and all that. I invited him many times to come and see the studio, see one of the films I've written. He would always say "sure," but he never came. The years and the fact that I didn't need him anymore had come between us.

No matter how I tried, I could never find a way to pay him back even a fraction of what I felt I owed him. His generosity was always greater than mine, and even the last time I took him out for dinner he snatched the bill from me.

There was little I could do for him other than visit every once in a while, send him postcards from my holidays in Switzerland and remember his birthday.

* * * * *

I'm sure he died with great dignity, And I will light a candle for his sweet soul, like any good ex-Catholic would.

"Angels can fly because they take themselves lightly," Chesterton once said.

Joe could fly alright, whether on skates or in his car, driving up Nicholas Canyon to gaze over the city, the radio playing THREE TIMES A LADY and the two of us sitting in silence, drinking apple cider and 'Black Velvet'.

Sometimes, words just get in the way.

And maybe I've already used too many.

Love,
Sarah

Thresholds

Bella Figura

by Kristina Schellinski

"*Ecco là,*" my mother-in-law-to-be placed one hand on my shoulder presenting me to a dozen close and not so close relatives who had crossed the Apennines just to see me, *la donna.*

"*Parla italiano?*"

"*Si, un pò.*"

"Brava, brava," they said when I explained I didn't speak much Italian but understood. Then, I could only make out the word *tedesca* — German — in the long sentence following. The nodding meant they accepted me for showing goodwill by trying.

A few curious Romeos, as the villagers of Rometta-on-the-Adria were called, crowded in through the kitchen door; nobody used the stately entrance door to the villa. "*Auguri, auguri,*" they shouted, enticing neighbours to their balconies. The word was always spoken as twins with eyes brimming with memories of their own weddings, twenty, thirty years ago. There was another pair, *bambini, bambini.* With innocent impatience they wanted to know when and how many children Luigi and I were planning to have.

Nudged along by the gentle push of Luigi's mother, I led the visitors to the *salotto.* Luigi smiled and made himself thin against the wall, letting all of us pass by. In the living room I faced them all by myself. The room had been turned into a wedding shrine displaying all gifts received so far in an impressive exhibit of Italian veneration for matrimony and family life.

"Who gave you this?" Aunt Assunta asked admiring an antique silver coffee set. I looked for help. Luigi's mother stepped up, read the card and from there on took over the guided tour of crystal and porcelain, lace and linen, vases, paintings and silver, silver everywhere. Silver cups, silver plates, silver bowls and spoons, silver spoons in every corner. Espresso spoons, ice-cream spoons, chiselled and plain, baby's first spoon and more espresso spoons as far as the eye could see. The piano, the sideboard, the shelves of the library, the coffee table and the window sills were all filled with shining gifts.

The guests sat down for an *aperitivo* with *confetti,* the pastel-coloured glazed almonds, served with sweet *amaretto* or a red soda water rightly named *bitterino* as it could have also passed for cough syrup.

"Can she cook?" someone asked, and another "can she sew?" Yards of shining silk lay among the gifts — a probing allusion to my talents. "*Si, si,*" Luigi's mother assured them. "*Bella!*" They nodded.

The room fell silent with expectation. Luigi cleared his throat; he was still standing in the doorframe; half inside, half outside. It was typical, I thought. Throughout the wedding preparations he had really not been there. Like sand, he slid through my fingers; it was happening around him, but not with him. Strangely, he had withdrawn into his shell ever since we arrived in Italy and I had been unable to tickle him out.

The gift! Oh yes, I was to unwrap the latest gift. When I felt the soft velvet cover I had an inkling. I unsnapped the fastenings and there was another set of twenty-four sparkling silver spoons!

"Beautiful. *Molto bello,*" I said. "*Grazie tanto.*"

I must have looked a bit helpless though because later Luigi took me by the side and said: "You must watch your face! You know, it speaks too."

"What do you want to say with that?"

"Oh, nothing."

"That's not true. You brought it up. Don't hide now." It was incredible how much he, like his family, shied away from any discussion, from any differences of opinion.

"No. It's just the gift. They meant it as a nice gesture." Luigi said.

"Hm. Gesture — I think that's the right word. But it's useless, isn't it?" I asked.

"Why?"

"Because we've got at least two hundred espresso spoons by now! It doesn't make sense."

"Do you always have to think so rationally?" There was reproach in his voice.

"It is useless!" I insisted.

"But it makes a nice gift," Luigi gave to consider.

"Oh, I see." It dawned on me that if this was what happened at every Italian wedding, a spoon-go-around system had been set up. The spoons you received in surplus you kept for the next best occasion.

"That's crazy," I said.

"No. After all it's silver, right? It looks good and is not expensive. So can't you just smile nicely and accept it?"

"Oh, that's the point . . .," I said. "*Bella figura*. That's what I am expected to do." First he had left me alone to face the inquisitive crowd and now he implied that I had looked ungrateful.

He took it calmly which made me even angrier.

"I hate being exhibited like this. Am I a trophy or what?"

His silence infuriated me; my German character rebelled.

"Also, I want you to know, right from the beginning that I'll never bring you espresso in bed!"

"Don't worry," Luigi said. "I don't expect you to be like my mother."

With that, the discussion was over for him. He snapped his fingers, calling his younger sister over. "Go and fetch my car key, will you? It's upstairs." I couldn't believe it: she turned to go!

"It's terrible how you let yourself be waited on! You'd never dare this in front of our friends. Why here?" I said in Italian, trying to incite his sister to mutiny but failing. For all her seventeen years, she had been used to fetching things for her brothers or her father; even her mother had done it.

Luigi withdrew; not into his sulky silence but he said he had to drive down and pick up something from a friend. He had managed to escape once more.

Our search for a church had been complex. His parents had taken us to the Sanctuary of San Gabriel, a famous refuge for pilgrims, the Cathedral of Teramo, the most prestigious of all, and someone had even suggested that we get married in a side chapel of the Vatican.

"I prefer a small church, Luigi," I had said, "with a soul. Not with a big facade." Finally, we had found San Antonio, a baroque chapel hidden in a red brick house down a side alley, within walking distance from his parents' house. Its modest wooden door was so low one had to bow to enter. We had waited a long time before making the big decision; meanwhile, the restorer had revealed the chapel's original beauty: light-blue alcoves along-side the whitewashed walls harboured golden saints and the sunshine danced on the rediscovered frescoes behind the altar depicting fruit and wine. The chapel, despite its shabby exterior had become an acceptable choice for a wedding.

Ever since Luigi had asked me to marry him, he had tried to convince me to convert to Catholicism. But I was twenty-eight and didn't want to revoke everything I had believed in before. After all, there was only one God.

"Do it for them," Luigi pleaded.

"No, I can't."

"It would make them happy."

"I really can't." Even if it had made his parents happy, I knew I could not have gone through religious re-education classes. "You are so stubborn, so German!" Luigi was rarely exasperated; but he probably had a sense of an impending conflict that would not go away.

The evening bells of San Antonio rang; it was dinner time. In the kitchen a big pot was on the gas stove; his mother threw in the pasta.

"Why don't you children set the table under the fig tree?"

Her voice sang out from the open kitchen door.

"How many?" I asked her, fetching the plates.

"We are eleven, no twelve with your father. Lay one set extra, just in case." With a large wooden fork, which disappeared in a cloud of steam, she stirred until the spaghetti gave up their resistance in the gurgling water. It was magical; there was always enough pasta and there was never any left over. They never knew how many they would be for dinner. People dropped by at all hours of the day, especially at dinner time. Luigi's mother was famous as a good cook. My mood mellowed. I could learn a lot from her, I thought. She pretended to be perfectly cheerful while it was obvious that Luigi and I had argued.

The sound of an asthmatic Fiat 600 filled the courtyard. Luigi's mother peered out the door but couldn't see the car. "*Qui è?*"

"Padre Michele!" Luigi responded. So we were thirteen.

Was it a coincidence that he had come once more, to save my soul? I put the thought of a scheme out of my mind. Be in good faith, I reminded myself as we sat down at the table with the warm summer air enveloping us all.

"*Cara* Susanna," Padre Michele paused to savour a sip of the wine of the house. "*Certo, un dio, solo.*" He looked at me to see what effect his agreement had on me. "*Ma — anche una chiesa sola santa cattolica!*" he added.

My Italian dwindled. "*Si, certo . . . ma non posso.*" Tears rose. The sympathetic looks of my new family didn't help. "*La povera,*" I heard, "poor thing." I think it was because my father's face was reddening that the subject switched to the ample thanksgiving they would celebrate the Sunday after our wedding. It had been a fruitful year.

That night I went to bed with a splitting headache trying to rest for the big day. The next morning I learnt that Luigi had gone out to see Signora Leona; he had spent more than an hour with her. When I came down for breakfast everyone hushed. I could touch the secrecy that hung like a cloud in the kitchen air.

"What's happening?" I asked.

"Nothing. Everyone's just nervous." Luigi explained. He smiled a bit and that gave him away. There were two things to know about Luigi; he was always serious and he couldn't lie. So, when he had a smile on his face, I was suspicious.

"Don't talk nonsense. Something's up."

He denied it; he tried to keep a straight face. I burst out laughing as a test to see whether he spoke the truth. He started laughing, too.

"There you are!" I said. "So what is all this?"

"I went to see somebody."

"Who?"

"Leona."

"Leona? Who's she?"

"An old friend."

"What?"

"Not what you think! An advisor, sort of."

"What did she advise you about?"

"She said it was okay."

"Okay what?"

"To get married."

The others guessed what we were talking about and agreed, big smiles on their faces.

"Well. Great. I hope you're all reassured," I said.

"Come on," Luigi tried to put his arm around my shoulder easing me out of the kitchen. "Let's go for a walk in the olive grove."

It started out a distant drumming, then the trumpets came closer to the house until one could no longer hear one's own words. They had come to accompany the wedding party from the house to the church. My father and I watched the procession roll down the hill.

"What a show," he said when we entered the chauffeured limousine from the fifties to be driven the five-hundred meters to San Antonio.

Walking down the flower-flanked aisle, I saw Luigi awaiting me by the altar, his hands locked behind his back. The myrtle and marigold mingled in the hot afternoon air to an intoxicating perfume. My hand passed from father to fiancé. We sat on high chairs, three steps above the congregation and listened to their muffled weeps of joy remembered.

Three priests officiated the wedding mass: Padre Michele to the left, Padre Salvatore, who twenty-nine years ago had married Luigi's parents, and on the right a young priest from the neighbouring village.

My hands clung to a pamphlet where all I was expected to say was printed in bold red between the black passages read by Padre Salvatore.

The organ led us to Eucharist and Rosetta, the village soprano abducted us to the heavenly heights of 'Ave Maria', a solo offered to God and the newly-weds. Luigi's eyes had become sheer.

The Lamb of God was offered — bread and wine prepared for the holy communion. That was when the silence and serenity behind the altar came to an abrupt end.

Padre Michele mumbled: "No. *Io, no.*"

The young priest to the right shrugged his shoulders.

Luigi and I knelt down. I glanced over to him, my eyes two question marks. "It'll be all right," he nodded.

All right? I wondered. By now the voices behind the altar were more audible.

"I am not going to give it to her," Padre Michele said.

There was no doubt. He pointed in my direction.

Padre Salvatore tried once more. "But how would that look? To give it to him and not to her?" Then he decided: "I am taking the responsibility." And with these words he took the chalice and bowl and walked towards us. First to Luigi, then to me.

The bells rang, the organ dictated a march and to a chorus of '*auguri, auguri*' we left the church.

They said we ran instead of parading in dignity. But we were glad to escape into the waiting limousine — photographer in tow — heading for the beach. The sun prepared the Adriatic sea for the coming of a late summer's night. A golden blanket stretched out over the sky-blue quiet waters. The umbrellas were closed and the striped beach-chairs placed in neat rows.

"You'll get sand in your shoes." Luigi's parents had protested when I wanted the pictures taken on the beach. "You should do it in the studio. As it's done here."

Luigi swooped me up with his strong arms, a trailing blaze of sun-drenched sand flowing away with the wind.

"Always," he said and kissed me. Finally alone, finally together. We played until the sun had set.

"Couldn't we just leave?" I pleaded.

"Not yet," he said, "it isn't over yet."

At the reception his father read a poem he had written for us imploring his son's homecoming with a wife, though foreign, a child of their own now. To accordion sounds, young girls in bright red and black costumes performed the local tarantella dance and then Sergio, the family's famous artist friend stepped up to the microphone and cleared his throat. His ample figure was more than half-hidden by a cloth-covered gift he carried. "*Sono molto commosso*," he started and paused for a moment to wipe his eyes.

"Welcome home," he said, "I offer you this with all my heart."

With one move of his hand he unveiled an oil painting: a large white dove crowning the aquamarine sea, a smaller dove following.

"Oh, how . . ." I started.

"Bello!" Luigi concluded, squeezing my hand.

The next day at the train station, my father kissed me good-bye. He whispered into my ear so that only I could hear it: "I never thought you'd make such — such *bella figura*." ♥

A Tale of Two Weddings

by Linda Singh

As an American-born young widow with two children, I met, and subsequently married, Darshan, a man from India. Ours was a small wedding attended by twenty-five friends and family members in a Lutheran church in a mid-sized city in Illinois. In our one-ring ceremony (Darshan didn't like rings), I wore a baby-blue knit dress that fell two inches above my knees, a corsage of pink roses and a hopeful smile. Darshan exuded joy in a new suit with a rose boutonniere and my gift to him, a tie clasp. The simplicity of our marriage ceremony was both beautiful and appropriate for us.

* * * * *

Four years and one child later, my new family went to India to attend the wedding of my husband's younger sister, Kopal. Although we had exchanged letters, it would be the first time for me to meet Darshan's family. It would also be the most elaborate wedding I had ever attended. In fact, the bride got married twice, first in an evening Hindu service with the wedding party, priests and guests seated around a fire and the next morning in a Sikh ceremony under a tent.

* * * * *

I became acquainted with Darshan in a local hiking club that met for Sunday trips of trail walking, picnics and games of volleyball. I got to know and love him gradually. My family at first questioned the wisdom of my marrying someone of another culture and religion.

* * * * *

Kopal's marriage was an arranged one. She met Vishnu, her future mate, only twice before their wedding.

But there were no qualms in Kopal's family about her marrying a Hindu, for her parent's marriage had been a mixed one; Kopal's mother was a Hindu, and Kopal's deceased father had been a Sikh.

* * * * *

40

My family gave Darshan and me a set of table lamps as a wedding gift. It was the second wedding they had attended for their second daughter.

* * * * *

Kopal's dowry, an Indian tradition, consisted of such items as radios, clothes, an electric washing machine, jewelry and money. Since the bride and groom would live with the groom's parents, all would benefit from the dowry. Until the day of the wedding, the groom's family continued to bargain to get more gifts. As a westerner unfamiliar with Indian customs, it seemed strange to me for the groom's family to be compensated for allowing their son to marry Kopal.

* * * * *

My husband-to-be and I drove together in an automobile to our wedding site, a Lutheran church where the ceremony was officiated by a Lutheran minister. A week earlier, we had obtained the required blood tests and marriage license. Lighted candles flickered on the altar. An organist played hymns. The ceremony lasted only ten minutes. Darshan and I kissed. The minister shook our hands and wished us well. My brother took pictures. Then we, along with all our wedding guests, went to a private room of a nearby restaurant for a catered dinner reception. We had provided for a vegetarian meal to be served to the one Hindu guest, a close friend of Darshan's. Traditional wedding cake was served. None of Darshan's family had been able to come to our wedding and dinner reception, but we had their approval via letters and phone calls.

* * * * *

At 5 p.m., the day of the Hindu wedding ceremony, Vishnu, the bride-groom, wearing an ornate headdress, his face partially veiled, with a sword at his side and accompanied by his family and a brass band playing, arrived at Kopal's home on horseback. Dressed in my new custom made *shalwar kameez* (baggy pants and tunic) of bright pink silk, and with Darshan, who had donned a turban (a Sikh custom he had shed along with his beard when he came to the U.S.), we helped greet the arriving wedding party. The groom-to-be got off his horse and walked under a canopy of gold-tinsel roping and colored lights strung high above the brick driveway to a tent to meet his bride. Kopal looked radiant in her red silk sari and gold jewelry. She wore a jeweled nose ring.

The wedding ceremony took place around a fire with several priests in attendance. Leis of orange marigolds were draped around the bride's and groom's necks. Kopal and Vishnu walked around the fire several times. Ghee (melted butter) was thrown into the fire. Ancient words of Sanskrit were spoken and after an hour the Hindu wedding ended. Food and drink were served and the groom stayed the night at the home of a neighbor of Kopal's family. Their second wedding took place the next morning under a tent before a framed picture of Nanak (the last guru of the Sikh religion), and with a Sikh priest presiding while seated on a dias. Guests sat on rugs spread on the ground with the women seated on the left side and the men on the right. Two priests played drums and sang.

* * * * *

At the conclusion of our wedding ceremony at the Lutheran church, Darshan and I and our two attendants, a couple who were mutual friends of ours, signed our wedding certificate. We visited with friends and family at the reception, then drove to a popular Wisconsin resort for a brief honeymoon. My mother babysat for my children.

* * * * *

At Kopal's wedding no legal documents were signed. She and Vishnu were simply recognized as being married by their families and community. There was no honeymoon trip. They moved into the groom's family home where they would live as an extended family. Their future children would be raised in the husband's Hindu faith.

* * * * *

After we were married, Darshan attended Lutheran church services with me, but would not (and I didn't ask him to) convert to my religion. Eventually, we transferred to a Unitarian church that seemed to meet better the needs of our intercultural, interreligious marriage. All the children call Darshan 'Dad'. Through the years I have grown tired of hearing people ask where I met Darshan, as if he came from some other planet. But I always smile and tell them. Though I don't care, I ask them where they met their spouses. I'm sure some of my friends and maybe even family members are surprised that my marriage to Darshan has lasted. Recently, we celebrated our twenty-first wedding anniversary. There have been compromises on both sides.

* * * * *

Sadly, fate decreed that after ten years of marriage and three children, Kopal's and Vishnu's marriage would end with his death in a motorcycle accident.

* * * * *

Sometimes I get out the picture albums and look at the wedding pictures of Darshan's and my wedding and also of Kopal's and Vishnu's. All weddings, whether simple or elaborate, celebrate the joining of two people. In this day when one out of two marriages ends in divorce, intercultural marriages have as much chance as any other marriage to succeed and be long-lasting. ♥

The Sparkle

by Kate Mühlethaler

I'd made a friend.

There I was, not long in Switzerland, lying in a hospital bed after an appendicitis operation, when I heard a gentle voice with a Swiss accent enquiring, "Alright, dear?" What a difference those two words made, for I could speak no German. I turned my head. Sister Verena was near retirement age, slight, modest, unassuming. Her serene face was framed by tightly-rolled grey-speckled curls.

I got to know her quite well over the weeks that followed. I wondered how she'd learnt to speak English so fluently. Once, as she reached out to take away the thermometer in her dainty hand, I almost gasped aloud. On her finger was the biggest diamond I'd ever set eyes on. It seemed almost indecent in contrast to her dour nurse's uniform. On noticing my surprise, the soft, hazelnut eyes sparkled with mischief behind her tortoise-shell-rimmed glasses, and she told me her story.

I learnt that, for as long as she could remember, she'd spent her annual holiday in London with Maria, her best friend from school days. Maria had gone there soon after finishing her apprenticeship at the same hospital as Verena. She'd been employed as a children's nurse and in due course looked after the grandchildren of the family. During one of her visits, Verena had been introduced to Colonel Dobson, an elderly, distinguished-looking man. They met him at the choir in which Maria sang, and he'd always fascinated them, with his piercing speedwell-blue eyes and mop of silvery hair which he was forever brushing impatiently out of his countenance. People said he was married, but he never mentioned a wife. He referred to the two friends as "My Swiss Misses" and was always game for a joke. He was known by everyone as 'The Colonel'.

That was why it had come as such a surprise to Verena to receive his letter, written in beautiful spidery old-fashioned handwriting, asking if he could visit her for a few days. Why she hardly knew the man! She wondered if people would talk, and what her family's reaction would be.

As she approached the airport parking lot, she began to feel somewhat apprehensive. Well, anyway, it'll be nice to practise my English again, she thought, and marched briskly towards 'Arrivals'. She didn't have long to wait. Colonel Arthur Dobson, a small case in one hand, a walking stick in the other, strolled smiling towards her. How frail he looks, vulnerable, almost, she mused as she moved forward to greet him.

"Hello, Verena, good to see you again, on your home ground this time, what?"

His voice was as strong, as resolute as ever. The twinkle in his eye had not disappeared.

"Good afternoon, Colonel." Verena motioned to take his case.

"No, no, I can manage, it isn't very heavy and do call me Arthur!"

She'd taken a few days off work and the time passed quickly. Arthur explained that his wife had died three months before. Verena had sympathised with him.

"Well, you see, she was ill for years, an invalid really, addicted to tablets. I tried everything, doctors, private clinics, the lot, but she never got free of it. We'd no family, a blessing, I suppose. So now I'm alone. I was always alone really, but there was forever hope to cling to, and I was busy looking after her. You know, she was like a child for me really."

"It must have been awful, a terrible strain."

"Well, I've quite a few interests, and the choir kept me going. That's why I used to joke with Maria and you when you came over. It helped me somehow to forget reality." He sighed. "That's life, you get your cards and have to play them. Now let's go for that last walk, you know I leave tomorrow already."

"Yes, and we haven't really done much at all. I could have taken you to Grindelwald or Zermatt, or at least shown you around Berne."

"Don't apologize, those places are full of tourists, and I've done enough travelling in my time," Arthur had quickly reassured her.

Yes, she'd be sorry to see him go. She couldn't really explain it, but for a former military man, he was so gentle, modest, and so appreciative of every little thing she did for him. "Oh, Vreni'll do it" had been the constant refrain in her life. And Vreni always had. She'd considered it her duty. But she'd never felt really appreciated. Until she knew Arthur.

They were both subdued on the way to the airport the next day, but they'd waved gaily enough before he went through the passport control. Well, that's that, thought Verena. They'd promised to keep in touch, and would see each other at the choir two months later when she was to go over to Maria's again. He was an extremely kind British gentleman, that was all.

* * * * *

Suddenly, in that quiet hospital room, Sister Verena took on a new vivacity. Lost in her memories, she'd completely forgotten my presence. It was as if it had all happened just the day before, and she remembered every word, every detail. She began to act out the conversations with even more vigour, and her story became a real life play.

* * * * *

The man bearing the telegram had whistled cheerfully as he walked up Verena's path to her front door.

"Maybe it's good news, Fräulein Ramseier," he'd said when he saw her concerned face.

What's up now? She sighed as she cut it neatly open. Her hands trembling, she read the words

"Would be honoured if you would become my wife.
Please reply as soon as possible. Arthur."

"Oh, my goodness! Well, I never!" She didn't know if she was coming or going. Her entire life had been planned out to the last detail. She'd exactly six years and forty-five days until her retirement, when she wanted to spend more time on her garden and have the kitchen renovated, and now THIS.

Suddenly she knew what she must do. Thrusting on her hat and coat, she locked the door firmly and strode along the lane that led up to the church. She gradually became more peaceful, but was so lost in thought that she didn't even see the neighbours' children who greeted her politely.

She sank down gratefully in front of the gravestones bearing the names Franz Ramseier and Martha Ramseier and began to talk to her much-respected parents. She knew that anyone seeing her there would think she was mad! She didn't care. She'd just wait until she knew she had their answer.

It was beginning to grow dark. At last Verena arose, her legs quite stiff. She knew what to do, she had her parents' permission.

The wording of the telegram caused her some difficulty. 'Yes please' sounded awful, like a child who wanted some sweets, too eager. 'I accept' sounded much too formal. At length she decided on plain 'yes', although she hoped he wouldn't think she was trying to economise with her briefness. She signed her name, just 'Vreni', and went to the next big town to send it off.

She knew there would be problems. He was so much older, eighty-four he'd told her, but he was still lively. Age is a state of mind, she told herself again. She'd never loved anyone before. None of the village boys had attracted her. And she herself had never had an admirer, at least, not that she knew of. She realised that she probably wasn't actually in love, whatever that meant. But it didn't seem to matter — she felt fully alive for the first time in her life. Verena had always been a practical person, and arrangements had to be made. She wrote to Maria, but told no-one else.

The postman brought a small insured package. It was from Arthur. The address on the little black box was a jeweller's in Bond Street. Inside, nestling against dark blue velvet, was the biggest diamond that Verena had ever seen. She caught her breath, hardly daring to try it on. Wonder of wonders, it fitted perfectly. She debated if she should wear it. "Why ever not?" said a small voice inside, "It's from Arthur, your fiancé." The word sounded strange. Her thoughts far away, she started to prepare lunch, scarcely feeling the need for food. No sooner had she finished eating, there was a loud rap at the kitchen window.

It was Martha, her eldest sister.

"*Mein Gott*, Vreni, I thought you'd be ready by now, you haven't even finished clearing off the table, what's the matter with you?"

Verena gulped. She'd completely forgotten. It was Tuesday, and every Tuesday afternoon they went to the village Women's Knitting Circle together.

"Yes, I'll just get my coat." She stretched her hand, up to the peg.

Martha's eyes bulged. "What IN HEAVEN'S NAME is that on your finger?"

Verena knew there was no way out. Martha was too shrewd.

"I'm, I'm, er, engaged."

"You're WHAT?" Martha folded her arms across her starched white apron. "And may I ask to whom — NOT that old man who's been staying here? Bertha saw you two walking about together, but, of course, WE knew nothing about it. I don't think it's right myself, you being a single woman and all."

"But I am fifty-five, Martha."

"Yes, and old enough to have come to your senses by now surely? You can't take on someone as old as that, he'll just use you as a cheap nurse and is only after your pension." Pausing for breath with her plump cheeks flushed,

Martha looked at her sister closely. "I thought you'd said you'd gone through The Change years ago. Your hormones aren't acting up funny are they?"

For Verena, something snapped. "I haven't got time to come to the Knitting Circle this afternoon, I have to write to Colonel Dobson to thank him for my ring."

Martha's mouth fell open at her sister's unusual outburst.

"What? He's a foreigner as well?" Then she managed to get a grip on herself. "You haven't heard the last of this you know, Vreni, — I'll have to call a family meeting. We can't have you making a fool of yourself, and the whole family becoming the laughing stock of the village, with your behaviour. You'd better take that ring off. It doesn't suit you. It's ridiculous — it's almost as big as that vulgar filmstar's, what's her name, Elizabeth something." Muttering as she walked away, Martha turned in the direction of home instead of the village hall. She'd completely forgotten about the Knitting Circle.

Martha's earthy Swiss farming dialect contrasted harshly with Arthur's gentle, well-bred Oxford English. Well, at least she wouldn't have to break it to them now.

She continued with her plans, ignoring all the violent protests from her family. She left for London in May for her usual visit to Maria. She'd see Arthur every day, but of course, it wouldn't be quite correct to stay with him, under the circumstances. He was delighted to see her. On the first day he took her straight to the smart jeweller's where he'd bought the ring.

"I just sent that one because I wanted you to be able to wear an engagement ring right away, dear. But now I want you to choose the real one yourself."

Verena had looked patiently at various rings an assistant showed her, but her mind was made up. "This is the most beautiful." She held up the ring that she'd worn the past two months.

"So, I made the right choice with that too." Arthur had seemed so pleased.

Verena knew that she could never live happily for long in London, even with Arthur. She was a country girl. And so they decided that she'd continue at the hospital, but only work half days, which would give them more time together.

Maria accompanied them back to Verena's small village and was Matron of Honour and only guest at the simple ceremony in the tiny church where the chaplain spoke some English. Verena's entire family boycotted the wedding, but she was too radiant to mind. She led Arthur to her parents' graves and silently introduced them. And then Maria had driven them home and prepared a meal before Verena took her to the nearest town to catch her train to the airport.

"How do you feel, Arthur?" Verena had asked her husband later as they sipped their hot chocolate. "Tired after all the excitement?"

"Not really," he answered, taking her hand. "You know my dear, even if I never learn a word of German, to say nothing of Swiss German, I feel as if I've come home for the very first time in my life."

* * * * *

Arthur never did learn the language. Their marriage lasted five years until he died peacefully at the age of eighty-nine. He lies near Verena's parents in the little graveyard on a hill in the Emmental valley.

Sister Verena paused for breath, looking down at her ring, sparkling brightly in the pale winter sunlight. She blushed suddenly. "Oh, my goodness, I must go and see if Frl. Schmidt is already out of Ops!"

"Tell me something, Vreni," I asked, still spellbound, when she returned. "How was your marriage? I mean, not only did you have the cultural differences to cope with, but also there was a terrific age difference between you, and you both had to manage all that at a late stage in your lives."

"Well, it's very simple really. We knew that what we had was so precious, and had taken so long to find, that we must do all we could to protect it. You see, we didn't know how long it would last, and we had to save our strength, so we had no time for trivialities like squabbles and so on."

I thought back to my own turbulent first year as a newly-wed, which we'd fortunately spent in a 'neutral' country, foreign to both of us, and I felt very humble. Yes, none of us knows how long it will last. Their five years of sheer contentment weigh heavily when balanced with a forty-year-old 'average' marriage. If only more people could hear Vreni's story, I thought, maybe they could learn something from it. So . . . la voilà! ◆

What's in a Kiss?

by Glenda Johnson Elam

Marzio and I first shook hands after hearing so much about each other through mutual friends. I was immediately attracted to him. He was so handsome: tall and slim with a deep bronze tan, his wild, curly black hair accenting his soft transparent green eyes.

"*Salve* (Hello), I'm Marzio . . . I'm so glad to meet you! I've heard a lot about you. You'll be renting a room with us for the whole summer, right?"

Two months later I was head over heels in love with Marzio and neither of us could explain how it happened. The long talks those summer nights felt natural, as did sharing meals and beer together at the restaurants on the Tiber River or on our balcony. It had become a comfortable habit. Listening to music and looking at Roman monuments at night seemed innocent enough.

One fatal night we kissed. For days our lips tingled.

I couldn't speak Italian. I looked up words in the dictionary, used verbs in the infinitive form and added the pronouns. It became a game for us. I would look up word after word as he patiently waited, repeating the sequence of words to be sure he got them right. His face would brighten when he understood and he'd answer using the few English words he knew and the many Italian words I didn't know. Many times I would nod my head saying I understood when I hadn't. Communicating became a real handicap.

At first it was 'cute' when people laughed uproariously because I'd mispronounced a word and given it a totally different meaning.

I'll never forget the evening I wanted to invite friends back to our flat for midnight spaghetti. I had learned how to make a decent thick tomato sauce. I asked everyone if they wanted to return to our place for a "*boccone.*" I'd pronounced the word with an 'i' diminutive which changed my offer for a 'bite to eat' into an invitation for oral sex. All because of a mispronounced 'e'! The guys were all for it. Fortunately, their dates were sympathetic and took my side when the kidding got out of hand. Marzio could tell many stories about my language flubs. I'd laugh but these mistakes made me feel small and stupid and I'd have to remind myself that I have a college degree.

Our personal life suffered because of the language barrier. I became frustrated when I tried to express deeper thoughts. Marzio's patience waned and he no longer tried to select words I could readily understand. He used words that best explained how he felt, often using the Roman dialect. He'd say, "But I'm Roman! I don't speak the Tuscan you're learning from that book, no one our age speaks like that. What kind of Italian are you learning?!"

Needless to say, these comments did not increase my confidence in the Italian I was learning on my own or at evening school.

When we were with friends and everyone would be telling jokes, Marzio would give me an inquisitive look when everybody was still laughing and ask if I'd understood. I'd glibly repeat the joke, only to learn I'd got the joke all wrong. Everyone would laugh again because of my version. After my many questions and their clarifications, I'd usually ask myself, "Why was it so funny in the first place?"

Now, even after eleven years in Italy, I'm still mixing up words in Italian. I occasionally say 'whisper' (*sussurro*) when I want to say 'sip' (*sorso*). I asked for my cuffed (*orlo*) pants at the cleaners and found out I'd said I want my pants given to me with a 'shout' (*urlo*).

I love Marzio and my loving him naturally meant I would live in his city, Rome. But language is not our only challenge.

When a woman loves a man here, it is taken for granted that her home and her social life revolve around the interests of her mate. Their friends are his friends. It is difficult to establish your own circle of friends independent of your husband's.

As an American, I was used to having my own circle of friends. This was a major obstacle for us. Friends presumed that when they invited Marzio to dinner that I would naturally tag along. In the beginning no one invited me personally to dinner, Marzio was asked since he was obviously the person who made the decisions. Marzio decided without even consulting me.

I insisted on my autonomy and the right to arrange social events as I liked. In the end, people who know us well have learned to ask, "Will you be coming with Glenda, or alone?" The best result of all is that this was a first step in establishing respect for my time and my activities as his wife who also has and needs to create space for herself in our life as a couple.

We had numerous arguments about midday meals. Marzio, and everyone he knew, felt it was quite normal for a wife to interrupt her day and prepare a piping hot meal of at least three courses for lunch. I was used to a whole-wheat sandwich and salad or a good healthy yoghurt. Once he communicated my preferences to my in-laws, all sorts of concerns about my 'damaging' American ways surfaced.

My in-laws were afraid I would turn their Marzio into a bloated human form like the ones they had seen in American programs on Italian TV. I was working too and lunchtime was a good time to conduct business. I had to convince Marzio that he was not deprived if he had a light meal instead of the traditional Italian lunch, especially since we had a full-course meal in the evening.

We agreed that I would prepare light meals as often as possible. He saw the benefits in keeping a trim midriff while his friends fought a never-ending battle with their bulge. He soon stopped repeating the criticisms about my cooking habits he heard from friends and family.

I began to create 'American' food variations my mother-in-law could not tolerate. I made a cheese sauce and added yoghurt to it instead of the usual heavy cream. Or I made *ragu* but not with ground beef but with ground soya nuggets, sprinkling cayenne to give it extra spice. I made chicken fricassee in beer. Marzio ate my variations with enthusiasm while my mother-in-law looked on with anguish wondering what kind of madwoman her son had married.

She tried to teach me to iron Italian-style by firmly pressing the iron onto the wrinkled garment. I watched her pull the cloth and strain the iron against it till the veins in her arm grew taunt. She supervised my easy-going ironing for a whole summer. She finally decided that the ironing could always be sent out or a person hired to iron our things at her house so she could at least supervise that person with better results. She decided I had weak wrists and was too used to synthetics to ever be a proper ironer. She made comments like, "What DID your mother prepare you for in life?" I can't bring myself to tell her that my mother thought a good education was far more important than a properly ironed shirt. Somehow it seems cruel.

I had married into a family that had hardly ever been outside Italy. They had read all the Italian best-sellers about America and were avid viewers of American TV-shows and movies. The thoughts and ideas they had about my home country were awesome. I found myself constantly defending our American informality, our casualness.

"Imagine they go barefoot in the house!"

"No, we usually have on socks or woolly mules and besides we usually have wall-to-wall carpeting."

"Did you hear that, carpeting, real dirt collectors. Can you imagine the diseases, etc. . . ."

"Well no, you see we have hermetically sealed windows and lots of air conditioning . . ."

"You see, it's true, all that air conditioning. No wonder they live in sealed cars and sealed apartments, the body loses its natural equilibrium. It's sad . . . Yes, you're lucky you're living here. Who knows what physical state you'd be in if you were still living in the U.S.!"

Finally, a few years ago, the grandfather went to Los Angeles. Ah ha! I thought, finally a point of view from someone in the family who has been there. I eagerly waited for him to return to disclaim many of the convictions all the sitcoms seemed to confirm: our rudeness, lack of respect for our neighbor's privacy, our undisciplined teenagers, and old people who shuffle in the streets!

The grandfather returned. He had seen only what confirmed his views. First he informed them that we actually did eat ice cream in dead winter, that the senior citizen ladies he met all had dyed hair of the strangest colors from a turquoise blue to a neon pink and they wore pants even if they had incredibly large buttocks. He pointed out that we Americans measured food portions by half-package contents or quarter jars of sauce, or by slices of bread or butter, something that is unheard of in Rome.

The grandfather described his harrowing experience when he tried to walk down an L.A. street to get a little fresh air. He was stopped by people in cars who asked him if he was all right or if he needed a lift. People warned him it was unhealthy to walk about on the street. He described the trouble he had finding a sidewalk on some streets and how long the streets were with not a soul in sight.

All this generated Sunday after Sunday debates about Americans being too big, about how human dimensions couldn't possibly be understood there.

I've been bombarded with their ideas of how different America is from Italy. My mother-in-law shakes her head in wonder, "Americans can uproot themselves from one city to another without any remorse and accept the reper-cussions of not having the familiar around them. I admire your courage to go out into the unknown, even to seek it because it will mean a better job or higher pay, or just a new experience. You've done that by coming here to live. It takes courage to do that. I couldn't." And with those words or similar ones, she'll wind up giving me a big hug and assuring me that I have a 'real' family I can count and rely on.

I think of my parents who felt that the most important thing I could learn was how to take care of myself and I hug my mother-in-law, hooking her arm in mine as we join the rest of the family waiting for us in the dining room to serve them their late lunch coffee.

Marzio literally forgot all his bachelor independence once we were married and lapsed into the pampered son he had been with my mother-in-law. It seemed as if overnight he forgot how to make pasta dishes, where the dirty clothes hamper was and that he had once been the model single man living alone. At first, I thought it was 'fun' washing dishes by hand because I had never had to do it. After a while as the domestic chores mounted, I found Marzio's convenient forgetfulness just a little too convenient and we started spending more time dining out than at home. At one point we were eating out every other night so that I wouldn't have to face a sink full of dishes.

Our cleaning bill tripled because everything went to the dry cleaners that charged exorbitant prices for things needing simple washing or cleaning. Chinese launders or self-service laundromats still do not exist in Rome.

Marzio insisted on having the old-style terra-cotta floors while I wanted carpeting to make vacuuming a breeze. He claimed that in a dust-ridden city like Rome, I was asking for all sorts of allergic reactions and unimaginable nests of indoor insects and colonies of parasites. In the end we chose a ceramic floor.

The way Marzio dressed became a direct reflection of my care. How he dressed was up to me. I am of the opinion that he can wear whatever he likes or wants to wear. He is old enough to choose for himself. My mother-in-law considers this 'neglect' on my part. The battle goes on even after five years of marriage.

All this could make anyone feel that a trip back home for good would be the best solution for everyone concerned, especially me! But when I sit at the table and look into Marzio's eyes and see his love for me, so clear and so obviously full of a comprehension I never dreamed of with any other man, I know that whatever the differences in opinions, skin color and culture, it is worth it. I feel loved and know what it means to love someone in return.

One evening he asked, "What are we going to do when we have a child and she (he's sure it will be a girl) has to deal with being half Black American and half Italian?" He shook his head laughing and reached out to take my hand in his. We both knew we can handle that and that 'she' will be just fine. ♥

A Moving Experience

by Sigrid K. Orlet

My grandmother was a wonderful comforter in desperate situations. Once when blood was dripping from my knees, she pressed me with her big arms against her soft and warm body. After the tears on my cheeks had dried into a small salty line, she said, "No matter how bad things are, in the end everything works out." The last time I heard these comforting words was shortly after my sixth birthday. My parents had decided to move within Germany. After hearing the news I ran into the garden to hide in an old apple-tree for the rest of my life. I would not move! However, my parents found me and in time everything worked out. But that was then!

Many years later, my boyfriend came to my mother's house one night, where we were baking cookies for the holidays. The sweet smell of cinnamon filled the house and large plates with warm cookies were standing everywhere, but he did not touch them. Pacing the floor he told me that he was being transferred from Germany to America and that he wanted me to come with him. At first I thought he was joking. But he was not. Silently he looked at me waiting for any reaction. Then he started pacing the kitchen floor again while I sat down and cried. I felt like hiding in an apple-tree.

Later that night we looked at a map of the United States and found the city he was being transferred to. It was a tiny black dot south of Detroit. Lying in bed, I tried to consider all the facts, the love of my family, my friends and my work. I had finally reached a point where I was comfortable with myself and my life. I definitely would not move to a tiny black dot on a map. Then the memories came, memories of the wonderful time we had and how deeply we cared for each other. We were convinced that destiny had brought us together. If there was such a thing as true love, we had found it. Tossing and turning all night, these thoughts played tug-of-war in my head. Neither side was winning! Kleenex tissues piled up on the floor and headaches and tears were finally followed by restless sleep.

I had a difficult time looking into the mirror the following morning, because my eyes were almost swollen shut, but miraculously I had made up my mind. I would move to America with my boyfriend and his daughter.

Two weeks later there was another development that was about to change our lives even more dramatically. Bureaucracy had caught up with us and demanded its price. The United States would not let me accompany my boyfriend to live in the States, unless we were married. No exceptions! Rain clouds darkened the sky while we were sitting in our car in an almost empty parking lot. Avoiding looking at each other, we could not believe what was happening. We had recently decided never to get married. My boyfriend had gone through the painful process of a divorce and I wanted to remain independent. We preferred a partnership with no strings attached. So far it had been wonderful, but this new turn of events was just too much. Bad enough that I had to give up my comfortable life in Germany, now I was pressured into getting married. I could not believe this was happening. Feeling sick, I left the car. My boyfriend came and embraced me. There we were, standing in misting rain on a parking lot with fog drifting by. Shivering, we held each other knowing that no matter what happened next, it would not be easy.

However, there was no time to be wasted. A decision had to be made fast. His personnel department had to have an answer the following day. So after another sleepless night with tissues piling up on the floor and another morning with swollen shut eyes, we went to City Hall to apply for our marriage license. We got married within two weeks promising each other a divorce when we returned to Germany. But for the time being, I was wife to my husband and mother to his teenage daughter.

Christmas came and went, we packed our suitcases, muttered good-byes and left. The traumatic experience of moving to a foreign country unraveled. This was not one of our happier moves. Each of us had moved before, but always within Germany. We never had to struggle with speaking a foreign language, learning different customs, or eating strange-looking foods. However, this latest move spanned continents. We were being transferred to America, a country we only knew from movies and geography classes.

Moving to a foreign country is not for the fainthearted and it was definitely not for us. Leaving Germany was very painful. Vacuuming the floor for the last time, my life rolled past me like a movie. Every room reminded me of things long forgotten. There I was standing in an empty home, feeling miserable. My grown-up world had come to an end. My English was far from perfect, I would have to start all over again just like a small child. Learn a new language, learn new customs, learn to be a mother and wife, pass a test to get an American driver's license, find the post-office, a new dentist and make new friends. There were so many obstacles and I was scared that the future would be bleak.

Our teenage daughter's life also had come crashing down. She had to leave all her girlfriends behind. Having problems with growing up and struggling to become an adult, she did not want to leave her comfortable and familiar surroundings. She needed the support of her friends, her school and her family. She did not want to move and suddenly having a new mother did not help either.

Emotionally and physically drained, we arrived at the airport of our new hometown in the snow-covered middle of nowhere. "Well, at least the snow looks the same as at home," said our daughter while we were headed towards the hotel. "Where are you from," asked the hotel clerk, because from now on our heavy German accents would mark us as foreigners and make us seem different from the majority of people surrounding us.

Falling into the stale smelling hotel beds, I remember thinking that this was not the way I had envisioned my honeymoon to be. And for that matter, there was none. Under all the pressures that come with starting a new job, my husband hardly had any time for his new wife. The new wife, on the other hand, tried to make friends with her new daughter, and often failed. In those long weeks I regretted my decision to move to the States and also the one to get married, and there was no one to talk to.

The first month passed and we were still staying at the hotel. Discovering how different we were from Americans scared us. Not only did we have a different language but body language, mimic, preferences in color, clothes, foods, opinions and humor were also different. Never understanding the laugh-ing-track in movies, we just looked at each other helplessly. Was this supposed to be funny? Ordering food was an adventure too. Often we did not get what we ordered. Or at least that is what we thought. And why was there always ice-water on the table? Who in his right mind would drink ice-water in the middle of winter, or stuff himself at all those all-you-can-eat buffets? Aimlessly wander-ing around in big shopping malls, we looked at styles of clothes, furniture, wall paper, bedding and drapes which all seemed to be so old-fashioned to us. In the parking lots were enormous cars, some of them in such bad shape that they were almost falling apart. They would never be allowed on the road in Germany. Life seemed to be so much more regulated where we came from. In our home country, stores closed at 6:30 p.m. and never opened on Sunday. No one would dare to call me honey, sweetie or dear, and only my family and friends called me by my first name. I was scared and intimidated. There was no way I would ever get used to all this. Never, ever!

The second month passed also and we were still staying at the hotel. Not a very comfortable situation since we had to go out for every meal and there was nothing to do. We were bored. While my husband was at work doing wonderful and interesting things, we stayed at the hotel. The weather was awful, it snowed, rained, froze and snowed. I did not have a car and was afraid of driving anyway. Traffic signs appeared to be different, the traffic-lights were on the wrong side of the intersection and cars were allowed to turn right on red. Unbelievable!

Then there was house-hunting! With snow falling relentlessly, driving was almost impossible. This did not seem to bother our real-estate agent, an over-weight man in plaid pants who called me 'honey'. He picked us up almost every day and showed us countless houses, until they all turned into a big colorful blur in my head. I refused to keep looking, but my husband wanted to see more. We argued in the car, we argued in the hotel elevator, we argued in our room. I left and slammed the door. There I was in the hallway of the hotel on the seventh floor without a room key. I had enough! I would not look at another single house, I was tired of the discussions with my daughter, I was tired of living in a hotel and I was tired of being in America. I wanted to go home!

In bed we had a long talk about our frustrating situation and about how difficult this was for all of us, but that things could only get better. We continued to look at houses the next day. They were so different, being made of wood and not brick. The kitchens were completely furnished, and the sound of kitchen-sink disposals kept frightening us every time the real-estate agent turned them on. There were no fences and I wondered how people knew how far to mow the lawn in summer. Some of the houses for sale were still occupied. Sometimes a housewife with curlers in her hair opened the door and TV sets were turned on all day long. There was so much to learn, and the American way of life seemed to be so much different from what we had seen on 'Lassie'.

After an endless search, we finally decided to buy the first house we had seen a few weeks before. It had three bedrooms and mustard-colored aluminium siding. We were not too excited about the mustard color, but there was a huge backyard and an old oak tree in the front. It was a pleasant neighborhood and the school district was supposed to be excellent.

So finally, on a clear February morning the moving van arrived with our belongings and with countless memories. The unpacking began. Seeing our things in America felt very strange and homesickness kept creeping up on me. I cried over every single broken dish I found and there were many.

A few days later, his daughter and I were still unpacking boxes and arranging furniture when we heard knocking at the front door. Motioning to her to be quiet, I went to the window, hiding behind the drapes. A man was standing in front of the house, looking rather grim. We did not know anyone in America so I did not open the door. He kept knocking for a while but finally gave up. We watched him walk away. Soon the heavily falling snow covered his footprints. When I put another log onto the fire my hands were shaking.

Later that day, we found out who our visitor had been. When my husband came home from work, he told us about a phone call he had received earlier. It was from a man who identified himself with OUR name, insisted that he lived on our street and complained about a moving expense bill he had received. My husband told us also that they had agreed to meet. Of course I did not believe a single word my husband was saying, but he insisted that we had an invitation to come to the Orlet house after dinner and he did not change his story. We knew this could not be true, because Orlet was a very rare name, even in Germany.

Playing along with him, we talked about our 'relatives' living nearby. We put on our winter coats after dinner and walked a few houses up the street. We thought my husband was carrying the joke too far when he walked up to a house and rang the door bell. A beaming man opened the door, introduced himself as Mr. Orlet and gave us hugs as if we were old friends. I could not believe what was happening. Pinching myself, I discovered that this was not a dream.

There we were, sitting in the family room, the fire crackling and Mr. Orlet and his family looking at us in amazement. Pacing the floor, he listened to our explanations, every other minute saying: "*Mensch Meier*," which is a German expression of disbelief. We agreed, this was incredible. Someone from Germany with his last name had moved almost next to his house and the mail carrier had delivered the freight bill to the wrong address. He told us that his family had immigrated from Germany when he was a little boy. Now a father himself, he lived his quiet and perfect family life in the Midwest, and suddenly three 'relatives' walked into his family room. He loved it!

During that stormy night with snow falling and spring still deep asleep, we made our first friends in America. Knowing someone in the neighborhood who cared helped us over so many hurdles. They came with us to enroll our daughter in high school, invited us over for dinner and put up with me saying all the time: "Well, in Germany we do this differently." I am sure they soon got tired of hearing this sentence, but they never said a word. They accepted us the way we were. Just like relatives, we were invited to all family affairs and we no longer felt as lonely in this huge country called America.

Nevertheless, I was still homesick. At the sound of the brakes of the mail truck, I would race to the mailbox, but more often than not, there was no mail from Germany. Unhappy with my life, I started to eat cookies, cake and ice-cream in excess, gaining fifteen pounds within the first four months. Being home most of the time, I lived the life of a housewife and mother, wrote letters, read books and watched TV. I was miserable, I missed my family, my friends and most of all my mother. Being this unhappy did not help our marriage either. We fought almost daily because of misunderstandings, about little things like who was going to do the dishes and big things like the behavior of our daughter. My husband did not understand what I was going through, he did not realize that being home all day drove me crazy, and that I was too scared of all the hurdles out there to change my situation. He was excited about his new job and our daughter had made friends in school and adjusted quite well. But I felt betrayed. Deep down I made my husband responsible for all my suffering. How could he do this to me? Walking around with so much anger bottled up inside me, I did not even realize that his seeing me like this hurt him.

But slowly the cold and death of winter disappeared and snow turned into rain. Standing at the window I watched the change of season, realizing that my life also had to change. The warm breeze of spring touched us all and things began to turn around. The snow melted, flowers started to blossom and cherry trees looked like puffy white clouds. I enrolled at the university and life got better, including our marriage. It felt like coming home after a long and sad journey.

I made friends and met students from all over the world. Sharing our thoughts, I discovered that everyone went through almost the same feelings of loneliness, frustration and anger I had experienced. It was something almost anyone had to go through after moving to a foreign country.

Without working on it, my mind eventually opened and began soaking up all the wonderful new things that surrounded me. I met people from Africa, Australia, Canada, England, France, India, Israel, Lebanon and Sweden, all living together in harmony. They all had different cultural backgrounds and shared it with everyone who was interested in it. What a wealth of knowledge! We learned about different foods, customs and ways of thinking. Appreciating all this, I grew more and more patient towards the people I met. I realized that living in a foreign country had made me change some of my views and become more open-minded. Life treated us so gently, we enjoyed being a family and we enjoyed all the wonderful things around us. The red painted barns in the countryside, fresh walnuts from the tree, and funnel cake with powdered sugar.

Three years passed all too quickly. After our initial struggles, those years brought my husband and me much closer than ever before. We had mastered some very difficult situations and our relationship was so much stronger because of it. When another spring came and bathed our old oak tree in golden sunlight, it was time to say farewell to America. I did not want to move! I loved our family picnics at the river, the strawberry festivals, potluck parties, all-you-can-eat buffets, Halloween, college football, Thanksgiving celebrations and carolling in cold winter nights. I loved the three old men playing dulcimer music in the park every Wednesday afternoon, and I would miss each and everyone of them. In our extensive travels during these three years, I had grown to love the open spaces and breathtaking natural wonders of America. Would I ever see them again?

Understanding the tears in my eyes while I was packing our china into carton boxes, my husband took me into his arms. We had been through rough waters in those three years of our unwanted marriage. We had come to America with so many fears and prejudices and left with the most beautiful memories. Memories of wonderful times and new friends. We learned that when we go out into the world and are open to everything new, life will treat us gently and help us through all kinds of obstacles. We get a different view of the world and become more patient towards every human being that crosses our path.

Oh, and yes Grandma, you were right. No matter how bad things are, in the end everything works out! ♥

Marriage Made in Heaven

by Verena Bakri

Slowly and very gently I folded the thick letter and put it back into the colorfully-stamped envelope. While I was gazing in deep thought at the snow-covered mountain peaks, I must have smiled like I had never smiled before. My mother, who was placidly sitting next to me on the bench in the crispy clean winter setting, just said matter-of-factly: "So he proposed to you!"

What? How did SHE know?

"Easy," she declared, "a mother can see these things on her child's face!"

That saved me time and energy trying to explain this new sensation of utter certainty, this long-nurtured secret love of mine. I had been carrying it around the world with me for over seven years — from Philadelphia to Florence, from Zurich to Sao Paulo and Heidelberg, from Crete to Copenhagen, Mallorca and Luxembourg, and now to Flims in Switzerland where I was enjoying a perfect winter vacation after my odysseys. She knew 'him' only from my fervent descriptions and treasured photographs, but had never met 'him'.

For me, those seven years since we had seen each other had seemed like an eternity. But the memories were fresh, as if it had been only yesterday that I waved goodbye to him from high up on the deck of a majestic ocean liner, east-bound from New York to Genoa. The band was playing a nostalgic farewell tune, and the sailors had started to get ready to turn in the gangways. At first I had been a bit disappointed that he had not shown up as he had promised. I had hugged my relatives and gone on board. As I was standing at the railing and straining my eyes to spot them, there he was in flesh and blood: Bakri Abdullahi, my friend, well-wisher and protector. He stood out in the crowd — tall, slim and very handsome, with his typical features of 'the people of the sun-burnt faces', an attribute Abyssinians were known by in history books of yesteryear. We saw each other at the same time and nothing could have stopped me from rushing back on land and seizing this last chance to hug and kiss him.

Later, someone next to me at the railing chatted excitedly and handed me some paper streamers. We passengers were expected to throw them out to our loved ones on the quay as the ship slowly started moving out of the harbor. Forget it, I thought, I might as well put it in my pocket rather than throw it. Anyway, it'll never reach him . . . But I did give it a try. Against all expectations, Bakri caught it with a radiant smile. This last sight of him never faded in my mind. A few days later I was overjoyed to find an enlarged picture taken by the ship's photographer of that precious moment when the ocean liner had left New York. I purchased it with my last dollars. This picture became one of my most treasured possessions — along with the crumbled bit of pink streamer that had remained in my hand.

Years came and went and our paths never crossed. Our long but infrequent letters were platonic, filled with mutual understanding, very cordial and spar-kling with humor. He had always treated me with respect. He was five years older and wiser than me and gave lots of good advice regarding all 'those foreign sex maniacs' in the 'City of Brotherly Love' — Philadelphia — where we had both studied. I felt like his little sister. And yet, deep in my heart, I always knew there was more to it, much more . . . if only we had the same religion. Bakri was a devout Muslim. I come from a strict, Catholic family and I knew he was out of bounds for me.

After corresponding like this for two years, in one of his letters, Bakri mentioned casually that he had returned home to Ethiopia and gotten married to a girl from his home town, by arrangement through both parents. I accepted the fact, congratulated him and we continued our correspondence. I was working then as a secretary in my home town of Zurich, and travelling, whenever I had enough money, to faraway places to see the world and learn yet another lan-guage. I fell in and out of love several times with people from my country, Switzerland, and from other European countries who had similar social and cultural backgrounds. I was high-flying one day and deeply disappointed the next. Sometimes I was upset by the strange attitudes of so-called Christians. I became much more tolerant of other religions in those years and learned to appreciate the differences while finding plenty of parallels between the various world religions.

Five years later, I received a letter from Bakri telling me that his marriage had failed and that he had divorced his wife some months before with the agreement of both their parents. He had tried to save the marriage for the sake of their two children, to whom he was very attached, but their educational backgrounds were too different. In spite of his goodwill, they could not come to a satisfactory arrangement.

Divorce always has a shocking effect on me, especially when it concerns people I feel close to. I was deeply disturbed at the news and wrote him more frequently, sharing with him more of my life's philosophies than ever!

Was it our long-standing confidence and friendship, or just my heart-felt words of sympathy about his situation? Or was there something he read between the lines of my letters that triggered off the proposal that followed soon after? Only Cupid knows . . .

And when that letter arrived that changed my whole future, there were no more tabus, no doubts, no questions — only the certainty that this was what I had been waiting for ever since we had parted at the New York harbor. I was convinced our love would work out. I agreed with Bakri who had put it so beautifully and so clearly: "I pray that God, who has joined us in spirit, will unite us in body!"

I could not ignore that probably my church and maybe my family would try everything to prevent marriage between this *'Mädchen aus gutem Hause'* and a divorced Muslim from a strange land. Surprisingly, my family and friends expressed more understanding and acceptance of my decision than I had dreamed possible. Apart from the occasional 'strange look' or 'sour remark' from people I could not care less about anyway, I was pleasantly amazed to discover a great amount of genuine interest and tolerance. Those who had their doubts were soon convinced of the strength of our relationship once they met Bakri in person.

Long before we set a date for the wedding, it seemed that everything could be worked out quickly with the church through the legal ecclesiastic office I had consulted. The priest in charge encouraged me to pursue the proper channels for a dispensation from the Vatican.

As a scholar, Bakri knew a lot more about my religion than I knew about his. Although his family practiced Islam, they were not fundamentalists and did not frown at his decision to marry a Christian. In fact, his aged father, who had never learned how to read and write but was a very wise and respected man in his community, gave us his blessing when he saw my picture shortly before he died. Bakri was well aware of my background and of my wish to remain a Roman Catholic, to have — if possible — a proper church wedding, and if we had children, to baptize and instruct them in the Christian faith.

My legal advisor confidently told me to go ahead with all the steps necessary to obtain a license from my Swiss municipality since I would not be able to get a visa to join Bakri in the States where he was supposed to return to complete his doctorate degree. We both had quite a handful of time-consuming, complicated, often frustrating and costly errands. We had to figure out the difficult ecclesiastic jargon that needed to be translated from my mother tongue, German, into English. From his side, documents had to be translated from English into two or three Ethiopian languages. These had to be submitted at both of our respective municipalities, council of elders or church authorities.

The distance separating us did not help. Although mail service was prompt between Ethiopia and Switzerland, it was trying for me to have to play the role of a 'spoil-sport' in our wonderful long-distance romance by asking detailed questions to fulfill the requirements of the ecclesiastic court. Negotiating that we should be granted a church wedding was tricky enough in German, let alone in English.

There were no printed forms to be filled in as might be expected for an important matter like that. Instead the priest in charge just jotted down what was likely to be of importance, such as, "Have you ever been baptized in a Catholic church?" or "Did you accept any money to marry your first wife?" All these questions had to be answered meticulously by Bakri and confirmed by three people of his community who knew him. I would have preferred to take this burden from Bakri's shoulders and go through the process of testifying and soliciting testimony myself. The legal ecclesiastic procedure in our case was called '*in Favorem Fidei*' meaning 'in favor of the believer' which explains the detailed answers demanded. We had all the information together in six months but were then advised to submit the petition package through the diocese where we would eventually be living together in the States.

While still in Ethiopia, Bakri won a scholarship to study German in Germany. We prepared ourselves for our reunion in Switzerland by clarifying our stand-points as systematically as possible to prevent misunderstandings due to language difficulties, tabus or lack of time. Night after night, I composed my poetic love letters, well aware that Bakri was writing his at the same time. We seemed to have some very vivid telepathy going for us.

Bakri was concerned about the impression his country would have on me and begged me to visit Ethiopia BEFORE I commit myself to marry him. I felt it was unfair to make a marriage depend upon the country of origin of either partners. I was convinced I could live anywhere in the world as long as we were together, accepting and tackling any challenges coming our way.

We both felt we should evaluate our feelings after we could meet again.

Who knows how much we could have changed physically as well as in character and behavior in those seven years of absence from each another? We wanted to avoid disappointments since we had both suffered from previous unsuccessful romances.

When the day of our long-awaited reunion finally came, we missed meeting each other at the airport in Zurich. His plane had arrived early and, not finding me, he had decided to call my mother and inform her he would wait at the downtown terminal. By the time I called her and discovered where he was, I was so excited, I could hardly think. That twenty-minute bus ride back to Zurich was pure agony. In the terminal, which had no more than two dozen seats, I rushed around, looking without seeing, listening without hearing, until finally he came up behind me, tapped me on my shoulder and said softly, "Are you looking for someone, Miss?"

We were in each other's arms instantly and did not care about the world around us. We knew immediately that our seven-year separation had not made a difference in how appealing we were to each other.

As I am typing this, the twenty-third anniversary of this historical reunion is just around the corner. We are surrounded by three lovely daughters. Each has inherited features from both of us. Aida, nineteen years old, our 'Sparky', has her father's fine features, sharp intelligence and natural self-confidence, as well as my love for languages, art and music. Lydia, our 'Softy', at fifteen, is big-eyed, like the angels in coptic icons, has Bakri's gentle ways, bright smile and terrific sense of humor, but finds it difficult to withhold her emotions, just like I do. Yobdar (an Oromo name meaning 'the horizon of beauty') is twelve years old. She's our 'Goldie', with her golden hair and brown velvety skin. She's known as the friendliest kid in class, carefree and charming, full of determination and perseverance. And all of them, just like their parents, love the unknown and the different. They have an insatiable longing for adventure and discovery and a genuine openness towards anyone regardless of his or her cultural background, religious convictions and upbringing. We have managed to instill in them the knowledge that 'home is where we are' and not some faraway place where we would like to be. This conviction has helped us all to settle smoothly whenever we have had to move.

Bakri and I have never made it to the altar in all these years. Nor was our wedding ceremony at Addis Ababa's Municipality in the presence of four witnesses a great ceremony to brag about. But we had a lovely party with friends. Our honeymoon too, was somewhat of a failure, as Bakri had to leave for the States the morning after the party so as not to forfeit his scholarship. He left me behind to discover his roots with the help of concerned and sincere friends. Those two weeks in Ethiopia were better eye-openers than any guided tour with a travel agency. The beauty of the people and landscape was fascinating. The hospitality was heartwarming. The gap between rich and poor was shocking. The wealth of ancient traditions was incredible. The variety of spicy dishes was delicious. The craftsmanship was fabulous. The confusing Amharic language and script and the many local Semitic dialects were frustrating since I could not communicate with the man on the street. Those were two weeks of impressions, feelings, amazement, questions, culture shocks racing through my mind and heart like merry-go-rounds gone berserk. I learned that life with a foreigner from a faraway land would never be boring nor easy, but always a challenge.

No matter how hard I tried, I did not succeed in completing the formalities for a church wedding. During the first ten years I involved seventeen priests. All of them showed consideration and understanding and made promises for a fast and efficient settlement of the case. But IT JUST NEVER HAPPENED! Was it because we moved to so many different dioceses within short periods of time that the ecclesiastic authorities lost trace of us? (No, a forwarding address was always indicated.) Was it that Bakri got tired of my even mentioning the fact and we did get into arguments about it at times? (No. Because I was determined to keep trying to have a church wedding no matter what the obstacles were.) Was our petition clumsily if not incorrectly formulated? (No, because high-ranking church officials were involved.)

After ten years of my trying to have a church wedding, the Vatican had not even acknowledged receipt of our petition. I decided to stop blaming and torturing myself and wasting tears. There would be no more begging for favors! I made up my mind after having spoken to a Jesuit father who had just baptized our youngest daughter in our living room. He went through a lot of trouble to get us a straight-forward answer. The answer was, "Yes, you may now get married in church," as the Vatican had meanwhile decentralized the deciding authorities into the dioceses. But it was too late . . . neither Bakri nor I wanted to go through the ceremony any more. It seemed to us as though we would have put our previous years of married life into question and we did not see why we should do so, since we had lived decently and not — as the common term suggested — 'in sin'.

The reverend agreed with us and said, "Your marriage has been blessed by

God and He has given you beautiful healthy children. You should not let it worry you any more." He encouraged us to continue being a good example to our children and to lead a God-fearing life.

Bakri has never for one moment tried to keep me away from church. All our children have been baptized and have been following religious instruction wherever we have lived. Every evening we pray together. The first communion and the confirmation ceremonies have been celebrated in the presence of good friends and are highlights for all of us. These ceremonies were not overshadowed by the fact that Bakri is not a Christian. On the contrary, in the true spirit of the United Nations, we have always been fortunate enough to have tolerant friends and all world religions were represented in our midst on those days: Christians, Jews, Muslims, Buddhists, Hindus and Baha'is have been among us to congratulate our girls on their great day, and a lot of views and explanations about parallels in other religions have been exchanged at those and other occasions, giving our children a true sense of belonging to the great race of humans, to the 'children of God', no matter what color or creed they may be.

Thus ends this tale of a 'successful', multiracial, multi-religious and multicultural, totally 'mixed-up' relationship. We thank God for having protected us and guided us in many difficult situations which any regular couple must expect during the course of their marriage. Our difficulties have been due to our often having to live under harsh economic, political and climatic conditions in the duty stations we are posted through the United Nations. Our misunderstandings and disappointments have never been caused by our differences in race or religion, but rather by trivial incidents like overspending the household budget or tardiness for appointments which is, incidentally, a classical case of over-adaptation on both sides. The proverbial punctuality of the Swiss is practiced by Bakri while I have become very lax in that respect. Our biggest challenges come from the influences and pressures from outside our family or from the hectic life we lead.

We are still madly in love with each another and if asked if we would want to replay the whole comedy, our answer would probably be a slow but growing broad smile. ♥

Love and Scrubbing Steps

by Nancy Steinbach

"Falling in love had been so easy," I said out loud to no one in particular. There was no one to hear my complaints, and I wasn't even sure why I felt so unhappy. After stooping down to rinse the mop, or what passed for one, I continued washing the floor. Why couldn't I buy a simple sponge mop in Germany, the kind that can be found all over America? When thinking about what it would be like to live in a foreign country, I had never considered mops made of strings. It was one thing to tour a foreign country but quite another to actually live there.

As I finished mopping the tiled entryway, I thought about how it had all begun. I had met Werner at a university in California three years before. We were both new to the area, only I had come from Arizona and Werner had come from half way around the world. His beautiful green eyes, black hair and sense of humor made me take an interest in him immediately. I found his foreign accent charming. What really captivated me was that even though he was an Engineering student, he enjoyed poetry readings and film classes — and I liked to go to technical museums with him and learn how things ticked. After a year Werner had to return to Germany.

I visited him for what was to have been a summer vacation traveling in Europe. We had Eurail Passes and traveled throughout Europe, going as far north as Scotland and as far south as Sicily. We lingered at the Louvre and every other museum we came across. We bicycled through southern Germany and we camped in Liechtenstein in the rain. By summer's end, we knew we didn't want an ocean separating us. After a simple wedding ceremony, we settled down in Heidelberg, Germany, where Werner was finishing his studies. But life just wasn't the same anymore. My feelings for Werner hadn't changed. Not exactly.

I finished washing the floor and carried the bucket to the bathroom and emptied the dirty water down the shower drain. We had been lucky to find this small basement apartment. We didn't have much money. I wasn't eligible to work even though I was married to a German. Besides, my German wasn't good enough yet.

Just as I was about to sit down, the telephone rang.

"Nancy? This is Jean. I'm back."

"How was New Jersey? Did you have a good time?"

"What a question. I gained ten pounds because I ate everything in sight. Which reminds me. I've got your chocolate chips and molasses. I can drop them off now."

"Thanks Jean. I'll make some tea and we can do some catching up."

When Jean arrived, she noticed the mop drying by the door. "You've been hard at work, I see," she said.

"I put it off as long as I could, but we're having guests over tonight. I sure could use a sponge mop. You want to bring me one next time you go back to the States?"

"Sure, I can fit that in with the twenty frozen steaks Christine asked for. Sometimes I'm almost afraid to mention I'm going home. If I filled every request from my American sisters here, I'd have to charter my own plane."

"What did Christine want with steaks?"

"You don't understand, you're a vegetarian. But the Germans just don't cut meat the way they do back home. Here are your chips and molasses. What on earth did you want the molasses for?"

"That's for gingerbread. I'm starting to crave things that I never thought much about back in the States. I'll make you some. With a lemon sauce it's delicious, mmm, mmmm."

"Spare me. I've got a few pounds to lose." Jean looked at her watch. "I have to leave. I have a class at two. Will you be at the university today?"

"No, but I took my German exam last week. I should know soon whether I passed or if I'll be back declining more verbs." I wanted to enter the graduate program in literature, but first I was required to pass a German language proficiency test.

"That's great news. I'm sure you'll pass. We can go to lectures together."

"That would be a help. I've sat in on a few already and I didn't have a clue what they were talking about!"

"It'll come. Just give it time," Jean said.

I walked Jean down our long driveway past the house where our landlord lived to where Jean had parked her car. On my way back to our house, the landlady, Inge, came out and greeted me with a smile.

"Guten Tag. Wie geht es?"

"*Gut, danke. Und Dir?*" I was glad that the landlady didn't mind the informal 'you' form. I had a hard enough time just keeping straight the content of what I said, much less all the grammatical cases and endings that made a German sentence seem like a work of art.

Inge walked me back to our apartment. We usually talked about the weather, gardening, or Inge's children. But Inge had something else on her mind.

Stopping in front of the steps that led down to our basement apartment, Inge said, "You see those green spots on the sidewalk?"

I saw some smudges that I hadn't noticed before. They looked like moss stains caused by the wet and warm weather.

"You'll have to scrub them off. If they stay there, we'll never get the steps clean," Inge told me.

"Scrub them?" I asked bewildered. The time the leaves piled up in our stairwell and Inge had asked me to sweep them away, I could understand. But scrub concrete?

"Yes, like I do it. I can lend you my brush. You need to use detergent. You should do this once a month. It makes it look well-kept."

"OK, I'll give it a try," I said. I hurried down the stairs saying goodbye to Inge. This was too much.

I closed the door behind me. I had seen many German women out on Saturday mornings with a bucket of soapy water and a brush, on hands and knees, scrubbing the steps clean. When I first toured through the country, I had been impressed by the spotless houses and beautiful gardens.

Now, I knew what work it was to keep up such sparkling entryways and attractive landscapes. I also knew about arguments between neighbors over each other's yards. Inge had been upset when a neighbor a few houses away let the weeds go to seed, and she complained the seeds all ended up in her yard. And Werner had overheard a neighbor telling Inge to cut down the chestnut tree in front of Inge's house because most of the leaves blew into his yard. The tree still stood, but in the fall Inge would rake the leaves every day.

I went to the kitchen to begin making dinner for our party. Inge's request couldn't have come at a worse time. I had never seen anyone in the States clean their entrance way, except maybe to hose it down once in a while. And with the drought in California, no one even did that anymore. The landlady had gone too far this time. I would have to have a serious talk with Werner when he came home.

I decided to make first the chocolate chip cookies for dessert. I rummaged in the kitchen cupboards looking for walnuts, but all I found were hazelnuts, the staple of German recipes. I still had time to run to the store and pick up a few items. I knew I might find walnuts at the 'Reformhaus', the equivalent of a health food store back home. If they didn't have them, I'd be out of luck. Usually the grocery stores carried walnuts only around the Christmas holidays. I grabbed my backpack and bicycled to the neighborhood stores.

Since there were no shopping centers nearby, most people did their shopping locally where there was a bakery, a butcher's, a small grocery store, and a health food store. Going there used to make me feel like time had been rolled back a century, but after the novelty wore off, it was something else again. Going to different stores was time consuming. And getting used to the opening and closing hours was difficult. Many small stores closed in the afternoon for a two hour lunch break. And almost all stores closed at two p.m. on Saturdays — except one Saturday a month when they stayed open to six. And the hairdresser closed on Mondays, the library on Tuesdays, and the doctor's office on Wednesday afternoons. The only thing easy to remember was that on Sundays everything was closed!

I parked my bike next to the health food store. I was pleased to find the walnuts, and I also bought some rice cakes and soya burger mix. I passed by a display that made me smile — peanut butter and popcorn. How funny to see the staples of my American childhood considered a specialty.

I was back by 3:30 which would give me plenty of time to make the cookies and get the salad ready. A batch of cookies were cooling off when Werner came home. He gave me a hug with one arm while sampling a cookie with the other.

"What are you making?" he asked, munching on the cookie. He spoke only German with me since we had settled in Heidelberg.

"Soya burgers, salad, and baked potatoes — with sour cream, since we're having guests," I answered as best I could in German. It wasn't easy concentrating on all those German endings that changed with each noun.

"Soya burgers? Nancy, I don't know if they'll like them."

"What's wrong with them? You like them."

"You know I like everything you cook. I thought you might just get some Wurst, you know, that's easy to fix."

I took the cookie sheet from the oven but it slipped out of my hand. "Ouch . . . I've burned my finger." I ran cold water over the burn.

"Are you OK?" Werner asked.

"It's not bad. Could you put the next batch of cookies in?" I went to the bathroom to find some ointment. Even though the apartment was small, every room had a door, including the kitchen and the hallway. When Werner was home, he had the habit of keeping all the doors closed. By the time I got to the bathroom, I had opened and closed three doors.

As I reached for the first-aid lotion, I knew I was upset. In the beginning, I had been amused by cultural differences. Seeing our toothbrushes reminded me how I used to tease Werner for washing his face with cold water and brushing his teeth with warm. For me, it only made sense to wash my face with warm water and my teeth with cold. But these differences were not so amusing anymore.

I marched back into the living room, defiantly leaving all the doors open. It seemed funny to show my anger this way; as a teenager I had shut my door to show I wasn't happy.

Werner was on the telephone. I went into the kitchen and left that door open too. I checked on the cookies. That was the last straw. Werner had turned off the oven. Without asking, he always automatically turned off the oven or burners telling me the stored up heat would finish the job.

Werner hung up the telephone. I strode up to him and handed him the apron his mother had made for me. "Here, you can cook dinner tonight. You can say I took suddenly ill. I'll stay in the bedroom and study," I said in English. Whenever I'm angry I switch to English because I can't get the words out fast enough in German. I went to the bedroom and flopped down on the bed.

Werner came after me. "What's wrong?"

"You're different here. In California you didn't close all the doors or turn off the oven. We had people over for vegetarian dinners and that was fine with you then. Now you're on my case if I leave a light on too long or heat up more than one room. I'm tired of seeing my breath in winter when I use the bathroom."

"I'll cook dinner tonight. OK?" He went to tickle my feet, but I pulled them away and sat up.

"Werner, I want to go home. On the next plane."

"Come on, what happened today? It can't be the wash. It's not even Sunday."

He was trying to make me laugh. That time had been an experience for both of us. We had come back from a trip and since we didn't have a dryer, we hung the clothes up on the laundry line to dry. Then the next door neighbor came over and asked us ever so nicely to take them down because it was Sunday. Every door and piece of furniture we owned ended up covered with wet wash. We had been able to laugh about it. But I couldn't laugh anymore.

"That's just the problem, Werner. I want to go back home where people aren't so particular about what other people do."

"But what's that got to do with dinner tonight? Don't you like Manfred and Renate?"

"I like them. How could I not like them? I don't understand a word they say." In all fairness, I knew that Manfred, Renate, and Werner would start out speaking in high German when they got together. The problem was they would soon switch to their Schwäbisch dialect which might as well have been Greek to me.

"But that's not all. Inge wants me to scrub the steps. On hands and knees. With detergent. Once a month."

"Oh, no. So that's it. Our landlady is on the warpath again."

"I like her. She's always having me over for tea, and she helps me with my German. But, Werner, I never want to live next to the people we rent from, even if they are our best friends."

"Sure, but we can't move back to the States just now. Look, we can take turns scrubbing the steps."

I sat up on the bed. "I've never seen a man out there yet scrubbing."

"Then you'll see one now, OK?" Werner said. "We can cancel dinner tonight and have it some other time at a pizzeria."

"No, let's have it here. It's just that I don't like it when the women do all the cooking, serving and cleaning up. I know you've got to spend more hours working out of the house than I do, but couldn't we share the chores more?"

"Sure," Werner said. He took the apron and tossed it in the trash. "How's that for a start? You want to stay in the bedroom tonight?"

"No, I want to see if you can really cook. This should be good," I said feeling mischievous.

"You've got to promise me one thing."

"What's that?" I asked suspiciously.

"You'll keep my social security number a secret."

I threw a pillow at him and we both tumbled off the bed entangled. There had been a few things, too, that Werner didn't like about America. He had told me the Germans had prevented their government from assigning everyone a number and using it to put personal information into a centralized system. He couldn't understand why Americans weren't bothered that the social security number was used everywhere: as a student ID number, military service number, on tax reports and bank accounts. Even his dentist had asked for it. Then there was the airy, tasteless white bread, weak American coffee, and . . . but that's Werner's story to tell. ♥

Expected Response Syndrome

by Claire Bonney

It is difficult to write about inter-cultural marriages, not having partici-pated in any other one. It is an important topic to think about though. When we have troubles in a marriage, we often forget to depersonalize them and to realize that at least some of these — not all — are due to cultural differences. I think that communication runs through different channels and that these channels are, for the most part, culturally formed.

If I had to pinpoint the single most difficult element in a dual-cultural marriage, I would define it as ERS — the Expected Response Syndrome. ERS means that whatever you expect to happen in a given situation is not going to happen and whatever you never dreamed would happen surely will. On our wedding day, I started to get an inkling of how ERS works when my husband and I were on our way to City Hall on the New York subway. Terror struck him. "What do I say when the judge asks me?" he gasped and sputtered as he nervously pulled on his new tie. "I can? I will? Yes?"

Then we visited my parents for our first American vacation. After my father had gone through the less personal topics of life insurance, apartment fire-safety regulations in Switzerland and business and investment prospects, he cleared his throat and said to Matthias, "So what are your plans and goals for this vacation?" I thought my husband would faint. What an absurd question! He looked at my father as if he hadn't understood and finally answered, "I don't have any goals and objectives. I'm on vacation." I thought my father would faint. What a strange answer. He had never heard of a vacation without plans and goals.

Following what is probably a biological process, dual-cultural pairs tend to attract other dual-cultural pairs as friends. My favorite guests are a couple from Los Angeles. Yve grew up on a farm near Lucerne in Switzerland; Josh grew up in Las Vegas, Nevada. They are our cultural mirror image — a mixed Swiss/

American couple and, like us, living on his home turf. The last time they visited here we took a drive together in their rented car and she backseat drove the whole way until he almost had apoplexy. I could easily see that this was a cultural pattern. Most Swiss women do not drive the car when out with their husbands, but nearly all are horrific backseat drivers. It is a national trait — but one that our American friend didn't know about. Both were mollified when I pointed this out.

On the other hand, Yve works miracles with my taciturn husband. My biggest gripe about him is that he never opens his mouth. Every bit of information I get from him seems excavated from archaeological strata older than those at Olduvai Gorge. "How was your day, dear?" I might ask.

"Fine," he says.

Or, in a more quiet mood, I might venture to query, "What are you thinking about?"

"The computer," is his answer.

But as soon as Yve shows up, those two wander off together way in front of everyone else on a walk and murmur mysteriously in their native language in low tones for hours. If I ask what they were talking about, I usually get a monosyllabic answer like "life" or "work" as a complete explanation.

Children are, of course, a fairly big issue in any marriage. In a dual-cultural marriage this theme tends to get a wee bit more complicated. Table manners used to be an issue at our house. I drilled away at my three-year-old nephew until I was blue in the face. I'd tell him "Say thank you, say please, don't use your fingers, ask for the butter if you want it," and so on. I got no support in this from my husband or even from my nephew's own mother. I harbored suspicions that they both didn't care about his future, that they were ruining his character and making dinner time unpleasant as well. Upon visiting friends with a three-year-old daughter in the U.S., I heard them harping away at her too — using exactly the same phrases and parentally-correct tone of voice that I had used. I realized then, finally, that what I had been enacting was an American pattern. I thought manners were manners, but it isn't true. Since then I have let up on my poor nephew. His manners are good enough, actually.

Speaking of my nephew, every woman has a stock of quick cheap emergency recipes for fast dinners for kids. We grew up on them, we know about them. Take tuna noodle casserole. My own mother made this with La Choy chow mein noodles out of the can, chopped celery and Campbell's Cream of Mushroom on special at the A & P for 15 cents a hit. Chow mein noodles are something I have never yet found in Switzerland in fourteen years of looking. Cream of Mushroom costs about $2.50 a can and stalk celery is a rarity. So much for that idea. How about creamed chipped beef on toast? We used to love that for lunch when we came home from school. But how do you say 'chipped beef' in German? We used to get ours in a red and yellow plastic bag. What should it look like here? And what about the toast? It is just not the same on 7-nut whole wheat or hearty *Dinkelbrot* or thick-slabbed *Soyamehlbrot* as it was on floppy white Sunshine bread. So why didn't it occur to me to make a cheese *Wähe* in the first place? I can't tell you. The force of memory I guess.

The loss of intimacy and the loss of historical dimensions that occur through the loss of a common language is sad. If I say something consciously old fashioned like "Four score and seven years ago" every nuance of that goes down the drain. It becomes a literal epithet. Try out "In Xanadu did Kubla Kahn ..." on your foreign spouse and see what kind of reaction you get. Old ditties on TV commercials that do so much to hold the American culture together — the lead song from the 'The Jetsons' on television or screaming "The Shadow Knows" in scary voice — stuff like that just does not exist between us. You learn to simplify your statements and you always have the feeling that your mind is simplifying itself proportionately.

As one dimension of the general language problem, books are always a topic at our house. We have too many. When I clean the bookshelves I know why. We have the big fat NAME OF THE ROSE in German and English. Why? We have both found that reading in bed is not fun in a foreign language. We have twice as many cookbooks and gardening books and bird and flower identification books as anyone else since these are culturally specific. And all the double dictionaries — French-English, French-German, Italian-English, Italian-German, Turkish-English, Turkish-German and the lexicons — WEBSTER'S THIRD COLLEGIATE DICTIONARY, the DUDEN in eight volumes, the TIMES ATLAS OF THE WORLD, the SCHWEIZER SCHULATLAS, Kübler's SPRACHLEHRE and Wilson and Follett's MODERN AMERICAN USAGE. And why do we have all these books? Well, we can't ask each other "How do you spell 'Caribbean'?" It just doesn't work. They spell it differently in the other language. Or, "What is a synonym for 'picaresque'?" Are you kidding? The other one never knows. The simple Sunday pastime of doing the crossword puzzle together becomes a bickering brain-wracking chore more exhausting than climbing the Matterhorn.

At times, the language problem can mushroom into billowing Hiroshimalike clouds. For instance, my sister sent my husband such a nice birthday card last year. "There are still some things older than you are," it said on the front. He opened it and there was a little gray pile labeled "petrified dinosaur turd" inside.

"What does 'petrified' mean?" he asked. "What is a turd?"

I was laughing so hard I couldn't answer. He was frustrated, stonily angry at being shut out of the union of my sister's and my commingled mirthful spirits. By the time I had answered, the joke wasn't funny anymore. This year the card was, "What do they say to the birthday boy in Merry Olde England?" The answer inside was "Happy Birthday (we speak the same language you know)." This got about as many laughs as the turd. Blank-o. Oh well, maybe next year.

Holidays are also odd — the collective humor is different. If I wear my pumpkin socks on Halloween, to him it is a personal quirk. Halloween does not exist, pumpkins are rare, the whole collective level is missing. However, our First of August party, the Swiss equivalent to the American Fourth of July, has become an annual tradition. We have an allotment just outside the city, a contemporary Liberty garden. We get it rigged up with the paper lanterns and the fireworks, the sausages and potato salad that are *de rigueur* here. We try to get as many foreigners to come as we can — last year we had a Russian couple, an Icelandic-German couple, one American, three Germans and four Swiss. It is the only kind of party at which I feel comfortable. If everyone is Swiss, I am uncomfortable and feel like an outsider. If everyone is American, it seems strange and limiting as well.

For example, we were at a party Americans were giving for someone who was graduating from the C.G. Jung Institute in Zurich. My husband was the only Swiss person there. An American woman, wanting to make conversation as they do, asked him, "So how do you feel about being Swiss?" At first I didn't understand why this bothered him but when I imagined myself at a party in Chicago with all Swiss people and being asked, "So how do you feel about being American?" I had to agree it might feel weird. The fairest solution would of course be to move where neither of us is a native and where we have to use a third language. Imagine that though — who would write the letters to the Social Security office, who would figure out the bureaucracy that nobody understands and who would help Junior with his homework?

Once, just once, I had a love affair. With an American of course. I basked in the luxury of reading poetry together, of hearing an old song I knew emanating from the shower. The old ERS was working fine. I knew when he would be touched, get angry, be restless, want to dance and so on. For better or worse nothing else in the relationship worked out. But that part of it was lovely.

"But what is good about being interculturally married?" I asked my husband this morning. We are thrown upon each other without really understanding each other, without our collective selves. Our telephone bills are high and our travel expenses leave our annual budget in shambles. He answered that the relationship is a little perforation in his otherwise grim reality. It creates fresh air and more space. He said that without this type of marriage, he would feel trapped in a static time warp. He actually convinced me that we have the feeling that our world is big and that we are world citizens in it. If we actually do get beyond language and free ourselves from our conventionalities, and sometimes we do, we find a much deeper bond holding us together. As if our very naked selves and souls, free of cultural baggage and foregone conclusions, do really want to meld. ♥

Children

Penny in Samoa

by Mildred Gaugau

"Honey," I called, "Penny is coming to see us. She'll be here next week."

Excitement filled me as I ran from the post office and waved the letter for Tavita to see.

Two years before, I had fulfilled a lifelong dream to come to the South Pacific. Not only did I visit my fantasy, but met, fell in love with, and married my very own native chieftain. We had lived on the island of Upolu, Western Samoa, since our marriage. Now my sixteen-year-old daughter would make her first visit to my island dreamworld.

Tavita smiled as he shared my excitement. "Great, how long will she get to stay?"

I looked into his eyes that always seemed to beam with warmth and affection. How was I so lucky to find this wonderful man, I wondered? Then I answered, "I don't know for sure. Probably quite a while. Six thousand five hundred miles is too far to come for a couple of weeks."

As we prepared for Penny's visit, I received word that one of my best friends and her family would come the week after Penny's arrival.

We had been hard at work building a thirty-two-foot catamaran for tourist excursions around the island. But all efforts ceased as we prepared for our visitors.

We met Penny at the airport, with *ulas* (leis) and excitement. She greeted us with determination. She was determined to hate Samoa and everything about it. There was no electricity, no TV. The waterfall, just outside our *fale* (house) made too much noise and the first night we were awakened by her screams.

"Help, help!" she cried, "I've gone blind!"

"Honey, I'm coming," I called as fear knotted my stomach.

The flashlight guided me to her bed. The mosquito netting billowed ghostlike in the dim light. I could see her sitting inside the net, her fists dug into her eyes, as she continued to scream. Only a few seconds had passed.

"Baby, what's the matter?" I tried to hug her through the filmy material.

"I can't see! she cried. "I can't s - - -"

Her voice died away as she took her hands from her face.

"Sweetheart, are you okay?" I asked.

"Yeah," her voice dropped. "Yeah, I can see. I guess I just didn't realize how dark it is here."

I held her tight and rocked back and forth. "Of course honey, I'm sorry. I forgot that you're not used to our total darkness."

How stupid of me! The thought had not crossed my mind to have some kind of night-light. After all, there were no street-lights, no city lights to reflect into the sky. I now remembered that many times, after the kerosene lamp had been extinguished, I had opened and closed my eyes and experienced no difference. I could understand Penny's feelings when she had awakened from sleep to the horror of absolute darkness — darkness that couldn't be penetrated, no matter how hard you strained your eyes.

"I'll go get one of my sister's little lamps," Tavita said. "We can use it to give Penny some illumination, but not light the entire house as our Coleman does."

"You don't have to," she mumbled, "I'll be all right now."

"No," he said, "we should have some kind of light anyway. My Samoan eyes can see through the dark, but you and Mom are not used to this total blackout."

"Thanks," she muttered.

I felt terrible. I had known that she always had trouble with nighttime. But I had been so wrapped up in my new little world, that I'd not prepared for this situation.

The next morning we were still in darkness. But this was the black mood that followed Penny. The food was gross. The water from the falls was too cold for bathing. The fish in the pool nibbled at her legs while she tried to wash.

"There's nothing to do," she wailed.

"Why don't you help me with the laundry?" I asked. "It's fun down in the river."

"Mom, really!"

Nothing helped. She didn't like Samoa. She didn't like Tavita. I wasn't even sure if she liked me anymore.

Maybe when Beverly, Sonny and Rhonda came, she would lighten her mood. She seemed to be a mixture of excitement and resentment as we completed our preparations for the Taylors' arrival.

The night they arrived, our little *fale* glowed from the kerosene lanterns and the friendship that was shared. We showed them how to crawl inside the mosquito net, without the insects following. We made plans for the weeks to come.

The days sped by as Tavita took our Audi and continued the tour business. I used the van and conducted personal tours for Penny, Beverly and family. We were busy from daylight to dark, either in the van or in the pool or ocean. We hiked up the mountain, went to *fia fias* (luaus). We explored landmarks by day and Samoan nightlife by dark. Even Penny seemed to enjoy herself.

All too soon, however, my friends' time was up and the airport was our next stop. The Taylors boarded a plane that was even smaller than the regular Apia-Pago Pago flight. Tavita, Penny and I waved until the tiny three-seater was long out of sight.

And then . . . magic was the only explanation! Magic had happened! Penny was happy! Right under our noses, a new girl had emerged. She helped with the chores. I no longer had to do her laundry. She scrubbed and bounced her clothes on the rocks in the river just like a true native. Her bathtime was now playtime as she tried, in vain, to catch the 'nibblers'. Pied Piper Penny! Her followers? The village children. They adored the girl with the long blond hair and eyes the color of new leaves. Every shell was brought for her inspection. Even some that were still occupied. They climbed the rocks of the lower falls to an outcropping about half way to the top. After several false starts, Penny jumped with the others into the pool. From then on, she practically lived under the falls.

"Stop there," I called, "I'll take your picture as you climb and then when you jump."

The two of us grew. We were closer than ever before. I didn't know what had brought on this change. I didn't care. Whatever had happened was wonderful. All I wanted to do was enjoy.

But once again, a trip to the airport was in order. Penny had to return to Oklahoma for school. A severed limb would hardly have caused as much pain as did her departure. For days, I reached for her and talked to her before I remembered that she wasn't there.

Tavita and I returned to our tours and work on the boat. Our life was full and busy. The love that we shared made working together a pleasure. I had never known the adoration that I felt for this splendid man. And in return, being cherished the way he did me, was beyond my wildest dreams. But still, I missed

Penny. She missed us too. After only six weeks, even with no electricity, nibbling fish, cold waterfall showers, gross food and all, she decided to return and attend Samoan school.

The night she arrived, I jumped up and down, trying to see her through the darkened windows of immigration. Tavita had already alerted the officials that 'his daughter' would arrive and they must speed her along.

What a difference. This time Penny exuded enthusiasm. She was tired, but her happiness was clear as she expressed her anticipation about her life in paradise.

Right away, through Tavita's influence, we enrolled her in the top rated school on the island. Though there was a waiting list, Tavita's know-how, and Penny's outstanding results on the entrance exam moved her to the head of the list.

One day after class, she came into the *fale* and said, "Mom, I don't understand."

"What don't you understand?" I asked absently as I continued to prepare our supper.

"Why do Samoan girls at school change their minds so often? One day they want to be friends. The next they act like they hardly know me. Then they turn right around and want to be buddies again."

"Sugar, I don't have any idea." I understood her puzzlement. I had been in the same situation in the village. I'd spun the problem around in my mind for two years and still didn't have an answer. "I guess Samoans just have different notions about friendship. The only suggestion that I can make is to be friendly to everyone, but don't depend on their friendliness in return. That way you'll be pleasantly surprised when it comes and won't be hurt when it doesn't."

In addition to her 'buddie' problem, we had sold the van and now had to depend on the village bus. Tavita still had the Audi, but if he wasn't going our way for one of his tours, we had no choice. The *aiga pasi* (bus) was always an adventure.

"Mom, the bus didn't come this far!" Penny shouted as she ran back to the *fale*. "It turned around in front of the Catholic church. What am I going to do?

Buses in Samoa never followed a schedule. The one for our village had filled before it reached the district limits and the driver had simply turned around. He would make his trip into the city, then return for the villagers left behind. I knew that the other area buses would be loaded when they passed and that Penny would never get into town, let alone to school before ten o'clock.

"Just stay home with me today. We'll just have to work out something with Tavita from now on."

Her days at school continued to be good and bad, friendly and objectionable. But our times together were full of excitement. Tavita's *suafa'i* was the MAIN highlight — the ritual of title. His honor came directly from the Head of State. Men and women from every village of Samoa came to the event. My eyes as well as Penny's ached as we tried to focus on everything at once. Speeches from high-talking chiefs; kava served by non-titled tatooed young warriors; ancient fine mats and kava sticks exchanged in the traditional ceremony; all these sights, sounds and tastes almost overwhelmed the two of us.

Tavita in his ceremonial *tapa* (a sarong made of tree bark in traditional style) with an heirloom *ula*, looked the part of his heritage. The title was from the first king of Samoa and Tavita was the first since that monarch to bear the title, *A'e*.

With permission from our new chief, Penny was everywhere with her camera. "Just wait until they see this back home," she whispered with wild excitement. "How many sixteen-year-olds get a chance to see a king's title given?"

After the rite of passage, Tavita's position thrust us upward in island society. "Ladies," he called as he returned from a trip to Apia, "we have an invitation from the Head of State. We've been asked to help entertain visiting dignitaries."

"Me too?" asked Penny.

"You too," said Tavita. "Of course you too."

While I contemplated rubbing shoulders with Heads of State, Prime Ministers, even Kings, I thought about how life on the island was diametrically opposed to the ho-hum existence I had led in Oklahoma. I had been divorced from my first husband for three years before I visited Samoa on vacation. I had earned my living from a small florist business and an even smaller farm that my sister operated. After my marriage and subsequent move to the Pacific, I found a peaceful tranquility that I had never known. When I washed clothes in the river with the other village women, I never missed all the 'labor-saving' devices that I had to 'do without'. When I cooked over a wood fire in the cooking *fale*, I sometimes dreamed of the ease of an electric stove, but soon forgot even that when Tavita and I worked together. I found unimportant conflict in the fact that on a social level, we dealt with rich influential leaders of the world but on a daily basis we lived the life of humble villagers.

Penny accepted this strange paradoxical lifestyle with ease. She blossomed in a way that was never possible in Oklahoma. But soon after the Head of State's reception, she made the announcement that I had dreaded.

"Mom, I have to go home." Her head was bowed and her hands twisted around each other. "I don't want to leave, but I worry about Dad, there by himself."

I knew that she not only worried about her dad, but missed him greatly as well as her sister Vikki, who had married the year before. I gathered her into my arms. "I'm going to miss you with a vengeance, but as you've seen, my life is here with Tavita."

"I understand, Mom, I can see how happy you are." She stepped away from my embrace and tried to brush tears from her cheeks without my having seen them. "Watching you and Tavita actually gives me hope for the institution of marriage."

Later when we told Tavita of her plans, he was as saddened as we, but he tried to lighten the situation by announcing, "We'll fly over to Pago Pago to see you off."

All our spirits brightened, thinking of making Penny's departure a little easier.

But no matter how hard we tried, grief still tore at my heart as we watched her board the giant DC10. When we returned to Western Samoa, a pall spread over me. I had never felt the pain of separation from my children so poignantly as at this time. Even when we left the States, after our marriage, loneliness hadn't hit me so hard. Had I really made the right decision? Was this man I loved with my life worth the terrible ache that I now felt. Could I live the rest of my life separated from my beloved family?

That was almost ten years ago, and yes, Tavita is worth whatever so-called sacrifices I've made. But I haven't had to be separated from my family. We live in Oklahoma now as we have at different times in these ten years. We enjoy both homes. Wherever we are, we work toward the goal of development of the land in Samoa. As we dream and project about the future, Penny continues to be an integral part of our lives and plans. She has made many trips to the island and always looks forward to being PENNY IN SAMOA once again. ♥

Chop Suey

by Ivy Humphreys

"Have you thought about the children being mixed?!" asked my prospective mother-in-law, desperate for some persuasion against our 'foolishness.'

I had every sympathy for my mother-in-law. I understood her alarm at the prospect of her fine Welsh son colouring his progeny. But with all respect for her point of view, I had to express my own opinion on the issue: "I envy my children," I said, "for the very reason they will be mixed."

Her battle was not with me but with her son, who would not be turned from his wish to marry me. I left him to argue with his mother. I did not wish to come between mother and son. I was prepared to leave him and still be friends if our relationship would hurt him and his mother. Besides, I did not want a husband who could not speak up for himself.

Our marriage was a credit to both of them. My husband was positive with his mother, and she set aside her anxieties in magnificent spirit. It was a triumph of her good heart and intellect against her cultural programming. I have never ceased to respect my mother-in-law, and I love her dearly.

We have four children, all girls. After the first two were born, which I thought was an appropriate number, my husband claimed, "Two isn't enough for a family." After three he said, "Three is an odd number." The irony for me is that I had claimed I wanted neither marriage nor children when I first became friends with my prospective husband.

Even my mother-in-law does not find that our children look unnatural. Like all children, they simply look like both parents, in greater or lesser proportion between mother and father. And like all families, we amuse ourselves with our observations of the permutations we have.

My husband is tall, fair and blue-eyed, with long legs and large bones. He comes from Anglesey and imagines he must have Viking forebears! I am a small Chinese from Singapore. My husband is 6' 1" and I am barely 5' tall. Perhaps because our children are all girls, the likelihood was increased that they should have inherited my lack of height rather than their father's stature. All our children are below the British average in height for their age-groups. They were not small babies, with birth-weights ranging from seven and one-half to eight and one-half pounds, but they do not look like they will grow tall. At fifteen my eldest is just 5' though pleased she has already achieved my height and even passed me a little.

I have laughed with friends on this matter of the odd physical match between my husband and myself by saying, "I only married Hugh to give my kids a chance!" Only as chance would have it, not one child looks like she will be as tall. "Just as well they are girls," is what we've said.

It amuses us even more that while they are short of inches in height, the children have big hands and feet — not especially what I married their father for, but nevertheless what they have got from him. Poor kids, to be otherwise small like me but with big hands and feet stuck on! My third daughter at age ten has already achieved my shoe size and her two older sisters are taller than me.

There is no evidence of my husband's blue eyes in any of the children. They all have brown eyes like mine although two of the children show a lightening in the brown of their eyes.

I call my eldest 'Black Beauty' because she is the darkest of the four siblings and the most like me in colouring, in her skin and in her eyes and hair.

My second daughter I call 'Snow-White' because she is the most Caucasian in her skin colouring and eyes, although her hair is as dark as mine. Her skin is pinkly pale but in her other features, a clear Eurasian is seen; there is no denying the oriental input in her.

Number Three is 'My Golden Girl' because she has an overall sun-bronzed look with the lightest coloured hair of the four girls. Her skin is like a tanned Caucasian's although I suppose it is in fact ethnically derived. She is browner than Number Two but is the one of the four children who would most pass for a complete European.

Number Four has me foxed for a name, partly because she never seems to look the same twice. This could be because she is still young and changing. She seems to have a bit of all the others in her — almost like the 'House Special' coming at the end of a menu.

It's like my husband says, "The best laugh from a mixed marriage is never knowing what your children will look like, and being wonderfully surprised each time!" ♥

Mothers Know Best — Or Do They?

by Polly Platt

Growing up in America as the treasure of doting parents who encourage you to develop an open mind, a critical eye and assertive self-confidence is a terrible preparation for a young American woman marrying almost any kind of European.

It was particularly terrible for the two kinds I married, an Austrian and a Yugoslav. And even worse for bringing up European children.

I'm still married to the Yugoslav, after 25 years, by the grace of God. The marriage to the Austrian lasted about ten minutes longer than the time required to produce three children.

There is still the quaint notion making the rounds that children 'help' a marriage. I was told this by the friends of Fritz, a charming Austrian, before we were married. I was to be his second wife and was dubious about the prospects of this marriage. His first wife, also American, seemed awfully nice.

"It will work beautifully," his friends assured me. "First of all, you have newspapers in common. You're a journalist. He's a newspaper publisher. Secondly, he didn't have any children the first time and was much too young anyway. You'll have children and live happily ever after."

Six weeks after we were married Fritz went to Egypt for the paper. I had always longed to go to Egypt. However, I was pregnant. American women do pretty much as they please under any circumstances, including when they're pregnant, short of karate or shotputting. I argued. I stormed. I threatened. I stayed home.

Three weeks later I was rewarded with photos of Fritz on a camel, Fritz in front of Cheops's Pyramid, Fritz on the Nile with the temple of Rameses II towering over him. There were always a lot of people around him, and always the same woman. Very pretty and not pregnant. I was told she was a research assistant.

The next trip for the paper, two months later, was to another place I'd always wanted to visit: India. More photos. Fritz at the Taj Mahal, Fritz riding an elephant, Fritz at the Ganges. The research assistant was always there too, along with a lot of other people. I thought she must be awfully good at her job. I told myself I could volunteer for the job myself after the baby was born. I would have a nurse (this was a long time ago) and Fritz was talking about going to Hong Kong.

Gabriella let it be known that she was ready to start her journey into this world at 6:30 one hot morning in August, two weeks early. My mother hadn't yet arrived from America. Fritz had always bounced out of bed by that hour and was revving up for work. He offered to drop me off at the hospital on the way. As I got out of the car, he told me to be sure to tell the doctor to let him know when the baby had arrived. Five hours later, the doctor told him he had a little girl and in due course he came to see us.

Gabriella was enchanting. The moment I got her home from the hospital I dressed her in a little shirt and diaper, then slipped her into the sweet sleeping-bag-dress my mother had sent me, and lay her, tummy down, in the bassinet. Since it was still terribly hot, I left the window open.

The Austrian nurse, who arrived a little later, was horrified. First she grabbed the baby, yanked off the sleeping-bag and wound a towel around and around her as tightly as possible, explaining that they must be swaddled so that they can't possibly move. This comforts them, she said. They like to be shackled, as in the womb.

Next she put the baby back in the bassinet, on her back. Gabriella screamed, but Nurse was firm. "Babies must always lie on their back," she hissed, "or they drown in their vomit."

Thirdly, she closed the window. I argued. I insisted and shrieked, but I was no match for her. She had been to Austrian nursing school, was about 80 years old (it seemed to me) and had handled all 'her' babies like this. Anyway, everyone in Austria knew that these were the rules. It had always been done like this.

I howled to Fritz that evening that the baby was going to turn into a jelly fish because she'd never have a chance to exercise her muscles. That lying on her back was not only not natural but would give her a hideous flat back of the head, like a Gingerbread Man. And that because of the stuffy room and it being 90 degrees outside, she would no doubt suffocate.

Fritz said the nurse was right, and added, "Lots of people have frozen to death," he said, "but no one has ever stunk to death."

Two weeks later, my mother arrived, threw open the windows and fired the nurse. Thus Gabriella was able to kick her legs, which she did with gusto, and to sleep cozily on her tummy. She was rescued from suffocation and a flat head.

Four months later Fritz said he was going to Hong Kong soon. I said wonderful, I'd go along as his research assistant. He said my German wasn't nearly good enough. I said I'd pay for the trip. He said he'd see. A week later I discovered I was pregnant again.

My mother arrived a month before Sasha was due, to be sure there was no nonsense about swaddling clothes and airless rooms. I told Fritz I thought it would be nice if he could be at the hospital while I was delivering. He agreed, and was there. Sasha was a breech baby. Four hours of grim pushing in the operating room, my mother mopping my brow, and the baby barely budged. The only way I could get any push momentum at all in this frustrating situation was by letting out bloodcurdling screams. Push — scream. Push — scream. Fritz was just outside the operating room door, in the hall. When the third baby, Andrea, arrived, he took care to be in Moscow.

When Sasha was three months old and Gabriella almost two, Fritz and I arrived back from a dinner party and discovered that Gabriella had snubbed the chamber pot and wet her bed.

Fritz was upset. I started cuddling her — she was a deliciously round cuddly tot, like a cherub — but Fritz wanted her punished.

"Why did you wet your bed?" he asked her angrily.

Gabriella was a linguistic genius and spoke both German and English in sentences at one and a half. She'd never heard that voice before. "I don't know," she said, terrified.

"What do you mean, you don't know?" said Fritz, almost shouting now. "What's the matter with you?"

He made a movement as if to spank her. I couldn't bear it and stepped between them. "Don't! She can't help it!" I said.

"She's two years old! She'll be wetting her bed when she goes to school!" he said.

"Not unless you go on at her like that!" I said.

Fritz was now furious at both of us. He put his coat back on and left the house.

I was furious too.

I was often furious at what I considered his medieval formulas for bringing up children, some of them right out of the torture chamber. I was definitely always right, and righteous about it. Now, so many years later, I wonder. I still think I was right about not spanking a child for wetting the bed, but some European mothers would disagree. And it was definitely the fierce old Austrian nurse who had it right, and not me, about swaddling and crib positions. Painful as it is for me to admit it, swaddling is definitely in for newborns, and lying babies on their tummy is out. Doctors are now saying it's a major cause of crib death.

It's curious how cocky we American mothers can be about our deep pools of knowledge in bringing up children. It doesn't disturb us at all that the pools get churned around to flow in the opposite direction about every ten years. Like about breastfeeding. Like about playpens, now considered a dangerous blow to a baby's ego.

The certainty that we are the sole custodians of truth means that we generally have little respect for centuries of tradition in other cultures. We dismiss them as old-fashioned. This is dangerous for intercultural marriages, particularly if we're wrong. Foreign husbands get hurt. If, in addition, we gang up with the children against the husband, another American-mother tendency, the husband understandably runs off.

That Austrian marriage of mine was clearly in trouble for lots of reasons. One of them was that I was married to an Austrian, living in Austria, and expected by everyone, Fritz included, to behave and feel like an Austrian — without the remotest possibility of doing so. Clearly, if I ever married another foreigner, it would have to be on a neutral cloud somewhere.

For his part, Fritz had had enough of Americans, and next time around, he married an Austrian. Evidently a good choice, as they've been married for 22 years . . . and have two sons.

Ande is a Serb who fought with the Royalists and lost against Tito and the Communists after World War II, thanks to Soviet and American aid, and was obliged to live somewhere else. He chose France. When we met, six years after my divorce from Fritz, he was head of an international organization in Vienna. I figured he had to be more cross-cultural than Fritz. He was a widower whose Rumanian wife had died in childbirth a year before with the second of his two sons. They were younger than my girls, and had been living with their Rumanian grandparents in Paris when we moved there.

Lots of people have things to say about their mother-in-law, but has anyone tried a **Rumanian step** mother-in-law?

At the time, moving to Paris didn't seem like such a big deal. I mean, all we were doing was uprooting three German-speaking, half-American girls ages seven, nine and eleven to France, when they didn't speak French, from a house with a garden in a quiet suburb to an apartment in a huge bustling city not known for its cozy friendliness. They would be far from Fritz, who had been a welcoming weekend father. They would be sharing their mother, whom they'd had to themselves for six years, with a macho south Slav step-father — who, dear as he is, would not fail to make his wishes sound strangely like orders — and with little brothers who only spoke French and had already learned that boys are best, younger or not.

Five cultures and no support group of any kind. On the contrary. This was one of the funnier things that happened: Soon after our arrival in France, we had Sunday lunch in a country restaurant outside Paris. I spoke English to Ande and the girls, and French to the boys. The girls spoke German to me, to each other, and to Ande. Ande spoke German to the girls and French to the boys and English to me.

After a while, a Monsieur at the next table leaned over and said, "*Excusez-moi*, Madame, but I have the impression that you are speaking three languages in your family, *oui*? Is this indeed so?"

I nodded.

"As I thought," he said. "I am a doctor, and I feel obliged to tell you that burdening small children with so many languages is **very** bad for them."

What does one conclude twenty years later? Was this intercultural marriage and the subsequent move to Paris hubris — heading too close into the wind, almost capsizing — or was it the mythic adventure described by the great teacher, Joseph Campbell . . . where you set out optimistically and naively for the unknown, are flayed and mangled by dragons and, if you survive at all, come out the other side another person, with another dimension?

There are sidewalks in Paris where I can't go; the tears are still there. But they are mostly my tears. The girls were integrated within a year with their little step brothers, their new father, and their new school, friends and country. They went through the excruciating French school system with distinction.

Today they speak four languages, and Gabriella, the linguist, speaks six. They have no principal language. The girls speak English to me and to each other (they switched from German after six months in France — it's called the Mother Tongue!) and French to Brani and Pierre, and whatever comes to Ande, who speaks seven languages. They love France . . . and America, and Austria and Italy, where we went every summer. They are vigorous, caring, effective members of the community — many different communities. They're at home anywhere. Moving — changing countries — seems normal.

Is this good or bad? Who can answer that? ♥

Adopting New Cultures

by Leslie S. Guggiari

While at graduate school, I once shared a house in Vermont with a married couple. She was American, he Egyptian. They insisted that in an intercultural relationship or marriage, it is important for both partners to agree that they could live in the other one's culture and country FOREVER! I have never forgotten that bit of advice. My Swiss boyfriend and I talked about this a long time. We did not want to drag each other anywhere, causing resentment later. In the end, we both believed that we could live someplace else together, maybe even forever. For us this meant that after getting married we would live in Switzerland.

One other important matter for me to discuss before getting married was children. I knew it was unlikely I could become pregnant. I was pleased that my Swiss boyfriend willingly went along with the idea of adopting children and agreed it was not important for us to have a baby that looked like us. We discussed adopting a baby from another country.

We got married and settled in Switzerland. It took some time for me to adjust to living with a new language, culture and customs and for the locals to get to know me. I wondered how my Swiss in-laws and friends would react to an intercultural and most likely transracial adoption.

We went to the adoption agency for a preliminary interview. Many documents had to be prepared. Only ten days later we were asked to come and see a photo of a six-month-old girl. My husband was ready to say yes immediately. I felt a bit scared and reluctant. I needed to talk to someone about it and regretted not having my own family nearby. That night I was so confused, I cooked a turkey upside down for our dinner guests. My husband was as excited and pleased as if I were pregnant. We had made the decision to have a child and from that day on we knew one would be ours.

Throughout the ten months from our first interview with the adoption agency to the day we arrived home with our sixteen-month-old daughter from

India, I depended upon my husband to make all the arrangements regarding the adoption. I felt overwhelmed with Swiss bureaucracy. There were over one hundred pages of documents to prepare. At least I could help in getting them all translated into English for the Indian government. We received little preparation from the agency. There were other families that had adopted from India that we could talk to but I was disappointed that there were no parent support groups in the area. I also felt the need to understand the Indian culture before traveling there and I found only one person who could tell me more about the region where our daughter was born.

Our documents were completed in two months and sent to India. We could only wait. I used that ten-month waiting period to read books about early childhood development and anything I could find on India. My husband enjoyed watching the diaper-changing scene in the movie THREE MEN AND A BABY and I enjoyed discussing motherhood with American women living in our community who had European partners. With them I could talk about child care and being a mother in a foreign country so far away from my own. My husband and I both felt very strange buying baby-bedroom furniture when there was no sign of a child in our home and, of course, no pregnancy to confirm it.

We had an unforgettable trip to India. There were moments when we worried that maybe it was wrong to take this baby from her home and culture. We decided she should keep her name. Besides the clothes she was wearing, it was all she possessed. Finally, we could bring our daughter home to Switzerland. That once-empty bedroom became full of life. But we also learned that taking sixteen-month-old babies from their only known environment and immersing them into another without even their permission is not easy. She was scared and tense for a few months but has now grown into a cheerful, bicultural, bilingual three-year-old.

As her parents, we too have grown, changed and learned every day. Like parents who come from the same culture, we have had some heated disagreements about how to raise this child. My husband draws on his experience coming from his Latino/Mediterranean culture and I draw on my American baby-boom, 60s and 70s culture. I want my daughter to become an independent, strong, self-motivating individual and woman. My husband concentrates on protecting her, letting her know she is always safe and will never be abandoned again. Most of the time our attitudes are complementing rather than conflicting.

The way we interact with our daughter reflects fully the different ways we were brought up by our parents. We have argued about her pacifiers, her sleeping in our bed, her toilet training, her eating from OUR laps instead of sitting on HER chair. These situations have provoked arguments, tension, silence and even some good laughs. At tense moments, I have felt alone, unheard, and sometimes invisible. At times I feel compelled to defend my points of view on how this child should grow up and determined to raise my daughter my way and not the Swiss way. My husband is usually patient with these outbursts. He is just as determined about his own way of raising children but he has less of a struggle since, living in Switzerland, she will be 'growing up Swiss' anyway.

Introducing a third culture into our family has made us sensitive to each other's individuality. We try to keep our daughter's Indian heritage alive by talking about India and her life before she came to Switzerland. Whenever she asks questions about her adoption, I try to have answers for her. Whether it be about our different skin color or why she wasn't in my tummy, I feel she is entitled to know the whole adoption story. We have many photos and videos from our trips to India and an album called her 'Life Book' with all the letters between us and India before her arrival, her Indian certificate of vaccinations, and messages from our friends and family after her arrival home. We know her life did not start with us.

It is easy to have a birthday party but for us it is also important to recognize the day she came into OUR lives which we celebrate as 'Homecoming Day'. We dress in Indian clothes, eat Indian food, and have an Indian film, video or music to help her learn more about her country of origin. Usually her Godparents and the Director of our adoption agency are invited and other Indians from our community. Her 'Homecoming Day' is part of our calendar like Thanksgiving, the Fourth of July, Swiss Carnival and the First of August celebrations. I have tried to go with her as often as I can to visit my family in the United States so she can get to know the American side of her family too.

We also want to help her establish contact with others from India. She attends adoption conferences with me and has a chance to be with children from all over the world. We get together regularly with the other children living nearby who have come from India. She likes being with these children. I wonder if then she doesn't feel so 'different'.

I speak English to her and my husband speaks his Swiss-Italian dialect to her. I'm glad she can speak English, not only for its usefulness for her future but because I want to be able to share my home culture with her. I knew she would automatically pick up the local dialect from her father and her Swiss grandparents and later learn Italian in school. At first, I did not understand why my husband spoke dialect to her instead of Italian. But as I have slowly begun to learn it myself, through my daughter, I see how much this dialect reflects the Italian-speaking Swiss culture. As adults, trying to learn second and third languages, we are envious that our daughter is growing up bilingual. She has helped us develop our own skills in crossing cultures.

Our daughter has brought us closer and at the same time accentuated our differences. This means she has brought out the best and the worst in us. Like perhaps most adoptive parents, we are at times overly concerned about her and try to make up for lost time with bonding, language, good nutrition, stimulating games and helping her make friends. When communication between us, the parents, breaks down, she suffers as well so we make a greater effort to listen to each other's needs and opinions.

Most of the time we enjoy the fact that our little family has three cultures and four identities under one roof. We have just recently welcomed a fourth member of our family, a two-year-old girl from the same orphanage in southern India. We are all looking forward to sharing our lives together, to trying to live in harmony, with respect and in honesty with each other. Our goal is to accept one another as individuals and profit from the synergy of our heritages. We hope to keep our differences from becoming obstacles. It will be an exciting lifetime job. ♥

Beauty or Beast?

by Marian S. Hong

When my husband and I were married, interracial marriages between Orientals and Caucasians were not as common as they are today. We often got strange looks or sarcastic remarks from people. Things really got interesting as our children came along. I was helping at my children's elementary school for their annual flower sale. Our youngest son, Michael, was four years old and I had taken him with me for the afternoon. Michael played with the other children, but came to me periodically for one reason or another.

An older woman noticed that he was with me and approached me as I was busy helping people select their flowers. She said, "I see you have a new arrival!"

At first I did not understand what she meant, so I asked her to repeat her statement.

She smiled and repeated, "I see you have a new arrival!"

I then understood that she thought my son was a Vietnam orphan. After the Vietnam War, thousands of Asian children were sent to the United States to be adopted by American families. I replied, "He's not a new arrival."

She then asked, "How long have you had him?"

"All his life."

She was rather confused. "I'm surprised, he looks so - so - Oriental."

"He is Oriental."

"How can that be since you aren't Oriental?" she asked looking more bewildered than before.

When I told her that my husband is Chinese, she was quite taken aback. She tried to recover gracefully from this embarrassing situation by stammering that he certainly was a cute child. She quickly walked away from me but turned back a few times to look at Michael and shake her head.

During those few minutes, in her eyes I had changed from a wonderful benevolent mother, who had given a poor war orphan a home, into an immoral, loose woman who would give birth to a 'mixed baby' that she must have felt neither race would accept.

We have laughed about the incident for years and wondered what that woman must have told her friends about her unusual experience at the school flower sale. ♥

My Little Polyglots

by Frances Favre

What is more impressive to the solidly monolingual citizen of an English-speaking country than children who can switch blithely and unselfconsciously from one language to another? We meet them all over Europe as well as in those parts of our own countries where immigrants have settled, and some of us feel ashamed at what we consider our lack of a 'gift' for languages. Is there some particular linguistic kink missing in the Anglophone brain? This changing back and forth among languages seems such an extraordinary feat. In fact, it is nothing of the kind.

When I married my Swiss husband, one thing I was particularly looking forward to was having bilingual children. I have always thought it is a pity not to acquire another language when living where it is offered and I wanted my children to speak both languages fluently, but I wasn't too sure how to go about achieving this. It was not going to be simple. Unfortunately, it is possible in Geneva for an English-speaker to survive happily without ever learning more than the most basic French.

"Everybody in Switzerland speaks English," I was told, but my in-laws spoke only French. With my own family on the other side of the world, it was quite likely that my children would never learn English properly and I was determined to avoid that. After all, to deprive children of the language of one of their parents is to rob them of half their heritage; and this is true of any language, the so-called 'useful' ones (e.g. French, Spanish, Japanese) as well as the not so useful (e.g. dialects such as Welsh). Children have a right to know the culture of both parents; it is part of them and I intended my children to profit from mine.

When my daughter was born, I looked into the question of bilingualism very seriously and was disappointed to find that there were very few helpful books or articles on the subject easily available where I lived. The local parental guidance institution could have advised me had I been Italian or Spanish, but they seemed to believe that English (and German) speakers needed no help. They felt we were capable of managing on our own.

There were a few highly technical books on bilingualism in the public library, but they were short on practical advice for mothers and made the achievement of 'true' bilingualism seem an impossible goal, especially for a small child. One book defined the bilingual child as one who is as proficient in each of two languages as a monolingual child of the same age! To my relief, I discovered in time that this is not the way bilingualism works. In fact, the two languages take turns catching up with one another, with one or the other dominating according to circumstances.

I decided to start off by talking to my baby in English, although this meant that she would hear two languages right from the beginning, as her father spoke French. Although I felt much more natural talking to her in my own language, I was not encouraged to make a long-term project of it by the monolingual people around me. They were full of dire warnings: exposing an infant to two languages at once would retard development in both, there would be confusion in speech, maybe even stammering, and later difficulties at school. Fortunately, I was heartened by other mothers like me, whose children chattered away in French and English with no trouble at all. I asked their advice.

For one thing, I was told that if I wanted my daughter to speak English, she must never hear me speak anything else. One friend said that her son had never known that she could understand French until he started school, which then came as a great surprise to him. Up till then, he had served as her private interpreter, a function that most bilingual children enjoy enormously. I don't know how she managed that; it would be quite impossible for me. I had to speak French with my in-laws, the doctor, my neighbours and the cashier in the supermarket; there was no way for my child to hear me speak only English. Well then, friends said, there should be a 'home' language (English) and an 'outside' language (French), and we should stick to that. The idea is excellent but hard on my husband, who is much more comfortable speaking French. So, what should we do?

What I did was to see that both my daughters heard as much English as possible on every occasion, while their father and Swiss grandparents related to them in French. To my delight and relief, there never seemed to be any confusion in the mind of my first child and she was very chatty from an early age. Of course she had her own special mixture for a while when it came to vocabulary: "Swans *là-bas*!" was one of her earliest comments on our lake. She tended to use whichever word was simplest for everyday communication, saying 'please' and '*merci*' instead of '*s'il vous plaît*' and 'thank you'. On the whole, she was aware of which language she should speak to whom, although for a while she seemed insecure with anyone who spoke only English: French was a sort of linguistic safety net.

So, when she was a baby, I spoke English to her nearly all the time and so did most of my friends and their children. I took her to the English church and to Geneva's American Library where a kind lady read stories every week. I sang nursery rhymes to her, bought her English records and cassettes and read her all the books of my childhood. For a while, English was indeed her mother-tongue, but from the moment she went to school the French language took over. All her little friends learned it too, and they would play in French together while we English-speaking mothers looked on. After a time, the children only used English as a 'secret' language when they didn't want their Swiss schoolmates to understand.

Although I persevered in speaking English to her, my daughter at this time nearly always answered me in French. I could have pretended not to understand or insisted on her using English, but this would have been tedious for me and discouraging for her. Not too happily, I found that I had to re-think my ideas on what exactly someone's 'mother-tongue' is. Is it the language spoken to mother or the language mother speaks? If 'mother' in fact has nothing to do with it, and it is the language most easily spoken, my daughter's mother-tongue definitely became French. I concluded that the language of the school and playground plays an important role in this development.

"Your mother tongue," a Dutch friend once told me, "is the language you count in." Her English and French were impeccable, but when checking accounts or a restaurant bill, she did it in Dutch. American friends whose children were born and educated in Geneva confirmed this. One of their sons, who is now married and working in Washington, D.C., and whose accent betrays no knowledge of another language, does any arithmetic in rapid and fluent French to the surprise of his colleagues. He still speaks French with his brothers and sister, as do the children of nearly all my friends among themselves.

I began to fear that my daughter would lose her early command of English. While my friends could take their children on holidays to England and America to visit relations, my family was in Australia so frequent visits were impossible. Also, whereas Spanish and Italian children could have lessons in their language in the Geneva primary schools, such lessons in English did not exist when I needed them. I was told there were not enough English-speaking children in our neighbourhood to make special classes worthwhile. So I tried teaching her myself. But I am not qualified and I found, besides, that lessons with Mummy were not taken very seriously.

Finally, with the help of friends and the church bulletin board, I found an excellent private teacher who taught in English just about the same things that my daughter was learning in school in French. These lessons were a great success and enabled my daughter to speak, read and write English as if to the manner born. She spoke, however, with the rather upper-class clipped accent of her teacher. This didn't bother me. But the son of a friend of mine, who also had been to a private teacher, came in for a good deal of teasing when he was eventually sent to school in England. Having spoken English only with adults, his accent and vocabulary were very different from that of his peers, and he had no knowledge of their slang. He soon learned, naturally enough!

Having progressed so far with my daughter, I found that trips to England and later to Australia presented no problems. Her initial surprise at hearing English spoken all around her amused me: suddenly English wasn't just the funny language Mummy and her friends spoke. Other people spoke it too! Back in Geneva, I still try to speak consistently with her either in English or French, although I tend to speak in one while she answers in the other. Occasionally we fall into the regrettable habit of talking the mixture 'franglais'. Although warned against this, it doesn't seem to have done her any harm and it is so much easier! Now that she is well into her teens, I am much more relaxed about the whole language business and don't worry that our family often mixes the two. My daughter certainly knows the difference now. At least we communicate!

Cheered by my apparent success in helping one child to become bilingual, I faced the prospect of doing the same for my second with optimism, only to discover, as happens in all areas of child-rearing, that what works with one is no good with the other. It is probably more a question of temperament than brain; my younger daughter is in no way less bright than her sister but she started to speak later (in both languages, but with French dominating). She had such trouble with reading and writing at school that extra English lessons were not practicable. Now, therefore, her skills in English are mainly in speaking and listening. Strangely enough, when it came to learning German in the course of their school careers, my younger daughter found it much easier than her more bilingual sister.

What is bilingualism, anyway? Much more is being written about it these days and there are many definitions, some more realistic than others. In my opinion, it is more than being able to speak two languages 'like a native'. It is the ability to deal efficiently with a variety of situations and to communicate with other people, in speech or writing, fluently and without mental translation. It is a matter of being able to cope with life equally well in either of two languages. This, fortunately, is not difficult to achieve, nor is it uncommon. It doesn't depend on intelligence, either, or on having a 'gift for languages'; millions of people, of all races and levels of education, are bilingual.

The possession of more than one language is always an advantage. A child can acquire two, and sometimes even three or more, quite easily. Much depends on the family's linguistic situation. The languages learned by the child must be those spoken or at least understood by both parents. Two seems to be the most practical number at first. I know a child who stopped talking altogether when a third language was introduced.

Were anyone to ask me now how to help a child become bilingual, I could only advise them from my own experience. What worked for me in Geneva would probably work in any other country. Constant exposure to the 'foreign' parent's language and culture helps the child to pick it up with great ease. Look for new books on this subject, books aimed at families rather than theorists, full of good practical advice, examples and case histories. These are not only very entertaining to read but can be an invaluable aid to parents who, like me, wish to bring up their children in a many-tongued world. ♥

Cultivating Clarissa

by Angela Conti Mølgaard

After a wild night with my lover, I reached over to run my fingers through his hair. But the hair was too soft and too long. As I opened one eye, I saw that it was blonde, not brown.

It was Clarissa, asleep between us. How could he let her do this? Maybe it was another nightmare or maybe she heard our love-making and decided to break it up.

It was six on a Sunday morning and Clarissa was parked under our sheets. There would be no lingering in bed reading the papers. I went off to the john and when I got back they were cuddling and giggling.

It sounded intimate, even though I didn't understand a word they were saying. He was holding her in his arms. It was like watching him hold his ex-wife, since Clarissa is the spitting image of her mother. He was speaking in a loving voice and nuzzling her. I felt sick. I tried to think rationally. He's known her longer than he's known me. The kid needs this. She is in a new country, a new house, a new school and trying to deal with me. She must be traumatized, suffering separation anxiety, culture shock, the works.

My analyst reckons I'm jealous because my own father was a rat bag and never treated me like this so now I want to deprive Clarissa. On the street, this ten-year-old wants to be carried in his arms. In restaurants, she must sit on his lap. She complains if we speak in English because she doesn't understand. When they converse in their language, it's me who doesn't understand. When he is feeling amorous in public, he is forced to slip me love messages written on bits of paper so Clarissa doesn't see. All I wanted to do was pack my bags and leave. It was the tenth time that month.

I must be in love. In fact, it must be the greatest love I have ever known since I decided to put up with this rubbish. Why else would I try to deal with a no-win situation with a hostile ten-year-old I can't even communicate with.

I eventually married this man whose name I couldn't pronounce even after six months of Danish lessons. Aage Birger Bjerregaard — it was a mouthful and I never got it right, so I just use "hon" or "honey". His first name sounded like

'Ova' like in ovum, which I hoped was symbolic since I was trying to get pregnant (to knock Clarissa off her pedestal). The closest I got to his middle name was something like 'brewer' as in Brewer's Yeast, and his last name was impossible. So Ovum Brewer's Yeast Bearguard, I take thee in sickness and in health, for breakfast, lunch and dinner, and to look after your brat.

Our first meeting was memorable, Aage was our interpreter. Clarissa said she had déjà vu. She had a dream six months before we met about me and my car. But the strangest thing was that she described my old car. She had no way of knowing what make or color my old car was. Was she psychic?

As an encore to our first meeting she dumped a bowl of spaghetti in my lap. I laughed it off. When it was obvious I was a permanent fixture in Daddy's life, she didn't look or speak to me for several months.

Aage proposed one night in the heat of passion and a little girl came screaming into our bedroom almost on cue. That's when I knew that in loving this man, I had to cultivate Clarissa.

I started by taking her shopping, to the cinema, the zoo and to McDonalds. I bought her clothes, shoes, cookies, her favorite grape juice. I knew her English had improved dramatically when we passed a toy store one day and she announced "You're a big business woman, buy me toys!"

But Clarissa wasn't happy, a day didn't go by without floods of tears. I read stories to her, sang her songs, made her pizza dinners, washed her little clothes, played Yatzee, watched cartoons, bandaged her wounds . . . and still she pined away for the company of her father. No matter how much I did, I heard the same song every night, "When is Aage coming home?" My presence wasn't good enough. I didn't rate. I was a maid, nanny, nurse, cook and laundress . . . everything but a kind of a mother.

As much as I loved Aage, I must say he had failed miserably as a single parent. Bringing Clarissa almost two thousand miles away from her mother and siblings did not help. We rarely agreed on her upbringing as Danes have a peculiar hands-off approach to parenting. Since Aage was a workaholic, Clarissa was basically subjected to my ethnic type 'mothering', replete with outbursts, guilt, hugs, kisses and lots of food. As I cultivated Clarissa, I learned to love her a lot.

One day two years later, I took Clarissa water skiing. This wiry young body of hers managed to get her balance only on the second try. When they fished her out of the water at the end of the lesson, she was shivering. She threw her arms around me for the very first time and said, "It's cold."

It felt good. ♥

Samir Between Two Worlds

by Marlies Knoke

The marriage lasted seven years — then it just didn't work anymore.

At 29, I separated from my husband whom I had met when I was 18. I not only left, I took our son with me. He was half a year old and a very much wanted child. Much wanted especially by my husband — who experienced this aspect of our separation as a shock. I was aware of that, but I felt I had no choice. I did not separate from my husband in spite of our child but precisely because of our child. He should not have to grow up in such a tense atmosphere as existed between us. And don't ask me why I had a child in this tense atmosphere. I tried to ignore the problems.

Well, that was the situation for us in Germany. Our baby was half a year old. I am German and his father, a Pakistani, felt he had been robbed of his life's happiness. I felt guilty as that's not what I had intended. I simply did not want to be with him anymore. Take his child away? No, I didn't want to do that. On the other hand, I was confident that our son would be better off with me.

The first few years after our divorce were difficult. My husband used all the tricks he could find to get me to change my mind. He begged. He threatened. He appealed to my conscience, to my sense of responsibility, accused me of being a racist and a bad mother who forced her child to be without a father . . . there was almost nothing he didn't try. He even threatened to take our child to Pakistan and he did this intentionally, as a punishment to me. "You took him away from me and now I'm going to take him away from you. You made me cry — now you'll have to cry." That was one aspect.

The other aspect was that from the beginning he had always been good at taking care of his little boy. He came to take care of him and play with him as often as he could, even when Samir was still a baby. For a long time I was suspicious that he mainly wanted to use these occasions to confront me. But even when I went away and left him alone with Samir, that didn't stop him from coming frequently for visits or to take Samir for walks.

I tried to suppress my fear that he might carry out his threats and take Samir away. I told myself that the more intensive his love and his relationship to our child, the less would be the danger that he would actually do something that could cause the little one pain. I refused to restrict his rights to be with our child as some friends and counsellors had advised when I confided my fears to them. On the contrary, I was of the opinion he should be with his child whenever he wanted to and as long as it was possible for him to organize it. As the little one grew, his wishes became of equal importance. Samir should see his father as often and as long as he wanted to, whenever it could be arranged.

It has worked out. Samir is now eight years old and goes to school. He spends almost every weekend with his father. Sometimes he is also with him during the week. Their relationship is a good one. What the little one likes about the big one is, for example, his way of cooking. Samir loves Pakistani food.

He does not speak or understand the Pakistani language. His father never dared to speak Urdu to him because he was afraid he would appear strange to his own child. Samir would have liked to learn his language. When he was in nursery school, he used the few Urdu words he knew instead of German words. Other parents whose children were there told me amusingly about how their children thought using these words was fun and imitated Samir. He would have liked to learn this melodic language, and he would still like to now.

Today my ex-husband is more active as a Muslim than he was during our marriage. He is engaged in a group that wants their own mosque and he celebrates their festivities, refrains from eating pork and prays from time to time. He also insists that his son should not eat pork and we try to respect this at our home too. Samir is not so interested in praying and apparently his father does not really instruct him in religious matters.

His father asked me to do this, but I cannot for two reasons. First of all, I have had a Christian upbringing and only know about Islam from a theoretical standpoint. Secondly, I am not a religious person and accept religions as only a kind of moral framework in helping to get along with others. I respect the fact that others may be of another opinion about this point and I have nothing against Samir's father passing his religion on to his son. However . . . see above.

In spite of this, the topic of religion once became a heated issue when Samir wanted to attend Protestant religion classes and I signed him up for them after having had a long discussion with the teacher. I had not asked Samir's father about this in advance nor had I informed him about it. Besides, I had the custody of our child and all the consequences. I had to organize and take care of his daily needs and manage financially. His father's child-support payments did not always come promptly nor to the full extent required. (I did not want to take him to court for this money because of the danger that this would have negative effects on the relationship between father and son.) His father is not available to take care of him full-time. Their contact is based on their spur-of-the-moment needs and is for me unpredictable. I can, however, accept this.

Up to now, I have been the one who is responsible for all the questions that occur regarding Samir's upbringing and daily care, and I have coped without having to ask Samir's father how to do things. This is why also at first I did not think too much about the question of religion classes particularly since in discussions with the teacher I became convinced that it would involve less the transfer of religion itself than in learning how to behave considerately towards others and practicing this behavior in groups for which there is usually not so much time in 'normal' school classes.

But in this case, Samir's father considered his son's being registered for this non-compulsory class as an open insult to him as a Muslim. He insisted that his son was a Muslim and what I was doing amounted to an indoctrination that was racist and irresponsible. It turned out that his father was also not doing very much to handle the question of Samir's religious upbringing. He claimed it was my responsibility as mother.

I am active on a parents' committee at Samir's school, and even before this confrontation I had taken a stand to re-evaluate the religion classes in Frankfurt's schools and to include children belonging to other religions. This meant putting more emphasis on the aspects of 'group dynamics', 'ethics', 'information about various religions, their histories and relevance today', etc. This would provide classes focused more on the children's exchange of information and their learning from each other than was the case in their regular 'learning' classes. These efforts of mine and a longer discussion about what would be taught in the classes Samir attended helped to iron out the conflict for the time being.

Another point where something like a bi-cultural upbringing has occurred for Samir, in spite of the fact that his father and I live apart, is that his father has intensive contact with Pakistani and Pakistani-German families. For a number of reasons, this would not have been possible if Samir were only with me. Through his father, Samir knows many children from such families, plays a lot with them and learns about their daily life in their families. In the summer, the fathers often take the children along to cricket games (Pakistani's national sport which is as important there as soccer is here in Germany). Fathers play while the children make their first attempts at batting at the side of the field.

In reality, Samir lives between two cultures: here in the rather chaotic household of his mother in a commune where he has for eight years felt comfortable spending his daily life, and there in the more structured, very orderly world of his Pakistani father where he integrates whenever he is there. I have the impression that this has made him very flexible, tolerant, curious and interested. I am looking forward to learning what life brings for him. In any case, I will continue to do what I can to help him retain his access to his father's family on the other side of the globe. Who knows, maybe someday he will need them. ♥

Food

Goulash

by Germaine W. Shames

My lover infuriates me. In many ways, too many to count. He stays up half the night, he hugs other women, his pate is greasy with hair tonic, he smothers his food in hot paprika, his political tirades border on fascism, he looses his emotions like a whirlwind over the smallest things . . .

Even before he senses my anger, he has his excuse ready. Always the same, arrogant excuse: "But, my dear, I'm **Hungarian!**"

And so he is. Though he left his country nearly thirty-five years ago in the wake of a failed revolution, though the United States has been his home for nearly two-thirds of his life, he is thoroughly and irrevocably Hungarian, and seems only to grow more so with each day spent distant from his homeland.

I am an American of sorts. And while I acknowledge that my national identity influences my behavior, romantic and otherwise, never would it occur to me to use it as an excuse to dismiss my idiosyncracies. "But, my dear, I'm **American!**" — so what? I reserve my passion for art, causes and lovers.

But my lover — let's call him Janos — feels passionately about being Hungarian. Like his reduced, dispersed little country, he has known multiple losses — property, friends, family. And, like Hungary, he has survived through a combination of astuteness, obstinacy and the unique ability to laugh and cry at the same time. All qualities I find infuriating.

Our romance is very much a goulash, full of zing yet hard to digest.

Janos lives at an emotional pitch that gives me chronic gooseflesh. He pulls me from bed at midnight to waltz with him through the over-decorated rooms of his apartment, impossibly cluttered with memorabilia from Budapest. He cries over album after album of decomposed family photographs then bursts into song. If I suggest we go to sleep, he snaps, "But, my dear, I'm **Hungarian!**"

Janos has the Magyar's eyes, slightly slanted with the capacity to shoot sparks. His high, taut cheekbones and pointed chin give him a look at once impish and imperious. His gaze can penetrate cell walls and secrets, laying bare my very soul. "Don't look at me like that," I plead, pulling back, already braced for his reply.

"But, my dear, I'm **Hungarian!**"

Whatever Janos may see in me, whatever fireworks my id might stir in him, the expressway to his heart is off-limits, blocked by a gastro-emotional freak of culture. I'll explain.

Janos has had many lovers but only one wife, Eva — a Hungarian, naturally. His choice of a mate was at once sentimental and culinary; no one but a good Hungarian wench can produce a true Hungarian goulash, he is convinced, as if his precious Eva carried the recipe in her bloodlines.

His craving for the stuff is epic, utterly. For no apparent reason he will suddenly recall a goulash he ate forty years ago in a Buda bistro, and, transported, his mouth will water, his eyes fill with tears. This hunger of his bypasses the stomach, it is in his genes, his history, in his very essence.

Well-intentioned if naive, I once tried my hand at a generic recipe — meat, potatoes, onions, carrots, paprika . . . nothing fancy. But there was a lesson for me in that hot pot, I knew, as I watched the ingredients sputter and fight each other, then gradually submit, and finally fuse in one pungent, viscous aggregate.

With what tender solicitation I placed a bowlful before my Magyar. I remember how he sniffed the crockery before inserting a fork into the steaming concoction. His nostrils flared, his lips curled — I took these to be good signs — and he ingested a big, hearty mouthful that sent streams of gravy down his chin. For a moment his face looked as placid as a nursing baby's. Then his nose puckered. The verdict was not good.

"Timid," he pronounced it, lacking that peppery '*je ne sais quoi*' only Eva and her tribe know how to give it. My creation was mere stew; it could not evoke a single sunset over Lake Balaton, nor the refrain of a half-forgotten rhapsody, nor the aroma of his mother's kitchen.

"You're impossible to please," I sobbed, defeated, clearing away the dishes while he poured himself a water glass full of Tokay.

His words of consolation? "But my dear, I'm **Hungarian**!"

There is no rebuttal. After six months of stewing over his habits and quirks, customs and manias, I have ceased to look for one.

Instead, I tell myself that like any good goulash, in time, our various ingredients will mingle, our flavors and spices coalesce. Janos will mellow, I will take on piquancy. What an exquisite meal love's alchemy will make of our differences!

But the process is slow and fraught with annoyances. Janos is determined to recover Transylvania, he still dresses like a refugee, his breath smells perpetually of onions, he uses too much aftershave lotion, his jealousy follows me like a spy . . . And there's no use complaining. No. He has his retort ready: "**But, my dear, I'm Hungarian!**" ♥

Ode to the Potato

by Susan Tiberghien

My French husband and I do not perceive the potato the same way. After some twenty-five years of marriage, when we visited the Krüller-Müller Museum in Holland and looked at van Gogh's "The Potato Eaters," I realized that the potato was proof of our different cultures. Pierre stared at the dark painting as intensely as if he were looking at the Last Supper. I skipped over it, thinking how strange such a solemn gathering around a platter of potatoes.

Coming from two cultures and two sides of the ocean, we have patiently tried to bridge our differences. And sometimes the smallest things, like the potato, have remained the peskiest. When I grew up in my family of four in New York, we ate at the most twenty potatoes a week. When Pierre grew up in his family of twelve in northern France, he told me they ate three hundred and twenty each week!

During the first years of our marriage, I found this fancy for the potato simple and quaint. I would cheerfully peel four or five potatoes every day. Boiled, scalloped, mashed, or browned, I complied. I could never find ones which baked properly. When we moved to Brussels, I even learned to French fry them like my Belgian neighbors did. But by the time we moved to Italy with three young children, I was beginning to feel the fatigue of peeling up to twenty potatoes every day. I suggested that when in Italy we should do as the Italians do and eat pasta instead.

Then our fourth child was born. For Mother's Day, Pierre handed me a large and heavy gift-wrapped box. He was elated. I unwrapped it. It was an electric potato peeler! Pierre remembered how easy it was at his mother's where an imposing potato peeler was permanently installed below the kitchen sink. At first I had thought it was a garbage disposal and from time to time I stuck orange peels down it. My mother-in-law finally told me it was not a garbage pail but a potato peeler.

Her machine could take a dozen potatoes at a time, and in three minutes it supposedly peeled them. It would spin, the potatoes would swirl against the abrasive sides, water would wash off the dirty peels, and when it stopped and the trap door opened at the bottom, out tumbled twelve spotted potatoes. Each one would then have to be cleaned by hand, with a paring knife to get rid of the spots and the eyes. And if ever his mother forgot and the three minutes lasted too long, the potatoes disappeared, all peeled and washed away, even the spots and the eyes.

In Italy, Pierre had found a smaller version for me. It did not attach below the kitchen sink, but stood on the counter or the kitchen table. It could take up to six potatoes and just enough water to cover them. Then when it was turned on, the machine would start to jump and skip and dance around the kitchen, spouting water everywhere. After three minutes, the potatoes still looked the same, but not the floor.

I thanked Pierre and used it faithfully. I told myself that it was the intention which counted. But when we moved to America for one year, with still another child, I hinted that there might not be room for the potato peeler. In fact I finally left it with my Italian neighbor as a souvenir of her American and French neighbors.

Once in the States, I put my foot down. No more potatoes for a year. I told Pierre that we didn't grow them, that they were too expensive, that I had no place to store them. And every now and then, when he kept asking for a pot au feu, with chunks of beef, onions, carrots, and lots of potatoes, I would buy little white peeled ones in tin cans. They were rubbery and tasteless. But I was the one shopping and staying at home and taking care of the five children, and I said no to potatoes.

Then we moved to Switzerland, having decided that we managed our biculturalism better in a neutral country. For one year Pierre had been blaming me for everything he didn't appreciate in the States, like not having fresh potatoes. And I remembered doing the same thing each summer vacation at his parents' home in the French Alps, once the local color, including the electric potato peeler, had worn off.

Now in neutral Switzerland, I discovered frozen French fries. It was so simple to fix them that we went back to eating potatoes, but only French fried potatoes. They were already peeled and cut. All I had to do was put them in hot oil for a couple of minutes before serving. The children loved them. Pierre, however, said they didn't have the same taste as the ones he remembered, the unfrozen ones, the ones I made once upon a time in Belgium. I took it in my stride. After all he wasn't cooking for a family of seven, soon to be eight.

And so our sixth child arrived. For Mother's Day, Pierre gave me another special gift. It wasn't as large as the last special Mother's Day gift and it seemed to weigh nothing. I couldn't guess. It was probably wrapped up in pretty pink paper with a pink ribbon. I don't remember. I only remember the contents, a box of instant mashed potatoes. After fifteen years of marriage and six children, my husband was giving me a box of potato flakes for Mother's Day! I wanted to throw the whole thing at him, the flakes and the box and the paper. But the children were all watching and eagerly waiting to taste their mother's mashed potatoes.

Soon afterwards, as I was alternating frozen French fries and instant mashed potatoes, our oldest son Peter introduced us to his first girl friend. She was French and went to the same high school as our children. Her father was a farmer, a potato farmer. He harvested six hundred tons of potatoes each year.

We met her parents and all of us became friends. They had six children as we did. Our younger children played together and their favorite playing place was the potato hanger at the farm where at the end of each summer the six hundred tons of potatoes were stored. There were mountains of them. The children would climb them, like bumpy brown haystacks, and then slide down.

Often we would go for dinner at their farm. In the middle of the table there would always be a platter of potatoes. Pierre would let himself be coaxed into refilling his plate innumerable times. Our friends wouldn't believe him when he said he didn't often eat fresh potatoes at home.

Together they'd talk potatoes all evening. Our farmer cultivated four different varieties but there were many more. Pierre learned to recognize each of the four by taste. I never had enough of an appetite. And when we went home, we'd invariably be given a ten kilo bag of Pierre's favorite variety that evening.

Now, some ten years later, I can smile about the whole story — the electric potato peeler, the box of instant flakes, the farmer and his six hundred tons of potatoes each summer. Pierre and I are again almost alone in the house. Only our sixth is still at home.

So from time to time I've gone back to cooking a few normal — unfrozen and unpowdered — potatoes for my French husband. Maybe it's because he has finally learned to peel them with me. Or maybe it's because I finally bought a second peeling knife. ♥

Of Bread, Rice and Spice

by Christa Pandey

'The way to a man's heart is through his stomach' is a saying we heard in our childhood. If it were true, the man I married should have run away after the first meal. In my tiny student abode, an attic room with two single-burner campstoves, I had prepared new potatoes, fresh white asparagus and boiled ham, all springtime delicacies in my native Germany. Melted butter, liberally poured over the boiled potatoes and asparagus was the only touch of seasoning. My Indian student friend ate it all with polite comments.

When he invited me to his place for the first meal, I got a whiff of pungency as I climbed up the stairs to the third floor where he lived in a room of a family's apartment. His landlady took a nosy look at the object of his attention and retreated. On a nicely set table stood a feast of fluffy white rice, a golden mix of cauliflower and potatoes, an egg curry and a salty yogurt dish he called *raita*. He had labored all afternoon on his one-burner stove to get this introduction ready for me. But I was as unprepared for the unfamiliar flavors as he must have been for the asparagus. Now it was my turn to eat with gusto and praise the cooking effort.

Much later I found out that my friend had learned to cook out of sheer desperation. As the son of a middle-class family in India, he had no need for the skill, even though he had chatted with his mother in the kitchen and had seen her cook. He had come to Germany to get his Ph.D., but nobody had warned him that the language of the university was not English and that German cuisine was even stranger than the country. As a vegetarian Hindu, he avoided meat. Initially, he often had to point to an item on a menu without knowing what to expect and many meals remained un-eaten for fear they might contain beef. After six months of struggle, which cost him most of his hair, he decided that the cows of Germany were not holy and that he had to acquire a taste for the local food. He also learned how to cook. When he invited me, his skills had progressed to five different dishes, four of which he wanted to share with me. I have to admit that I did not develop an immediate craving for this type of food, but I did like the cook.

* * * * *

Within our limited student quarters we could not cook elaborate meals very often. Our courtship progressed more on an intellectual and spiritual level than through our mutual cooking skills. I learned the Hindi names of some spice mixes, but was lost — so was he — as to their translations. Not that it mattered since their ingredients were alien to me even after I discovered their translations. An occasional meal at an Indian friend's house remained my only exposure to Indian food, since even our big city had no Indian restaurants in the mid-sixties.

My future husband became adept at eating German food and began to develop a liking for some dishes, especially cheese cake and Torten. At one of our visits to my parents' house, my mother served meringues with the afternoon tea. He praised them so much that mother would later buy them whenever she knew he was coming to visit. I discovered much too late that in his eagerness to please, he had overstated his case. In later years he would never eat another meringue. Mother's supply of cashew nuts, on the other hand, was a different matter. She genuinely won his heart with them.

After our graduations and wedding, we moved to the U.S. Gone were the days of student cafeteria food. Instead, I had my own kitchen and was expected to cook every day. I had found an Indian cookbook in an antiquarian bookshop and started experimenting with some of the recipes. My husband, ever the polite gentleman, praised my efforts and gave me a sense of accomplishment.

Soon I felt encouraged to invite a few Indian friends for a dinner of Indian food. With his advice I had selected a menu and labored most of the day, following recipe after recipe to the letter. Last-minute tasting by the expert assured me that I had not strayed from the book. The guests arrived and I proudly set out rice, *dhal* (Indian lentils), several vegetables and a chicken curry. One of the guests surveyed the table full of dishes and remarked: "Is this supposed to be Indian food?" There went my glory.

Obviously, I was not aware of the vast differences in the regional kitchens of India. My South Indian guests were accustomed to seeing *idli* and *sambar* rather than the more North Indian *dhal*, *bath*, *tarkari* on a dinner table. My husband tried to console me, but I did not invite Indian guests for dinner for a long time after that.

* * * * *

After two years of marriage we went to India for the first time to meet my husband's family. So far, I had seen only photographs. He had taught me how to wear a sari and I had succeeded well enough to get married in one. Before the trip he demonstrated for me the correct greeting of not only folding hands as you would greet a stranger or an equal and saying '*namaste*', but greeting the family's elders by bowing down and touching their feet with a '*pranam*'.

Still, I was not prepared for my reception. Streams of relatives arrived to inspect this alien creature. While my husband tried to catch up on eight years of family history with his father and his brothers on the outer verandah of the house, I was left in the inner court with the ladies and the children, none of whom spoke English. They also could not understand my bits of bookish ill-pronounced Hindi. It was my turn to feel culture shock.

During the initial days of our visit, anywhere from 25 to 40 people could be expected at mealtime. The meals were served on the swept verandah floor, where blankets served as seat cushions and eaters were lined up in long rows. *Thalis*, those large round metal plates, were set before each eater and one's hands served as utensils. Since my husband had always used knife and fork rather elegantly, I had never suspected that this might be a recently acquired skill not practiced in his home.

First the men were seated by rank, with my father-in-law presiding at the head of the row and being served first. The next round was served to the children, boys first, then girls, seated by age. Finally the women could eat. As the youngest, I should have sat at the end of the row or even served the meal, but as a first-time visiting daughter-in-law, I was accorded a guest's place near my mother-in-law, who always sat separately, at a right angle to the row of daughters-in-law and female guests, with a pillar of the verandah as back support.

The cook heaped huge amounts of rice on my plate, followed by side dishes of vegetables and pickles. After I watched the others mix bits of vegetables and pickles with some rice between the fingertips of their right hands and lift them in mouthfuls, I followed their example. But sitting cross-legged on the floor without spilling food on my sari required more flexibility than my untrained back and legs tolerated. Much later I learned how to sit sideways and lean my left hand on the floor for balance.

Most of the food was very tasty with the plain white rice counteracting the spiciness of the side dishes. Familiar vegetables like beans, peas and potatoes were disguised in new flavors and made me curious to see how they were cooked. But would I be allowed in the kitchen? After all, I was not a Brahmin

Hindu, only a Christian. In those days the kitchen was a separate open building, which you entered barefoot, as much of the cutting and cooking was done on the floor. I tried to peek in from the outside, being too alien to be invited inside. Through my husband as an interpreter, I could glean some ideas about spices and procedures.

My persistent interest paid off. Towards the end of our month-long stay I was finally allowed to sit in the kitchen and watch. I felt like helping, but I could not operate the tools. Especially the vegetable cutter was a fearful instrument. My mother-in-law operated it with such precision that it frightened me. Squatting in front of it and holding the fixed wooden board with her foot, she would lift the curved blade to an upright position. Then she pressed vegetables, potatoes and onions against the standing blade, cutting them into thin pieces without ever cutting her fingers. When I borrowed my husband's pocket knife to help at least with some cutting and peeling, SHE became so frightened at MY way of using a knife that she almost forbade me to help. On my next trip I carried a real kitchen knife, but she still had the same misgivings about my knife as I had about her *hunsuwa*, as that cutter is called.

* * * * *

During several more trips to my parents-in-law and other parts of India, I have picked up a real taste for their food and improved my American versions of the same dishes. I can even test *chapati* dough for the right consistency and roll out a round *chapati*. But those time-consuming flat or puffed fried Indian breads like *chapatis, rotis* and *puris* are my least favorite dishes of the Indian kitchen. Growing up on *Schwarzbrot, Grahambrot* and similarly solid slices of baked bread has given me a perception of bread that is hard to shake. Even moving to the States has been a cultural shock in this respect. The white squeezable bread which shrinks to negligible size in the toaster has made only guest appearances at our house. Fortunately, during his five years in Germany, my husband developed a taste for German bread.

Over the years our mutual adjustment to each other's food culture has given us an opportunity to create new combinations and flavors that would be unthinkable in either ethnic kitchen. Honoring each other's needs for certain foods while experimenting with others has become an expression of mutual tolerance and love.

We were very comfortable with our mixed kitchen until we invited several nieces and nephews to stay with us (as their *chacha* and *chachi*) and study towards advanced degrees at our local university. Coming straight from India, they needed the comfort of home cooking in their balancing act of adjusting to the new country. Suddenly I had to cook Indian food every day. After doing it for different batches of relatives for several years, I finally learned to cook Indian food like a pro. Even our Indian friends were impressed when we invited them for a big party and served only Indian dishes. Assuming that my nieces had cooked most of the food, someone asked: "Who has cooked all this?" To which my niece replied. "*Chachi*, of course!"

One of the challenges of culturally mixed marriages is the celebration of festivals. Since we have no children and live in a western country, we celebrate the Christian festivals, mainly Easter and Christmas, at home and leave the main Indian festival, Diwali, to the Indian community celebration. As the only Christian, I organize the festivities and select the food. For years we invited Hindu and Muslim friends on Christmas Day, since neither of us had any relatives on the American continent and the holiday felt empty without sharing. To follow American custom and serve a ham was out of the question for religious reasons, so we made turkey our traditional meal. But the fruit-and-nut stuffing my mother used to make did not find a friendly reception among my Indian eaters. Over time we found a well-liked potato-and-onion stuffing. For our vegetarian friends, we served several spicy vegetables and left a bit of stuffing out of the turkey.

As much as they liked cloves, ginger and cardamom in their vegetables, they could not appreciate those spices in our traditional German spice cookies such as *Lebkuchen, Spekulatius* or *Printen*. There too I had to invent some new traditions. Now I bake pecan sandies, coconut macaroons and various nut cookies, not my mother's Christmas fare, but appreciated by my Indian holiday crowd. Only *Dresdener Stollen* remains of my German Christmas. I bake it almost every year, even though some ingredients are hard to find. But then, intercultural cooking is an endless exercise in adaptation and substitution.

Since our Indian nieces and nephews have settled in our area, we are pressed to develop new festival traditions, especially for their children. Following the custom in my parents' home, we have our main family feast and gift-giving on Christmas Eve when we try to serve a simple but delectable meal. We have found a most delicious way of marinating and baking a leg of lamb Indian style and have made it our newest tradition, in spite of the association of lamb with Easter. On Christmas Day we still invite students, post-docs or some lonely person to share the traditional turkey served with rice and Indian style vegetables, cranberry sauce or a cranberry mousse for dessert.

The blend of cultures in our home has enriched the lives of the younger set and has broadened their view of their adopted land. It's broadened ours too. ♥

Language

Words as Bridges, Words as Snares

by John A. Broussard

He wrote to her with pride and satisfaction that he was, 'a one-woman man'. That ended the relationship.

We had already been go-betweens for thousands of men and women seeking spouses outside their own country, so we weren't surprised when this man wrote to us for help. What had gone wrong? He, a respectable American, had been writing to this lovely Filipina for almost six months. They'd exchanged photos. She was interested. They'd even begun to talk of marriage, or at least of a face-to-face visit. Now he was asking us to find out what happened. Why no letter back after five weeks? Why the abrupt breaking off of the relationship that had seemed so promising? "What did I do wrong?"

So we sent her a letter on his behalf. In a few days the reply came and left us more convinced than ever of the pitfalls in communication across cultural barriers — even one like this between a literate American and a woman from a country that prided itself on being the fourth largest English-speaking country in the world.

Yes, it was the phrase 'a one-woman man' that had caused all the trouble, but before we tell you why, a word about how we became involved.

For some ten years my wife and I ran a marriage-oriented pen pal club. At first, our major participants were American men looking for Asian wives. Over the years the business expanded and we received mail from almost every part of the world. Since English was the major form of communication, my wife wrote a book for our clients, one which emphasized the problems that an American would face in trying to communicate with a potential spouse whose first language was something other than English. And, more surprisingly to many of our clients, she pointed out how difficult it would be to communicate with someone familiar with the language, but using it with nuances of meaning slightly different from normal American usage.

We had spotted many problems early on. Any man writing to a foreign woman who labeled himself as 'easygoing' ran the risk of having her think of him as 'lazy', as likely to move all too readily from one job to another. We recommended 'good-natured' as a far less ambiguous substitute.

Disaster loomed for the man who, after a lengthy correspondence and arrangements made for his fiancee to take the long trip from Manila to Milwaukee, wrote impatiently, "I can't wait to see you," and received a cold and terse reply indicating that if he couldn't wait, she wouldn't come.

And woe to the woman who spoke of herself as 'homely'. And more woe to the man who took that to mean that she was plain or ugly, when she in fact was telling him that she was home-loving. And it was difficult for us to decide who suffered most from the confusion over the term, 'broad-minded', used by many Americans and Europeans to invite sexually-oriented correspondence, when in fact the term is used far more commonly in the rest of the world to mean simply the opposite of 'narrow-minded'.

Even where English is clearly the major language of the country, we found some startling misunderstandings. Why were so many New Zealand women reporting to us that they were 'machinists'? We, and I'm sure the American men who made up most of our clients, had visions of grease-covered women working drill presses in grimy machine shops. The answer was simple, but we had to ask one of our 'down-under' correspondents for clarification. There, a sewing machine operator is, quite understandably, a machinist.

But writing helped the potential mates to iron out many of those communication difficulties ahead of time. We urged them to question, to ask — to try and clarify. And for many it worked. For some it didn't. The misunderstandings were sometimes trifling, sometimes insurmountable. There was the Taiwanese woman, with a good mastery of English, who wrote enthusiastically about her love for music, who enjoyed a constant background of 'the classics', and her American engineering bridegroom who put down as a plus this shared enthusiasm for Bach and Beethoven to go along with everything else he so admired about this woman who became his wife. There were other cross-cultural factors that led to the eventual breakup of this marriage, but near the top was the endless playing of 'classical' Bing Crosby and Frank Sinatra songs.

And so we urged the correspondents to iron out all the difficulties ahead of time, to anticipate misunderstandings and resolve them prior to marriage. We knew there would be homesickness, unfulfilled expectations, disputes over food preferences, endless cultural obstacles to be surmounted. And for many, on both sides of the ocean, the letters were not only a pleasure to receive, but fun to write.

For one couple, letters became **the** way of communication. He was from the American Northwest. She was from the Philippines. They wrote for over a year. And the correspondence was extraordinarily satisfying. There were misunderstandings, but the written word resolved the misunderstandings. Finally, a decision was made. She would come to the United States on a fiancee visa. If they hit it off, they would marry. If not, she would go home.

They did hit it off. They survived the wedding bells and the honeymoon with all the success of the average American couple, and they soon after faced the small difficulties, also typical of that average American couple. And one day he went off to work angry. They'd quarrelled. Nothing serious, perhaps, but she'd cried the night before. He'd tried to talk to her but couldn't. Then at noon, the clouds cleared. He'd opened his lunch box, and there was a note from his wife — not a note but a letter, in the same style as the many he'd received during that year of courtship at a distance. What they couldn't handle face-to-face now seemed so easily resolved by these words on paper.

And when the skies darkened again, there were not only letters in the lunch box for him, but notes left for her at home. We passed that solution to the problems of intercultural communication along to our other couples who met and married through our services.

Oh, yes! We did solve that problem for the 'one-woman man'. His correspondent had been horrified at the thought of writing to someone she'd suddenly discovered was a strange and self-admitted hermaphrodite. ♣

Saying No

by Moo-Lan Siew Silver

When I was growing up in Malaysia, I was often told by my parents, who were immigrants from China, that I must be respectful, non-aggressive and non-confrontational. Part of this was learning the art of saying 'no'. A plain, blunt negative or refusal was crude, ill-mannered and left the other party no room to maneuver. It was considered acceptable to make excuses, to smile gently with a slight shake of the head, to demur, or even to say vaguely that you will do something and then do nothing. A person could also plead that a particular course of action was 'not convenient'. No one thought of the excuses as lies since they served the purpose of saving face. These responses worked in Malaysia because we all knew what the real message was.

Apart from making excuses, we could also resort to certain idiosyncrasies in our Malaysian English to soften a negative. Both Chinese and Malay use a final particle 'lah' or 'le' to denote the completion of an action. Incorporated into English, 'lah' took on a life of its own; it was ubiquitous and helped to round out an utterance in a pleasant way. We say: "No, lah!" or "Sorry, lah!" "I don't have any, lah." "Not nice, lah." "Got no time, lah!"

When I went to the U.S. to marry Charles, I brought along with my cultural baggage my inability to say no plainly and directly. I found, to my discomfort and indignation, that people did not accept my excuses. How rude Americans were! How insensitive! Couldn't they tell that I meant 'no' even though I didn't come right out and say it?

Two months after we were married, Charles and I piled our worldly goods into our rusting blue Volkswagen named 'Pigpen' and drove to Ohio where he had a job at a small, liberal arts college. It lay in the middle of flat farming country. The town had one movie theatre which closed in the summer. A treat for the students was being able to get to the next town for thirty-one flavors of ice cream.

One of Charles' colleagues was a woman with two young daughters and a husband busy with his dissertation. Lynn ran classes in consciousness-raising and sensitivity training. She needed a babysitter so she could be liberated and teach other women to be liberated too. I looked like a responsible adult, I could speak English, I was free, I was available! In short, I might do quite nicely as a babysitter. The fact that I did not WANT to babysit for her children mattered not at all. Of course, I never went as far as telling Lynn outright that I would not babysit with them. They were good kids, and I couldn't reject them and hurt everyone's feelings, could I?

"Would you like a job?" Lynn asked, looking intently at me.

"A job?"

"Well, it's not really a job." She gave a little laugh. "More like playing and having fun with my children. Going for walks with them, reading to them, telling them stories. Why, you could even have lunch together!" (We all ate at the same student dining hall.)

"Uh, I don't have much experience with children." (This was not an excuse; it was the truth.)

"Oh, you don't need experience just to play with children and keep them company. They have lots of books and I'll send some along. And they love being read to. It's easy and it's fun, you'll see. How about tomorrow at eleven so you can have lunch with them too?"

I had to think fast. "Charles and I are having lunch at home tomorrow." (Home was our little apartment in the student dormitory. Sometimes, we ate at home instead of in the dining hall.)

"That's fine! I'll bring them at quarter to one then. I have a class at one." She went off, black curls bouncing.

I babysat with them. As Lynn had said, it wasn't hard, but it did not change the fact that I did not want to do it. She came to pick them up about four hours later.

"And did you all have fun?" she inquired.

"Yes, Mummy!" they chorused, "Can Mrs. Silver babysit with us again?"

Mummy looked at me, a smile playing on her sharp little face, took out her check book and wrote me a check for four dollars and twenty-five cents. I was a tax-deductible expense.

Charles was exasperated. "If you didn't want to babysit with them, you should have said so! Why do you have such trouble saying no?"

"I can't do it. It makes me feel bad to say no."

"So you're going to do whatever she wants and feel sorry for yourself afterwards?"

"But I DID say I had no experience with children. Isn't that enough? I thought she would understand what I meant."

He snorted and went back to his book. I do not know what Charles said to Lynn or if he said anything at all, but she never asked me to babysit again.

Some years later, Charles had a new job and we moved to Indonesia. I was back in Asia and thought life would be easier because the Indonesians and I would have some cultural traits in common and we would understand the nuances of one another's speech.

It was a common practice for household help to borrow money from their employers. The American Women's Club had recommended that loans not exceed two weeks' salary because the deductions from their pay, continuing over a long time, would be demoralizing to the borrowers.

We had a nightguard who doubled as a gardener. Kunteng didn't do much guarding. After socializing with other guards at night, he would lock the garage, set out his reclining rattan chair inside and go to sleep, secure in the knowledge that no intruder could get at him. A month after coming to work for us, Kunteng asked for a loan so he could pay two years' rent on his house.

"Here in Indonesia, we have to pay our rent in advance. Where can I find the money?" He sighed.

Charles and I talked it over. I was not really a stranger in a new land. I was in Asia, a more familiar territory, so I should be able to deal with a simple request for a loan. But a new element had entered my life to complicate it — middle-class guilt.

"It's not as if we absolutely cannot afford to lend Kunteng the money," I reasoned, "but two years' rent . . . well . . ."

We ended up lending Kunteng half the amount he had asked for and congratulated ourselves on our negotiating skills. We happened to mention the matter to Don, our neighbor and an American. He stared at us and guffawed.

"You did WHAT? You should have said no! That amount is enough for TWO years' rent, not one!"

Did we get our money back? Yes and no. The deductions from Kunteng's pay went on for some time, but then he stopped working in the garden. He complained that we did not have the right tools although he bought them himself. It was too wet to work; his head hurt; his stomach hurt; he had to visit his sick brother. I finally fired him.

"But I can't pay you back if you want me to leave!" he protested.

"Never mind the money!"

Kunteng slung his denim jacket over his shoulder and walked to the garden gate, pushing the overgrown bushes out of the way in order to pass through, complaining as he went along that I wasn't giving him a chance to repay the loan.

A foreign family moving into a neighborhood is visited by numerous '*tukangs*', vendors and craftsmen of various sorts who come carrying their wares, tied up in large squares of cloth. You sit out on the front porch, the *tukangs* unwrap their bundles and display their goods. The two parties spend the next hour bargaining, swatting mosquitoes, and the vendors puff away on their clove-flavored cigarettes. It is a leisurely and civilized process.

The *tukangs* soon find out what the family is interested in — ceramics, batiks, batik chops, woven Sumba cloth, wood carvings, brassware, puppets. Some *tukangs* drift away and you are left with a few who become regulars.

Since I was interested in having some things made in wood, I had a special *tukang kayu*. 'Pak was a dignified, middle-aged man. Over the course of a few months, he made me a number of articles, amongst them was a large, mahogany spice rack. Never mind the fact that its appearance was marred by the bright blue hooks that were all that 'Pak could find in the local hardware stores. He also made me a dictionary stand for WEBSTER'S THIRD EDITION. It was beautifully carved and darkened to a deep brown with kiwi shoe polish over which he applied shellac. I thought one of its legs was shorter than the others but maybe the surface we put the stand on was uneven. I decided some carved chopstick rests would be useful and described what I wanted to 'Pak.

He asked to be paid in advance as his wife was ill and, by way of proof, he waved a sheaf of hospital bills in front of me. Since 'Pak had been reliable so far, I decided I would give him the money. A warm glow swept over me as I handed him the rupiah notes. I never got the chopstick rests nor did I see 'Pak again.

If I had trouble saying no, my American friends did not, or at least, not to me. I asked Jackie if she would be willing to make cookies for a school bake sale.

"No."

Just like that! No! Couldn't she at least have said "sorry" or "no, I can't" and offered some explanation? I was taken aback and a little hurt by her answer.

I made the same request of Sue, another friend, who said, "I'll think about it and let you know." Sue took a long time thinking. She was still thinking after the bake sale was over. Well, maybe an unembellished refusal wasn't so bad after all.

After having been away seven years, we returned to the U.S. A woman I had become friends with overseas was back at the same time, and we saw each other occasionally. Hyun often gave me homemade *kim chi*, the hot, garlicky Korean pickles usually made with cabbage. I loved them when they were three to seven days mature. After that, they were too ripe for my taste. The phone rang one morning.

"Hi," came Hyun's cheerful voice, "I have a large jar of very ripe *kim chi*. It's too strong to eat plain so I'm going to put some pork in it and make a stew. It's really good that way. Would you like to come for lunch?"

I thought of the self-imposed exile I would have to go into for the next twenty-four hours while the garlic worked its way out of my pores. My family would be deprived of my company while this process took place. Hyun was waiting for my answer.

"No, thank you. I really can't. I'm busy today."

I had actually said no! That dreaded word had passed my lips! And I had said it without much hesitation either! Was it possible that I was behaving like an American after seventeen years of marriage to one?

Charles would be so proud of me. ♥

The Tangled Lines of Communication

by Christine Miyaguchi

If you are like most husbands and wives, you probably, on occasion, find yourselves engaged in battle with each other. Some battles might be just small border skirmishes, while others could be classified as World War III. Aren't there some days you wish that someone would declare your house a demilitarized zone and send out the ambassadors for the peace talks?

And if you are like most husbands and wives, you know how tangled the lines of communication can get between the two of you. At times it seems as if you are each speaking a different language. But imagine the confusion when you each come from totally different cultures, and you actually are speaking two different languages to each other.

When I met Andy (I still haven't learned to pronounce his given Japanese name correctly), we were working for the same Japanese company in New York. Somehow we were able to communicate to each other that we were in love, and we decided to marry. We received a lot of advice from family and friends on how to have a blissful marriage. One of the last things my married friend Janine told me before Andy and I made the plunge was: "Just remember, Christine, always talk things out. The most important thing in a marriage is to keep the lines of communication open."

I tried to remember her words as we muddled through the first few months of our marriage. But what I soon realized was that we weren't dealing with a typical marriage and its typical rough spots. Our problems were complicated by our very different cultures and languages. The culture part of the problem is easy. He likes the American way of doing things and I like the Japanese way. But when it comes to the language part of the problem, well, that's a whole other story.

Our basic language of communication, if you can call it that, is English, or 'Jinglish' as Andy likes to call it. But somewhere between what comes out of our mouths and goes into each other's ears gets scrambled along the way.

Now when I think back on our dating days, I realize that I should have had some indication of the miscommunications ahead of us. I was never ready on time when Andy would come to my house to pick me up. While I would be getting ready, Andy would sit watching television or talking with my mother. I couldn't help but giggle a bit when my mother told our dog Mandy to go outside in the backyard. Andy jumped up from his chair, headed for the back door, and asked her what he had done wrong. It hasn't gotten much better since we've become man and wife. A typical conversation between us can go like the one that we had last month.

"Andy, do you remember that girl Susan at my office that I've been telling you about? The one that I don't get along with."

"Who's Susan?"

"Andy, I've told you about her a hundred times. The one who is always looking over my shoulder to see what I'm working on and reading everything on my desk when she thinks I'm not looking."

"Oh yeah, now I remember."

"Well, she did it again today. I was sending a fax to one of our local offices. I had to leave it to take a phone call. When I returned after my phone call, guess who was reading the memo? Susan! You know, one day I'm going to tell her just how much she annoys me."

"What did she say when you said that to her?"

"Said what to her?"

"That she annoys you so much."

"I didn't say that to her. I said that I WANTED to say that to her."

"Why?"

"Because of what she did to me."

"When?"

"Today. I already told you."

"But you said that . . ."

"What?" Both of us ended up saying at the same time.

"Andy, just forget it."

As in many of our conversations, by the time we are finished trying to interpret what the other was trying to say, we usually end up forgetting the original topic of conversation.

Thank goodness this only happens with trivial matters. We have all the major decisions agreed upon.

"Andy, how many children would you like to have?" I asked him one day.

"I don't know. I never really thought about it. How many do you want?"

"I guess three sounds like a nice number." I knew that Japanese are superstitious about even numbers.

"That sounds good to me too," he answered.

"Let me get this straight. We both agree that we want three children?" I held up three fingers.

"Yes, three." He held up three fingers of his own.

"Fine. Now we both sign this paper to that effect just so there is no future misunderstanding. Agreed?"

"Agreed," he said as he stamped his *hanko*, the Japanese equivalent to a signature, on the bottom line. I can't understand why the major powers of the world can't come to agreements in this peaceful and civilized way.

Another cause for a misunderstanding occurs when we're having some sort of heated discussion about each other's way of doing things. He says I don't wash the dishes correctly — I use too much soap. I can't understand why he still hasn't found the 'real' closet in our bedroom — he thinks it's the floor. These type of disagreements usually end with him walking into another room. Before he makes his grand exit, though, he will mutter some Japanese word or phrase, leaving me standing there, not knowing how to answer. I am sure this is his exact intention. When I question him about the meaning of this mystery word or phrase, he hesitates to translate it, always telling me there is no direct translation. He's not stupid. He knows how I'll react if he does tell me the true meaning; it usually leads to a bigger fight.

Take, for example, the Japanese word *wagamama*. As soon as he used this word to describe me, I didn't need a translation. I knew we were headed for an enormous fight.

"What does that mean?" I asked.

"I can't translate it. Get your dictionary."

"How can I look it up? I can't even pronounce it?"

I finally found it. Directly translated it means selfishness, caprice.

"See," he said to me. "It's a totally harmless word. It's cute to say to someone."

Sure, I think, maybe to someone who is Japanese it's cute, but you just don't say something like that to an extremely oversensitive American woman like me. He tried without success to convince me that it was a harmless word. It wasn't until weeks later, while I was having lunch with some Japanese women friends, that I found out that Andy was telling me the truth. My friends were using it to describe some of their male acquaintances.

"Do you know what that word means?" one girl asked me.

"Well, I've heard it a few times. Why, what does it mean?" There was no way that I was going to admit that my husband had called me that.

"It's a harmless word. If you're close to a person, it's a cute way of calling them childish." And they all laughed.

"Oh, is that all?" and I laughed along with them. It looked as if I had some apologizing to do when I got home.

I had every intention of apologizing to Andy when I arrived home that day, but the apartment was dark and empty upon my return. That was nothing unusual to me. He was probably working overtime again — just another of the Japanese working habits he brought from Japan. As I started to take off my coat, the phone rang. It was Andy.

"Hi, Andy. Where are you? Still working?" I asked innocently.

"Working? No, I've been waiting for you for over thirty minutes. Where are YOU?"

"The last time I looked I was in our apartment."

"I know that! You said that you wanted to meet me after work tonight at The Corner Cafe for a drink and a bite to eat."

"No, I didn't. I said that if I wasn't so busy at the office, I'd love to leave on time and go out. But I told you that I had to work a little overtime tonight."

"That's not what you said last night."

"Yes, I did, Andy. You just misunderstood me."

"No, that's wrong. You always say that when we have a disagreement. Why can't you just admit that you told me the wrong thing?" The operator interrupted, asking for additional money. "Listen, I'm running out of coins. I'll be home in fifteen minutes."

I could tell from the tone of his voice that when he did get home, he was going to threaten, as he did after all our arguments, to start tape-recording our conversations; that way we could have instant replay like they have in all the sports games.

"Okay, Honey. See you soon," and I hung up the phone. Oh, the joys and misinterpretations of an intercultural marriage! And I wouldn't trade a minute of it! ♥

Words of Love

by Germaine W. Shames

Once I had a lover — let's call him Juan — whose English was, at best, rudimentary. But Juan spoke the 'universal language' like a master. On his silver tongue, even the most garbled expressions took my breath away.

Juan and I met in Mexico, his country of birth, my temporary residence. Land of the *'piropo'* (verbal tributes to feminine charms), of love songs and laments, Mexico was the perfect setting for a storybook romance, and Juan, as I said, was well-suited to the role of Don Juan.

"My love, my heart, my life," he'd croon, looking deep into my eyes with a fiery gaze that made my heart smolder, "I love you with every breath I take, I can't live without you. You are the queen of my existence, and I your slave."

Whether or not I believed Juan, I can't really say. So dazzled was I by his declarations of love, so mesmerized by the burning look that accompanied them, that discernment failed me. Juan made me feel desired, cherished, worshipped. His words entered my bloodstream like an elixir and made my heart cha-cha-cha. In love with Juan's verbiage, I let it work its magic and asked no questions.

"My light, my soul, my treasure," he'd whisper endlessly, growing bolder, drawing me closer, so close I could see the facets in his eyes glow like hot coals, "I love you more than I love myself, more than your own mother loves you, more than — may The Virgin forgive me! — more than God Himself could ever love you. I swear I would die for you."

Fortunately, for most Juans few loves are ever actually put to the test. No doubt, Juan banked on not having to make good on his claims. He was only telling me what I wanted to hear, after all: words of love. But, as fate would have it, circumstances intervened — drastic circumstances — that thrust my very life into his hands. I'll explain.

One weekend Juan took me to a small seaside resort outside Playa Blanca where we intended to spend a few quiet days romancing to the rhythm of the waves. The setting — white-hot sands, placid sea, a caressing breeze — had all the promise of a sultry summer daydream. Shortly after our arrival, however, a nasty storm blew in, and the tide rose like a waterfall in reverse.

For two days Juan and I kept to our sweltering hotel room, glued together by our own perspiration. Whatever the misquitoes spared of me, Juan nibbled at unceasingly, until every pore of my body stung. By day three — the last of our little holiday — raw, dehydrated, half-incinerated, I decided to have a swim, come what may.

Out I ran to the beach with Juan calling after me, "My love, the sea she's mean. Don't go!"

He was right. I was no match for the waves, and they had their way with me. Tossed about like a dummy, sucked down into the drink again and again, I quickly felt my fight give out. I was drowning.

"Help me, Juan!" I screamed. My mouth filled with brine each time I opened it. "Help me! Help! Help . . !"

"Sweem, *Mamacita*, sweem!" Juan cried back.

"Help! I cried desperately, a dozen times, a hundred, though Juan had no doubt heard me the first time.

"Sweem, *por Dios* (for God's sake)! Sweem!" he repeated, matching me yelp for yelp.

The poor man was beside himself, clearly. He ran up and down the beach, weeping, wailing; he tore his hair, waved his arms, fell to his knees . . . and never so much as wet the tips of his toes.

When a wayward wave finally heaved me onto the beach where he waited, dry and safe, I couldn't help but feel sorry for him. Not meaning to, I had exposed him — his words had been so much flotsam.

But Juan showed no sign of embarrassment. To the contrary, his face lit up and he shed tears of joy.

"My goddess, my angel, my adoration . . ." he cooed, riveting me with his searing gaze as he led me away. ♥

At Home in Two Languages

by Susan Tiberghien

When I married a Frenchman and moved to France, I slowly slipped into a French-speaking pattern — thinking, dreaming, and raising children in French. Only when the children grew up and left home did I have the time and space to venture back to an English-speaking pattern.

It took awhile to adjust and make the edges fit, then one day I found myself American once again. Pierre, my husband, appreciates the variable metamorphosis, like having both wife and mistress. And I have the choice, will I live the coming day in French or in English?

If I decide on French, I'll greet my husband with *"Bonjour, mon chéri, as-tu bien dormi?"* There will follow an intimate exchange about whether we slept soundly, if we were too hot or too cold, how many times we woke, and so forth. Our breakfast will be short and precise — coffee, bread and butter. I'll question him about his day, he'll question me, it will all be rather rational, one subject after another, well-constructed, like a dissertation.

And my day will continue as such. In my head I'll make lists of things to do and go about my morning, proceeding methodically, not losing time. I'll avoid odds and ends of conversation with people I meet, especially with people I don't know and obviously never will. At the same time I'll be unfailingly polite, *"Bonjour Madame,"* *"Au revoir Monsieur,"* *"Vous êtes très aimable, Madame,"* *"Je vous remercie, Monsieur,"* be it with my neighbor, the mailman, or the butcher.

Back home, in the afternoon, when working at my desk, I may loosen up and temporarily slide out of this French-speaking pattern. But if the telephone rings, I'll sit up straight, pick up the receiver and reply, *"Allo?"*, without the slightest encouragement to whoever is at the other end of the line.

In the evening, I will relate my day to Pierre and ask about his. During dinner we will talk seriously about something in the news, politics, a concert or movie, a book, about our grown children, our friends, the company we wish to invite soon. If we are planning a large dinner party, he will suggest that I send invitations rather than phone everyone, "It's less familiar." And I will explain that I prefer to call, "It's more personal," even if I sometimes mix up the '*tu*' and '*vous*'.

Still today, we have certain close friends whom we address with the formal '*vous*', as we also address Pierre's parents, aunts, and uncles. Mailman and butcher or close friend and favorite uncle, they all get the same '*vous*'.

Now, however, if I decide to live my day in English, I will greet my French husband with something like, "Good morning, dear, time to get up," pulling off the covers to make sure he's heard me. I'll dress in a purple track suit and go fix orange juice to awaken our appetites for eggs and bacon or pancakes. I'll take my time, talking to Pierre about whatever comes into my mind. He'll try to get up from the table once or twice, but I'll ask him not to rush off, reminding him how I used to enjoy long breakfasts years ago in the States.

And when he's gone, I'll stay right there and reread yesterday's newspaper in English, making myself a second or third cup of coffee, and maybe adding some water. Before doing my work, I'll perhaps call and invite a friend for lunch. When I go shopping, I'll bump into somebody I haven't seen for weeks and stop and chat. By the time I get to the post office, there'll be lots of people waiting in line. I'll smile at whoever looks at me, and then I'll smile and talk with the clerk who's been there for several years. Finally I'll skip the shopping and serve whatever I have in the fridge. My friend won't mind, she's used to my improvised meals.

In the afternoon I'll work at my desk. When the phone rings, I'll lean back in my chair — or take the phone and lie down on my bed — and answer, "Hello, this is Susan." If the weather's good, I'll go for a short walk, down the road opposite our house, near the empty fields which remind me of New England. I'll find a stone and kick it along for company. I'll say hello to the people I meet, they'll look startled and most likely won't answer, but I'll keep trying.

In the evening, I'll tell Pierre about the old acquaintance I met at the shopping center, the clerk in the post office, my friend who came for lunch, the people who telephoned, and then this woman who was walking her dog and who wouldn't look at me, at least the dog did, it even wagged its tail. I'll laugh and make him laugh. He'll tell me about the people he met and we'll ramble on this way. Then I'll start telephoning our guests for Saturday evening and I won't give a hoot about '*tu*' and '*vous*'.

Bilingualism or split personality? Once the two patterns fit, the choice is mine. I wake up and write down my dreams in the language I dreamed them. I read the newspapers in both. I live my day as it comes along. I say either '*tu*' or '*vous*', which ever one I wish. And I make "I love you" sound just as beautiful as "*Je t'aime*." ♥

Coping with

Differences

Touching Experiences

by Vasco Esteves

When I came to Germany for a longer stay in order to study, it took me some time to become aware of a specific phenomenon. During the first months I felt like a happy tourist. Everything was new and exciting: the language, the people, even the snow which I was seeing for the first time in my life. But it seems that I had underestimated just how much this cold climate changes and leaves an impression on people in time. My first six months in Bavaria did not really put me into 'culture shock' — perhaps because the Bavarians, like the Portuguese, are also Catholics. But the next four years in Swabia and the following eighteen years in Hesse finally opened my eyes to a form of 'collective blindness' that is now all around me and cannot be avoided. What do I mean by this?

I gradually began to notice that Germans never looked into my eyes, except when they had to speak to me! I was, and still am, aware of this, particularly in public places. When walking around streets in town, for example, people stroll along as if they were alone in the world! Even in public transport one can sit or stand opposite someone for the entire ride without ever making eye contact! This is not a special discrimination towards me personally, it is also valid for Germans amongst themselves. For me as a Portuguese, this is all rather unusual, if not to say downright spooky. How is it possible that people can ignore each other *permanently* in this way as if they had made bets not to look at each other? Where are the people who turn around when a new person enters a room or when a beautiful woman walks by? I can try again and again to establish eye contact in Germany, but most of the time nothing happens!

At first I thought this was only a 'coincidence'. But unfortunately I soon realized that statistically it would be highly unlikely, for example, that on a Saturday shopping spree in a pedestrian zone, everyone (except the foreigners, of course) always looks only at the empty 'holes' between people! What is more likely, as I also realized from careful observations, is that apparently almost all Germans *intentionally* avoid getting caught in a stranger's glance. Meanwhile, I believe they have developed a skill of disrespectfully (or respectfully?) ignoring other people and concentrating on the essential matters: only looking at the show-windows of shops in the shopping zone, only at the food in the restaurant, only out of the window from streetcars, etc. Today this is called in the industrial working-world 'goal-oriented' behaviour. In retrospect, I have to conclude that it is no wonder that the German economy is so effective.

At first I also had problems with speaking. In Cafés I couldn't really carry on a discussion with my Portuguese friends because it was so quiet all around us — even though the Cafés were actually well frequented by grandmothers. It was like that in the trams too. I always had the feeling I would disturb others (or did *they* disturb me?) if I talked in public places. The explanation was admittedly very simple: it wasn't my talking that was objectionable, but my talking *loudly*.

It is indeed objectionable and impertinent to start talking to someone in public you don't know without an important and urgent reason. To the question "Are you also going to Frankfurt?" you'll probably get a response like "What makes you think I am?" or at best a very matter-of-fact answer like "No, I'm getting out at the next station." It is obviously not understood (or it's not accepted in Germany) that such a general question is only intended as friendly small-talk or as an expression of interest in the person you are speaking to. The answer will always be a rational reference to the subject of the question. And what business is it of mine if other people are "also going to Frankfurt?" I had a lot to learn.

Slowly but surely it became clear to me that we (the Mediterranean types, North Americans and all the extroverted peoples of this world) actually infringe upon German people's *private sphere* and interfere with their individual freedom by speaking too loudly or without justification! Until I discovered this, I had already committed this inexcusable nuisance a thousand times and probably caused irreparable damage! What kind of an impression must all these 'assaulted' and suffering Germans now have of the Portuguese? At any rate, I learned that speaking softly and remaining quiet were not signs of a misunderstanding but that this behavior was an achievement of civilization, at least of central European civilization. In this case, having to conform to these norms was fortunately not as difficult as having to abstain from direct eye-contact as mentioned previously. I had already had some practice in Portugal in behaving cautiously or even conspiratorially in public places because of Fascism and the secret police who were then in power.

But for me there is something is even worse, namely the thing about body contact — which is, of course, related to exchanging eye-contact and speaking. German people hardly ever touch each other. Touching is taboo! When greeting each other here in Germany, at most, one just shakes hands, but there is no kissing of cheeks or anything like that, not even within one's family! I still recall clearly how a German girlfriend of mine considered the cheek-kissing and hugging that took place within my family or when meeting friends as sexual molestation!

While I was studying, I sometimes shared a flat with other students. Body contact was allowed but only when it was 'good weather'. Once during an argument with a flatmate I put my hand on his shoulder and said in a forgiving way, "It's not so bad, we'll solve the problem." How surprised I was when he brushed my hand from his shoulder and unforgivingly answered as he turned away, "You're only trying to *bribe* me with your friendliness!" This meant that the problem had first to be settled objectively (verbally) and only after that would it be allowed for my flatmates to express their feelings! There was a sharp 'separation' between feelings and reason.

How often did I experience myself, or hear from others, how after a quarrel German women say to their partners, "I can't make love with you until we've straightened this out!" A reaction like that is not so much a cover up for blackmail towards the other person as I assumed at first, but an absolute, optimalized and goal-oriented and therefore radical separation of heart and head, separating what is private from what is business.

I remember another example that I experienced shortly after the 'wall' came down in Germany. I had a new colleague from former East-Germany. When he first joined the company he would shake hands with all his colleagues every morning. He told us that was customary where he came from and then excused himself for it because he quickly noticed that this way of greeting was not customary in our part of Germany. After two or three weeks he only shook my hand. He seemed to realize that I (a non-German) was apparently the only one who found shaking hands a good idea! Later he even stopped this with me: he had quickly become integrated into the working world of the western part of Germany.

But what do people in Germany do who, as 'foreigners', need absolutely and urgently this spontaneous and natural body contact because it is a form of communication that allows them to feel appreciation and affection? I often ask myself that question. Should I perhaps join a dance or sport club and keep waiting until the next scheduled event? Coming from the Mediterranean region, I was so spoiled during my childhood with this kind of loving attention by my Mama and by the behavior of my countrymen that I now feel like someone trying to swim without water. But where am I to find water if there is only a dry desert all around me? Since I've had a steady relationship and since I've been married, my wife has to make up all *by herself* for this emotional 'withdrawal' and has to give me double rations of the tenderness required daily. When she is away, I suffer instantly and mercilessly from terrible withdrawal symptoms. And when I think of all the foreign men and women who suffer from the same deficiency as I do but who don't have a partner, then I can actually only express the following advice: stick to the 'ghetto of foreigners' or arrange as soon as possible to have a *bedpartner*. In this country, that is the only acceptable and institutionalized possibility of receiving real physical appreciation! I see no other alternative.

The bad part of it is that if you are a foreign man or foreign woman, it is not so easy to get used to completely new kinds of behavior when feelings are involved. It is certainly also not so easy the other way round: far from regarding frequent body contact as an enrichment of their horizon of experiences, many Germans are more likely to consider it as an unbearable interference, an obtrusiveness, a shamelessness and a threat! Do we Mediterranean types need this physical appreciation from others only because our sense of self-worth is not — as many people believe — exaggeratedly high but exaggeratedly low? Or is this craving for physical contact merely what is generally referred to as being 'macho'? If so, how can the feelings of foreign women who have similar experiences be explained?

Perhaps, however, having less eye-contact, keeping silent and having less physical contact leads to fewer relationships and obligations. After all, relationships established through non-verbal contacts are above all of an emotional nature. But isn't it only through their emotions that people really get to know each other, make new experiences, become acquainted with foreign things, receive motivation and creativity for their work or are eventually able to change themselves? I often wonder if independence of physical contact is a sign of human 'freedom' or of human poverty. Does concentrating one's curiosity about physical contact to only one (or very few) people during one's lifetime represent an effective productivity-inducing 'means of rationalisation' or a sign of 'civilized progress'? Or is it, on the contrary, a restriction imposed on human development?

In any case, I refuse to believe that smiling or speaking to someone you don't know or touching someone is only a bad, sexually-inviting gesture, or that it's treating someone like a sucker or even trying to bribe someone or rob them of their freedom. Therefore, Dear Reader, lady or gentleman, do not be surprised if I start chatting to you directly when we meet by chance during my next train trip. If I don't, then it's because I'm especially tired that day or because I'm being especially considerate towards you. ♥

Christening in a Kimono

by Masako S. Uzawa

I was just tidying up the children's rooms. We still call them 'children' even though they have all married and moved out. In the recess of a commode I came across a baby kimono in a box that had been tucked away all these years. It had been handmade by my mother in Japan. It was the tiny silk white kimono all our babies had worn at their christenings.

My memory seemed to mingle with the moth crystals as I touched fondly the silky white damask lined with a pearly pink that could be seen through its sheer luster. It was amazingly well-preserved, unyellowed, unwrinkled and fresh as I remembered it many years ago. In the room full of reminders of their childhood, and of my motherhood, I felt as if I were turning the pages of my unwritten diary in my mind back to the spring of 1960.

This tiny kimono brings back memories of some incidents that now make me smile, but it was no laughing matter at that time shortly after my first coming to live in Switzerland.

An elderly clergyman visited us to talk about christening our first-born child. I don't know if he visited every newcomer in his church community or just us because I was a foreigner. In the early sixties there were hardly any Japanese living in Basel. I was the Japanese wife of a Swiss and our child was to be baptized. I imagine the pastor was curious and concerned about me as a stranger in town. He probably thought 'foreigners' were no problem as long as they were Christians, but Japanese? He came to check on the spiritual welfare of our family.

The interview was carried out in Swiss-German, with my husband as a spokesman and I as a quiet listener. The man from the church had a form to be filled out. He asked my name, address and nationality and since I'm Swiss by marriage, these questions were no problem. Then came the next question: religious affiliation. That's where the 'trouble' started.

"The father of the child, Protestant, and the mother?" The clergyman directed his question politely in High German in my direction.

As I hesitated, not only because of the language, my husband volunteered, "Buddhist." After a moment of dead silence, while his pen hung in the air, I realized that I had to say something. My husband acted as interpreter.

I tried as best I could to explain that I was born in a Buddhist family but Buddhists don't baptize or confirm children like Christians do. I told him I became well-acquainted with Christianity in Bible courses in the Japanese college where I studied English. In fact, we had to learn by heart to recite from Genesis, Corinthians and the Psalms. I had nothing against these good teachings. I wanted, therefore, very much for our child to grow up just like any other children and belong to the Swiss community. I had not been prepared for this kind of inquisition, but I poured my heart out.

"In that case, we shall baptize the mother and the child at the same time."

His final, forbidding sentence struck me numb. I felt like I was facing judgement day.

He said we should think it over and that he would come back another time.

During the next few weeks, my husband and I looked together deeply into our souls, so to speak. We had never before talked about religions so seriously. We were married in a non-denominational church in America, with no questions asked as to my religious affiliation. We named our first child Caroline, after our Alma Mater where we had met. It had been nice and romantic and we thought we were cosmopolitans beyond all the petty cultural differences. Now the time had come to sober up and face reality.

If necessary, I was willing to become a Christian so that our child could be as Swiss as our neighbors and to help her avoid having to encounter many differences later in her life. But the vision of a mother, likely clad in white, carrying her baby in her arms to be baptized together in front of all the relatives and congregation was too much for me. I just couldn't do it.

My husband was also upset. "It is said, 'the twain shall never meet', but we did meet. It was no mere coincidence. Our children are children of East and West. You keep your Eastern culture as I do mine. For it is their privilege to have both heritages."

At that moment he looked a foot taller to me.

He introduced me to Arnold Toynbee's book, CHRISTIANITY AMONG THE RELIGIONS OF THE WORLD. Toynbee was a historian, not a theologian, but his views were a revelation and personal gospel to me and most welcomed in my muddled mind. That book rescued me by helping me realize that by adapting to my new surroundings, I was giving in, giving up and losing my footing in my own cultural background which was undeniably a part of me. I discovered my failing faith in myself as a Japanese and recovered the last bit of my self-confidence. The shield of his doctrine gave me strength and I was ready to confront my clergyman.

It would have been a most enlightening discussion for a new Toynbee disciple and possibly for my clergyman also, if it had taken place. But it was not to be. The pastor had become ill and retired and instead a younger successor came who spoke English.

He repeated the procedure, up to the inevitable question about religion. Then he asked me if I was not AGAINST our child being raised as a Protestant Christian.

I told him, "Of course not!"

"In that case," he said, "you are a Christian IN SPIRIT." He would write down 'Protestant' in the space for religion. "It's simpler that way."

That was all. Just like that. How broad-minded he was. I felt weak with anticlimax, disappointed rather than relieved. I disarmed myself of the weight of my armor and felt miraculously light-hearted.

Were all the serious, soul-searching discussions in the past weeks in vain? No, it was a meaningful and enriching experience that we would not have gone through otherwise. As much as the first pastor was forbidding and the second forgiving, I was grateful for both of them. Perhaps the former belonged to the old school and the latter was influenced by the ecumenical movement. The confrontation of two religions helped me find my own identity.

It became clear to me that assimilation into a different culture does not mean I was to conform blindly to it but keep my own sense of values. The differences in cultures could also be constructive factors in an intercultural marriage. I still cherish the feeling of togetherness my husband and I felt in going through that crisis together as a couple. It laid an important foundation for our parenthood. Her christening in the kimono was a happy event for all of us.

* * * * *

Six years passed quickly and our daughter went to primary school where she also had lessons in religion. One day she came up to me with a big question written all over her face. She held up a small statue of Buddha in her hand that had been a souvenir of our trip to Japan. She had kept it among her Japanese dolls and it meant nothing more to her than a doll. "The teacher said this is an idol and that it's a bad thing," she told me.

I was caught unaware at this idea coming from the mouth of my little girl. I did not know what to say or how to react. I stopped ironing, sat with her and lit a cigarette to gain time. Then I told her a story as well as I could.

"You see, our dear God is up there in heaven. He has to see to it that all the people on earth are good and kind to others and live happily together. It's such a big world to take care of so he sent three prophets to the different parts of the world: Christ to the West, Buddha to the East and Mohammed to the Arab countries. Christians built churches, Buddhists temples and Moslims mosques, according to their customs. It's right for you to believe in Christ in a Christian country such as Switzerland, just as the Japanese believe in their religion. The same goes for the Arabs. You cannot say only you, Christians, are right and call others pagans, can you? That wouldn't be fair, would it? If you call this an idol, they will say the same thing back at you. Then there will be quarrels and fights. Dear God does not want that, but for us to respect one another . "

I wondered if she understood me. It must have made sense to her little mind, for I saw the Buddha statue back on her shelf again. I hoped she would not be too near-sighted but widen her view over the horizon of the Swiss Alps. After all, she had been to Japan where her mother came from and had been exposed to the different culture on the other side of the globe.

Some years later my daughter attended a Buddhist mass in Japan held in memory of her late grandmother. The atmosphere of the temple with all the gilded statues, candle lights and fragrance of the incense seemed to her as a ten-year-old to be like that of a Catholic church. The chanting of the litany in Hindi sounded mysteriously similar to Latin in her ears. She was right in a way. There are some basic similarities in many apparently superficial symbols of different religions.

When my mother visited us in Switzerland, I decided on one of our excursions to show her the Catholic church in Mariastein nearby which is known for a miracle which happened there. A child had fallen from a steep cliff but was unharmed. It was the right kind of outing for a seventy-year-old with leg trouble. I felt, as usual, like an intruder in a Catholic church and stayed behind, while my mother, a devoted Buddhist, seemed to have no qualms about it. She walked straight up to the altar, lit a candle and knelt to pray. I watched in wonderment at the figure in a kimono mingled with other believers in worship. She walked the long steep stairs down to the sanctuary, admiring the discarded crutches on the wall, offered as proof of miracles. As an afterthought she said, "It's the same all over, Buddhist or Christian."

* * * * *

Twenty years passed since my daughter had worried about her small

Buddha statue being an idol. It turned out that the man she chose to marry was a Catholic. I warned her about the difficulty of divorce and other strict dogmas.

She teased me laughing, "I am talking about getting married, Mummy, not getting divorced!"

I suggested she consider having an ecumenical wedding so their children would be free to choose.

She explained that religion was very important to her husband-to-be and his family. His uncle, a Catholic priest, would be marrying them as he had done all his nephews and nieces.

I felt how lucky the young generation is, as religions have become more tolerant of one another in the last decades. For a moment, I was lost in thinking how some dogmatic differences in religions had brought unhappiness in life, instead of blessings; unhappy marriages without divorces, lonely ageing women, once young and in love, unable to be joined with the men of their wishes, and some of my Japanese friends marrying the Swiss only by civil law, giving up their young dreams of wearing bridal gowns, to the disappointment of their mothers . . .

My thoughts were interrupted by the cheerful voice of a happy bride. "I am broad-minded, not too strict in religion. You know that, Mummy!" The ripple of her contagious laughter came over me in crescendo. I was pleased that the seeds of tolerance had taken root sometime during the past twenty years.

I remember so well how adorable she looked in this little silk kimono, and feel again the pride that I could pass on this little symbol of my heritage to her. She wants her baby, due any day now, to wear it at christening . . . as probably all our grandchildren will. ♥

Hail Britannia

by Elayne Clift

I still have difficulty in determining whether some of my British husband's habits are part of the national character, or uniquely his own. Certainly his sense of honour (or as we say, honor) suggests something noble beyond individual attribute. It was one of the first traits that drew me to him over twenty years ago, out of curiosity more than admiration, I must admit. Here was a man who by the third date hadn't made a move. My ego was sufficiently intact to believe it was his problem, but as a conditioned American woman, the situation certainly suggested pathology. In the nick of time, he convinced me otherwise.

This same code of honour nearly got me in trouble in other ways. Shortly after we became engaged, for instance, we took a train journey. On the return to London, the conductor neglected to collect our tickets. Feeling as though I had just won at Ascot, I suggested we turn them in for a rebate, as any full-blooded American would have done. My husband-to-be was horrified, however, that I would even contemplate cheating British Rail. The episode nearly cost me my engagement ring.

Now, honour may be one thing, but humour is quite another. Can it really be that all British men are so . . . I grope for the word . . . puerile? I mean, here is a man who actually thinks Benny Hill is funny. A man who once convulsed himself with mirth at the spontaneous suggestion that Dr. Christiaan Barnard was really 'a heartless fellow'. Even our children cringe now when they see their father chortling quietly to himself as he listens to John Cleese tapes.

Personal habits are another thing I wonder about. Do all Englishmen, for example, take a glass of water to bed with them with religious regularity and knock it over in the middle of the night with absolute predictability at least twice a month? And do they tuck a handkerchief under their pillows at night, forgetting always to remove it in the morning to the horror of wives and hotel chambermaids? (And in the age of KLEENEX, who needs to save it in the first place?)

One learns to live with this sort of thing in the end. But there are other idiosyncrasies far more threatening to the Anglo-American marriage. Take formality. The Anglos have it; the Americans don't. In the early days of our married life, my husband (who came to America as a diplomat) positively cringed whenever I suggested that our guests help themselves to another drink. And God forbid, I took paper plates on a picnic! Potluck dinners were definitely out. Consequently our social life dropped off to nearly nil; everyone lived in mortal fear of having to reciprocate.

We worked through the entertainment crises over the years, but other challenges remain. We still argue over whether it's hot enough to turn on the air conditioner (my husband is the only human being I know who thinks of Panama as temperate), what to pack for holiday ("But, Dear, you simply won't be able to get through the whole of Proust in two weeks. Besides, do you really need to take it all in hardback?"), and how many hand-me-downs can reasonably be carried transatlantic on one trip.

But I wouldn't trade it for the world, and neither would my American children, who have grown up with Mr. Men, Beatrix Potter, Arthur Rackham, Marks & Spencer, Mothercare and the Queen Mum. These biculture kids know what bacon and bangers are all about. They were weaned on tea and scones, followed by trifle and Queen's pudding, and they can tuck into a joint with Yorkshire pud. They are in love with Big Ben, Madame Tussaud and the West End. And as my daughter once said with enormous pride when she was five years old, "I speak two languages, English and American."

As for me, I no longer 'get my knickers in a twist' over the little things, and I don't mind anymore 'having the mickey taken out'. After all, no American husband I know calls his wife 'Darling', unless he's sending a greeting card. Most forget their anniversaries, and few remember to tell their wives on each birthday that they look 'absolutely smashing'.

More importantly, after twenty years, I value Britain's virtues, tolerate its foibles and cherish new traditions built on the best that both sides of the Atlantic have to offer. For, to borrow from Alice Duer Miller's splendid "White Cliffs,"
"I am American bred,
I have seen much to hate here — much to forgive,
But in a world (without Englishmen),
I do not wish to live." ♥

Squeezing In

by Dyanne Fry Cortez

It's the day before Christmas. The kitchen and den are dim in the early morning light. Nothing is stirring but the TV, which has probably been on all night. And my stomach, which has led me down the hall in search of breakfast.

A variety of creatures occupies the den. There's a teenager on the couch, frizzy brown hair streaming from one end of the yellow blanket, one long foot sticking out the other. A college student is curled sideways in the armchair, still in the gray sweater he wore last night. A patchwork of quilts on the floor between the couch and the Christmas tree appears to contain three kids of assorted sizes. No, four. One of the long lumps has a head at each end.

Signs of life appear as I spoon cereal into my mouth. A section of quilt rolls over. A small hand gropes for the nearest body, pats it once or twice. The sweater unfolds, extending its arms in a luxurious stretch. The oldest of my brother-in-law's seven offspring tips his head back and blinks at me.

"Good morning," he says.

I married into this Mexican-American clan two years ago, not knowing what to expect.

It's not as if I'm on foreign territory. My husband and I grew up in small towns a hundred miles apart: almost next-door neighbors, by Texas standards. Some of his schoolmates looked a lot like me, Anglo-Saxon Protestant with a dash of German. Some of mine looked a lot like him; we ate lunch, studied, and played in the band together. But until Javier brought me to meet Mama Cortez, I had never visited a Mexican home.

On some levels, things aren't so different. Like my own family, my in-laws eat turkey at Thanksgiving and exchange gifts at Christmas. The kids are just as hooked on TV. Everybody speaks English at least some of the time; for the youngsters, it's the language of choice. And food? Hey, this is Texas. Even a white girl knows how to unwrap a *tamale*.

What I can't figure is how these people co-exist so congenially in such close quarters.

* * * * *

I shared my childhood home with two parents, one brother, and a dog. I had a room of my own, which suited me fine. The kid brother was okay, in his place — but he wasn't to enter MY place without permission. Riding in the family car, we were each entitled to exactly half the back seat. We had two bathrooms for four people, and still got into arguments about fair use.

At the Cortez house last Christmas, we had one bath for fourteen people. A cousin from Mama's side joins the party on occasion; his wife and kids mean we add up to twenty-one.

Holiday meals are served on a long, patched-together table stretching across the kitchen and halfway into the den. When we're all seated, only one person at a time can squeeze through the passage between the kitchen and the hall. At the table, you have to keep your elbows reined in. It's like eating lunch in the coach section of a commercial jetliner. Except, of course, that the food is better. And there's more of it.

I keep wondering how people can spend much time in this crush without stepping on one another's toes. The answer, I begin to see, is that they aren't too particular about their toes. Or their elbows.

They appear to move without constraint, avoiding collision by means of some mysterious radar acquired in early childhood. If someone does get bumped or jostled, no offense is taken. These people enjoy contact. In fact, they seek it out.

There are never enough chairs to go around. But you don't notice it much, because no one stays in one spot for long. Seats are never 'reserved', and I'm gradually catching on that any space big enough for me to squeeze into is big enough to sit in. Personal space is measured in inches, rather than feet.

There's a sort of pecking order, but it operates so smoothly, you seldom see anyone pecked. Take this morning scene in the den, for example. Big kids on the furniture, little ones on the floor.

It never occurred to me until last night that I, the childless aunt, had a place in that pecking order.

* * * * *

My brother married at the age of nineteen. I hit thirty, still single. We still came home at Christmas, still slept in our separate rooms. We got along fine — until his first child was born.

"There's a crib in your room," Mom wrote me one day. "It'll be handy when the baby comes to visit."

The next time we were all home together, I slept on the hide-a-bed in the front parlor. There's no door, but the room is fairly private. Most of the traffic is in the central living area.

The following Christmas, they moved me into the living area. The front parlor was occupied by the tree.

"I set it up differently this year, so the baby wouldn't stumble into it, and the hide-a-bed won't unfold," said Mom. "Don't you think you'd be more comfortable here by the fireplace?"

Comfortable enough — except that Brother and his small family hit the kitchen at dawn, making breakfast for the toddler, who was talking up a blue streak. I pulled a pillow over my head and tuned them out. Then Brother came to sit on my couch and turned on the six o'clock news, cranking up the volume to compete with his son's voice. I removed the pillow and scowled at him.

"Good morning, Dyanne," he said kindly. "If you want to sleep some more, there's no one in your room right now. The kid will be up for a couple of hours, at least."

It occurs to me that my in-laws would find this story incomprehensible. No one was using the bed in my room; why didn't I sleep there in the first place? Better yet, why didn't Mom put the crib in my brother's room, where he could keep an eye on his child?

I don't know. Neither question ever came up.

Actually, Javier tells me his brother and sister-in-law have never owned a crib. "For as long as I can remember, those kids have slept in a pile on the floor," he says.

If one toddler could displace me so thoroughly in my own parents' home, I could well imagine where Javier stood in relation to his older brother. Seven children, and number eight expected next month!

I knew about the importance of family and parenthood in Hispanic culture. I knew the Roman Catholic position on family planning. Sons without sons — especially in their late thirties — were sure to be second-class citizens.

We'd spent last Christmas in his old quarters, a tiny room cluttered beyond belief with high-school memories and his mother's out-of-season clothes. He slept on the ancient twin bed, which sagged to the point of spinal damage. I found a roll-away in the corner.

When we stopped by for a weekend in the fall, we found the room transformed. The back-breaker bed was gone. In its place was a wooden-framed double with matching nightstand, dresser, and chest of drawers. It's now one of the nicest rooms in the house, and I wasn't kidding myself that we'd get it this holiday.

In fact, I expected nothing. Javier knew the rules here. I'd wait for him to tell me where to sleep. But he lingered past midnight, watching TV and talking with the men. A space appeared next to him on the couch. I took it and fell asleep on his shoulder.

He shook me. "Why don't you go to bed?"

"WHERE?"

"The new bed in my room, of course. Where did you think?"

I stumbled down the hall and collapsed. When he finally came to join me, I woke up enough to try to tell him what I had thought.

He stopped me in mid-sentence. "Do you know how many grandchildren it takes to equal one child?"

"I — uh, no. How many?"

"A lot more than eight," he said. "Do you know how many grandchildren it takes to equal a child and his spouse?"

I looked at him groggily.

"Darling, you alone outrank any two of those kids in there."

"But . . . " I tried to tell him about my brother's child, about Anglo friends who'd had similar troubles at home, about the textbook importance of family in Hispanic culture. He cut me off.

"That's just it," he said. "White people like the IDEA of family. We Mexicans know what family is really about." ♥

En Vogue

by Janet Rüsch

I had been in Switzerland only a few months when my husband promised to introduce me to the thrills and delights of skiing. This topic was not particularly foremost in my mind when I was making my marriage vows — a thought definitely worth considering for future brides-to-be of Swiss men!

If you have ever practised any sport in Switzerland, you may have noticed that it does not really matter how well you do it, but how good you look doing it. Visit the local tennis club, for example, and you will probably see almost everybody sporting the latest fashions and colours produced by the leading names in sportswear design and brandishing the most modern and expensive rackets.

Fresh from England, I was not prepared for this fashion culture shock. I had played tennis during my high school years — quite well I should add — clad in a blouse I had made myself in the needlework class, and a pair of not very short shorts given to my mother by a friend of hers. Since the said friend was about five times my size, my mother altered them to fit me. In later years, I was still playing with the same racket, restrung a couple of times. Its obscure trademark was by then hardly legible. Skiing? Well, I had never even dreamt about it!

My husband eventually informed me that he had booked a week's holiday in a very up-market ski resort. "But," he said, "I am not buying you the equipment because you might not like this sport. We will hire the skis and poles when we get there. In the meantime, see what you can do about borrowing the rest of the outfit from a friend or someone."

Fair enough. But when you are as 'petite' as I am, it is a bit difficult to borrow clothing that fits. A friend lent me her boots. They were a size too big but I was assured that with two pairs of socks they would be just fine. Leather boots that had to be laced up were rapidly going out of fashion at that time, but that didn't matter, I thought.

She also lent me a pair of corduroy *Keilhosen*, the style of which was running out at the same breakneck speed as the lace-ups. These trousers were of a corded stretch material, vaguely reminiscent of my present riding pants, but a thousand times less sexy. They were three sizes too big for me. "Well, if you wear a belt to secure them, no one will notice under a sweater," she advised. I borrowed an anorak — four sizes too large — from another friend. I had to wear several thick sweaters to fill it out.

One must bear in mind that the aforementioned friends were also English. I don't think the Swiss fashion culture had quite got to them either at that time. What I wore on my head, I shudder to think. Luckily, I have forgotten. The boots were black, the pants brown and the anorak navy blue.

Thus attired, I presented myself at the ski school, nervously clutching my hired skis. Normally, the skis should be about as long as one's own height. I am about 157 cm and the skis were two metres with front ends curling up like the shoes of a court jester — how I must have looked the part once I had laboriously donned them!

We assembled into groups, according to our abilities, at poles stuck into the ground numbered from one to whatever. The tiny tots had poles supporting heads of various Walt Disney characters instead of numbers. My beginners' group was allocated a rather dishy skiing instructor — a young Englishman. This is great, I thought, at least I will be able to communicate with him. After one glance at me, however, he actually seemed embarrassed to talk to me.

We started on what the Swiss so very aptly refer to as the 'idiots' hill'. I'm still not sure if this is because the slopes are so easy any fool can master them, or because of the antics you see being performed there. At first we had to learn how to climb up the slope sideways by digging the edges of our skis into the hill — a not too difficult task if the ground is covered in snow, but on a sheet of sheer ice, it is an utter impossibility when wearing loose-fitting leather lace-ups! After what seemed hours of physical and mental torture, we graduated to higher ground. Mercifully, the slopes there were snow-covered and we had to learn how to 'snowplough'.

The instructor informed us that bending our knees and pushing out our heels would act as a brake. So, skis pointing down-hill, I made my first attempt. I thought I was bending my knees and pushing out my heels but I was definitely not braking. As I gathered speed, I just froze, not only with cold but also in terror. At the bottom of this slope, the ground levelled out at the foot of the 'idiots' hill' where I had started out earlier that morning. Fortunately, the spot was by this time deserted. Even the tiny tots were way up high, skiing around like scores of colourful little gnomes who had been skiing for years.

I did brake eventually because I ran straight into one of the poles and ended up on my back. As I opened my eyes, I saw Mickey Mouse grinning down at me with obvious great pleasure. That was too much for me. I groped for my sunglasses that had, of course, flown off on impact, put them on and let the tears roll down, unashamedly.

I met my husband at the appointed time and place. I had seen him gracefully waltzing down the mountain in his blue cosmonaut-style boots, blue ski suit and matching gloves and hat, everything *ton sur ton.*

"How did it go?" he asked, smiling enthusiastically.

"I want a divorce," I answered. "Immediately. Now."

Actually, I had been made rather unhappy once or twice by people's remarks about the English having no idea how to dress. With this and the new added burden of skiing, I was beginning to feel doubtful I would ever fit in at all.

It took much coaxing and pleading from my husband to make me agree to give skiing another try. I finally gave in, deciding 'if you can't beat 'em, join 'em' — but under one condition — that he buy me the complete outfit from head to toe, everything brand-new and matching, even the lipstick.

If I was going to make a fool of myself, I was going to look good doing it! ♥

Family

Influences

Life with the Family

by Michael H. Sedge

There is a ritual in our home. Each evening tea and a snack are prepared and served in front of the television on an elegant, Sorrento, inlaid wood tray. To most Italian men, this is the way a 'perfect wife' should treat her husband — just like Mamma would.

Unfortunately, I'm the one doing the preparing and it's my wife that gets served. As she puts it: "If I wanted to be the typical stereotyped Italian housewife, I would have married a Sicilian and not an American."

Don't get the wrong impression. In this contemporary intercultural marriage, both my wife and I work as partners. We're realistic in that not every American man is Rambo and not every Italian woman is Mamma Lucia.

Italy's new breed of housewives are much like those in other industrialized nations. In fact, 'working mothers' rather than 'housewives', would be a more appropriate term to describe them.

My wife of seventeen years is up at seven, has the kids off to school by eight, and is out the door to her own teaching job by eight-fifteen.

Myself? I am a writer, an independent writer who works at home. In America, this translates to being 'freelance'. In Italian, it translates to being 'unemployed'. In their eyes, I stay home all day rather than leave the home to go to the office and, therefore, must not have a job. Despite my explanations and demonstration of a degree in journalism, to them I am unemployed.

Eventually, as my income increased from year to year, my wife accepted the fact that I was truly a writer. The bills got paid, money was in the bank, and that was proof enough for a modern Italian woman. Convincing her family was another story.

If there is one thread of truth in today's films about the Italian people, it is that of the unbreakable link between family members. It would be safe to say that when you marry an Italian, you are, in reality, marrying the 'family'.

Over the past fifteen years several family members have tried to help 'the

American' get a job. For example, an uncle, concerned that I 'do not have a job', once arranged — through a friend-of-a-friend — for me to work as a translator in a chemical plant. This, naturally, made the 'family' very happy. Imagine their shock when I said: "I don't want it. I already HAVE a job."

Finally, so it seems, the family gave up on me. Now they are somewhat amazed that I have the money to drive a new, top-of-the-line Fiat, travel to the United States several times a year and keep my wife and kids in the most popular European designer fashions. They no doubt are asking themselves: "Did he finally get a job?"

Children of intercultural marriages benefit the most. My daughter and son both enjoy good relationships with their Italian and American relatives. Each has been to the United States on several occasions and easily fit into either culture.

Raising children in an Italian atmosphere with an American mentality, however, has caused some . . . well, let's call it friction — particularly with 'the family'.

Italians have a way of over-protecting children. When I was growing up in the natural settings of Michigan, children would play in the rain, spend hours in the snow, and generally enjoy what nature offered. Italian kids, for the most part, receive what Americans call 'golden spoon' treatment.

"Don't let the kids go out in the rain," I recall my mother-in-law saying. "Put a cap on." "Don't forget your gloves." "Don't go on vacation there, it's too cold." "Don't go to the beach, it's too hot." "Stay in the house today, it's too windy."

I fear someday she'll tell the children to stop breathing because there is too much pollution in the air.

Having lived in Italy for over eighteen years, I've come up with my own theory regarding the over-protection of children: Find an Italian child that is constantly sick, and you'll find a child that has been overly protected.

Fortunately, my own children have taken their father's perspective on the subject. That is, listen with respect, then go ahead and do what you planned. This does not always work out to the best advantage, though. I recall the time my daughter, not heeding her grandmother's advice, went out on a cool evening and spent the next three days in bed with a fever. Of course it will be MY FAULT for the rest of my days.

Another problem I have, as an American, is accepting the closeness of the Italian family. In the United States, children leave the nest early to lead their own lives and create their own families and homes. Italians, on the other hand, seem to roost at home until a late age, then, upon leaving, return on an almost daily basis.

Such is my case. We're in a constant 'family' state: morning, noon, night, during weekends, during meals, during holidays.

Knowingly or not, our children have learned to take advantage of this. Whenever they want to do something, they ask their grandfather — knowing very well that I would probably say no. Since he rarely refuses the request of his grandchildren, this has created some misunderstandings. As much as I insist, however, I have to keep in mind that this is the Italian 'family' system and he is the head of that system — right or wrong.

Another problem with such close living is that one rarely gets a chance to make an independent decision nor does he or she get to 'grow up'. It amazes and amuses me, for example, that at age 38, and as modern as my wife confesses to be, she is just as caught up in the Italian family syndrome as I am. Her mother constantly criticizes her manner of dressing; insists on knowing where she is going; influences her decisions on home decoration; and generally maintains that air of 'mother probably knows best so do what she says'.

In the case of my wife's father, it is somewhat different: "I do know best so you will do what I say!"

Having lived with an American for as many years as she has, my wife does not accept such suggestions easily. She points out that times have changed and so, too have the ideas of Italian women. Sometimes this line of defense works, more often, however, it does not.

To say that the Italian family culture creates only problems would be to paint an untrue picture. There are also positive aspects to this tradition. It is comforting, for example, to know that whatever difficulties life presents, the family will be there to help. When I travel, I know my wife and children are not left alone. If my wife and I decide to go out for the evening, it goes without saying that the grandparents will take care of the kids.

Over the years I have learned to accept the cultural differences between Americans and Italians. I try to make the best of those that are enjoyable and overlook, as much as possible, those that may seem irrational. When I return to the United States, my parents, brother and sisters say that I have lived in Italy for so long that I look and even act like an Italian.

Perhaps, to them, this is the case. To my Italian family, however, I'll always be an American. After all, what self-respecting Italian man would be preparing tea while his wife sits comfortably in front of the television talking about her hard day at work? ♥

Maryam and Me

by Susan K. Perry

"He'll fall! He'll hurt himself, stop him!" my mother-in-law exclaimed worriedly, but not in English. Although I could speak only a few words of Arabic, I was beginning to understand enough of the expressions used by my husband's seventy-year-old mother to wonder if I hadn't been happier when I understood less.

When my first baby, Simon, was ten months old, my mother-in-law Maryam flew from Lebanon to stay with us for an extended visit. My husband John had just purchased a coin laundry that required his attention many evenings. Since he was also gone all day at his regular engineering job, Maryam turned out to be my responsibility, day and evening. By sharing the care of one small, active boy, we came to know each other unusually well.

In college, my Lebanese boyfriend and I dated for four years, while I concentrated on Middle Eastern studies. (Love sometimes leads to strange majors.) After we married, we spent a month visiting John's childhood home in Lebanon. I thought I knew just about all there was to know about his culture, until his mother spent four months in our house.

Never having traveled abroad before, Maryam must have thought our ways, our social life, and our supermarkets were incredibly strange. Though I expected adjustment to be difficult, somehow I thought she would do most of it. Instead, perhaps because of my youth, my lack of self-confidence as a new mother, or because I feared offending her and incurring John's irritation, I had to do what seemed like an inordinate amount of compromising. Many of our conflicts revolved around child care.

Maryam reared eight children to adulthood in a village of three thousand people in the hills of North Lebanon. One son had ten children, a daughter had twelve, and Maryam helped out often with her grandchildren. Maybe she did have a right to believe she knew more than I did about childrearing. After all, I was an only child who had rarely baby-sat, and I got most of my parenting knowledge from books and magazines. Yet, there I was arguing, in sign language and gestures mostly, that I knew what was best for my little son. When my husband was home (not too often), he tried to mediate. Mostly he threw up his hands in exasperation.

Simon had begun walking the month before Maryam arrived and was pretty good at it. In fact, he was running, climbing up, and jumping down all day long. Yet wherever he zoomed, there was Maryam, chasing after him with her arms outstretched, ready to catch him and protect him from calamity. She was aghast that I allowed him to play in the dirt.

I wanted him to feel free; she wanted him to be safe. She insisted he was simply too young to be doing what he was doing. She thought I was a careless mother. Yet I was struggling with my own urge to overprotect. I wanted Simon to grow up independent and unafraid — unlike me, who went through childhood plagued by fears. Try explaining that in a foreign language! I couldn't.

When Simon was ill with a stubborn fever and ear infection, and seven visits to the doctor and much medication failed to cure him, Maryam took matters into her own hands. Without a word of explanation, she set about gathering some unexpected items. While I watched, increasingly horrified, she snipped a lock of his hair, tore a few threads from one of his old shirts, clipped one of his fingernails, and set the whole collection on fire in a tuna fish can. She walked around him several times, muttering some words. I was worried she might do something dangerous. Her incantation complete, she put out the fire, leaving me wondering and more than a little annoyed. The next day Simon's fever broke. To me, Maryam's smugness was a wordless "I told you so."

Maryam and I disagreed over food. She thought fat was healthy, while I was pleased that my son was lean and energetic. More than once she followed him all over the house with a spoonful of rice, "just so he eats." It was pointless to explain that he obviously had FINISHED eating.

She seemed to hold it against me that I had stopped breastfeeding Simon when he was nine months old. She had fed HER babies whenever they cried. (It was actually John who had urged me to discontinue nursing when Simon was fully mobile. I couldn't win.)

She also was sure Simon would grow up lonely and not liking his parents because he was no longer allowed to sleep in our bedroom. I smothered him with hugs and affection, yet she tried to make me feel guilty for abandoning him to his own room at night. In the middle of one long night, when Simon was crying (he craved company at all hours) and John and I were trying to ignore him so he would learn to put himself back to sleep, Maryam got up from her bed in the guest room, went to Simon, and finally slept on the floor next to his crib. His aloneness worried her.

Aloneness: a condition I hungered for but rarely experienced for the duration of her visit. The long evenings stretched unbearably until bedtime, especially when John was away. I thought she would enjoy watching television, though it was quite a strain for me to sit with an Arabic-English dictionary translating enough so the programs would make some sense to her. But how can you translate a whole culture? She "tsk-tsk"ed her way through many shows, especially when men and women kissed, or worse, were shown in bed together. Maryam was two generations and a world away from the Los Angeles in which I lived.

Because of her poor eyesight and arthritic hands, she couldn't enjoy turning out the handicrafts that occupied so many of her younger relatives, and she was illiterate, so reading was not an option either. Thus we sat, evening after evening, I trying to concentrate on a magazine, she just sitting and looking off into space. I was immensely uncomfortable.

Besides that, she was used to much more hard work back home in the village, so that now she wasn't even tired enough to sleep at night. Also, she told her son, "I don't want to go to sleep before Susan and leave her all alone. She'll feel lonely."

Though I begged John to explain that I didn't mind being alone, he didn't want to take a chance on hurting her feelings.

Daytime passed more quickly. I did more housework than I was used to doing, since I felt more comfortable keeping busy than trying to read while she watched. She wondered how I could feel good about sitting still while the dishwasher did the dishes for me. The worst of it was, my husband half-agreed with his mother, which caused me to feel cornered. Maryam never came to trust the washing machine, and continued to hand wash her own things.

I had to admit that her energy was amazing. Once I mentioned feeling tired after writing several letters. She said, with a certain air of superiority, "Tired? From what? Writing letters is work?"

The days we went to the zoo, the park, and the homes of friends were the most pleasant, though she criticized me for letting Simon sleep in the car, sit in the sun, and even sleep in public in his stroller. She mumbled something about "antagonizing the evil eye."

After the first month of her visit, I began attending a weekly class for new parents, a kind of support group. I loved it. Maryam took care of Simon while I was gone. I thought it was working out beautifully until she complained to John about these "meetings" with which I was wasting my time. When he didn't come to my rescue immediately, but actually requested that I stop going in order to please his mother, I rebelled. I ranted and raved that it was unfair. I won, sort of, and continued to attend. But my resentment was overflowing.

One day my husband's cousin and his American wife, Nancy, came for lunch with their four children. I pulled her aside and poured out my frustration about what was happening to my privacy.

"I know just what you mean," she said. "Having in-laws living with you for months is a strain on even the best marriage. But it will be over before you know it, and you'll look back and remember the better days. Simon's having a great time, isn't he, with all the extra attention?"

I told her that Simon seemed to be the happiest one in the family these days.

"I thought so," she said. "Hang in there, and don't forget what your mother-in-law must be going through. Your husband is her youngest son, the only one who lives ten thousand miles away from her. She needs to return home knowing he's in your good hands. Simon's just a baby now, but wouldn't you want to know HIS wife was willing to give up a little for YOUR peace of mind?"

When our company left, I wanted to be alone in my room. Nancy is one of those special people who can make suggestions without leaving you with a negative feeling. What a lucky family she has, I thought. Then I figured I had better do some clear thinking about my own family.

In my insecurity, my newness at mothering, I had been competing with my mother-in-law. Did I think she could take my son away from me, or reduce his devotion to me, just because he added her to his collection of beloved people? How foolish. Simon was a particularly sociable creature, with room in his heart for loving many people. Once I let myself recognize it, I noticed how happy he was in Maryam's embrace, how he reflected her sadness on the days she suffered from homesickness.

I had also been putting my husband in the classically awkward position of choosing loyalties: his mother or his wife. But she would be gone soon, back home ten thousand miles away, and all he would remember was how I complained about her. Yet I would have liked him to remember how kind and unselfish I was during this once-in-a-lifetime visit.

I thought back to our trip to Lebanon three years before: we were given a room of our own, while several members of the family slept on mats in the living room for a whole month. Yet I never heard a murmur of complaint. The whole household, especially Maryam, had gone out of their way to make me feel at home. It had been a warm, large-family experience for me. And now was my only chance to repay them.

The remainder of Maryam's visit went smoothly. The dictionary stayed handy, and she delighted in my attempts to speak Arabic. I smiled a lot and she smiled back. I permitted her to follow her instincts with Simon more often, since it gave them both so much pleasure.

The day eventually arrived to drive her to the airport. We all hugged her for several minutes before we let her board the plane. Tears suddenly poured from my eyes, startling me and surprising Maryam.

Not until we arrived home and John returned to work did the shock of her absence hit. Simon and I were depressed for about two weeks. He and I moped around in the silence, wondering what to do with ourselves. I had the privacy I had been longing for, yet all I felt was loneliness. It took a while for the emptiness to dissipate.

When Simon was eight, his father took him to spend a month in Lebanon. The stories he brought back and still occasionally tells recall the warmth and hospitality of his huge foreign family, and especially of the unselfishness of his grandmother. I am grateful to her for showing him such an unforgettable time in his other home.

John and I divorced two years after that trip. I've heard that our cousin Nancy and her husband split up too. Simon will graduate from college this year and hopes to visit Lebanon again someday.

Maryam died last month. When the news finally reached me — even bad news doesn't travel fast out of Lebanon these days — I felt a surprisingly sharp pang of loss. Now my intercultural mother-in-law blues are only a memory. ♥

Castaways and Breaking Conventions

by Suzanne Sablan

Twelve years ago, I married a man from Guam. Guam is a tiny island in the Pacific and is approximately a ten-hour flight due west from the Hawaiian Islands. My husband Joe's culture is a mixture of Philipino and Polynesian heritage, while my ancestry is European from countries such as England, France, Germany and Italy. These differences guaranteed that we would have some compromises to make regarding values and our respective roles in the household, as we began living together as husband and wife. That task, by itself, is enough for any couple to have to deal with. But I soon found out that marriage to Joe meant marriage to his entire family and to new cultural expectations. I was frequently reminded in the first year of our marriage that our up-bringings were indeed quite different. The biggest cultural dilemma stemmed from Joe's parents' inability to accept our blended, intercultural relationship, and from their frequent attempts to control our lives.

There were some major cultural differences regarding religion and male/female roles. My parents were Episcopalians. My brother, sister and I all attended the same church throughout school and we were all part of the choir or youth group as adolescents. Although my parents perceived religion as an important basis for the development of our moral values, we were not an orthodox family. It was understood that, if we were in need of moral guidance at any time, we did not have to run to church to obtain it. Prayer in our bedroom was as significant as our incantations in church on Sundays. In my middle-class family, my mother insisted that girls and boys receive equal treatment. Special privileges were determined by academic, sports, or music achievement, as well as by dedication and effort. My mother had a stronger educational background than my father, so she encouraged us all to excel in our areas of strength, and recognized the significance of education. In addition, household chores were designated to all who lived in the house, regardless of sex. Thus I grew up with the belief that I could do anything I strived for through perseverance, education and intelligence, and I was not consigned to a life of baking cookies in the kitchen.

This greatly conflicted with my husband's upbringing. Although his entire family had moved to the States many years ago in search of better job opportunities, they still clung fervently to their cultural mores and expectations. They also felt no ties to any particular area of the States and moved to Hawaii, California, Washington and North Carolina before ending up in Florida in 1978. The Sablan family, like many Pacific Islanders, was Roman Catholic. Church was a requirement every Sunday and holy day. It was unheard of that their children would marry outside the faith: his parents had even initially insisted that I convert to Catholicism, which my husband disputed. There were also more traditional gender roles in his family. The women were designed by God to procreate and maintain the domicile. The men earned a living and had the final say about any decision made for the family. Children were to be seen and not heard, and their primary allegiance was to their father. Education was not valued, especially if it conflicted with after-school jobs. It was understood that at least 75% of each child's paycheck went to the father. This was actually 'generous' of my father-in-law because, as I understood it, many children in Guam who still lived at home surrendered close to 100% of their paychecks to their parents. Unmarried females could not go out on a date unless accompanied by a brother or parent who could chaperone. Women were treated as the inferior gender.

Considering these differences, one may ask how I ever became attracted to my husband in the first place! I have never been drawn to any male who is just interested in how many babies I can produce or how well I can scrub a toilet, as are so many of the 'macho' men I grew up with in New York. I had taken a cashiering job at a Florida hotel between college semesters and Joe was my supervisor and trainer. He was the farthest thing from macho you can imagine, and he treated me with respect and integrity. He valued my opinions and he never assumed he was a wiser or better person because of his gender. He was quite different from the rest of his family, as I frequently observed before we began dating. Since then, I have often joked that they switched babies at the hospital when Joe was born, because he is so unlike his siblings or parents.

From the beginning, my in-laws did not approve of our relationship. They insisted that I was 'too pushy' and based this myth on the reputation of people from New York. They also decided that I was much too outspoken because I spoke my mind eloquently — and often. Joe and I finally decided to elope when trying to accommodate his entire family became an impossible task. Joe, the third eldest, was also the first of the eight children to 'leave the nest' and his parents used a great deal of emotional blackmail to try and convince him that we were wrong for each other. It did not help that his seven siblings, ranging in age from seven to twenty-two, were all virtually tied to his parents' apron strings, emotionally and financially.

As we tried to organize our lives during our first year of marriage, Joe's parents were a continual source of interference. They did not respect that ours was a marriage of equality, and not one of subordination. My in-laws felt that I had no right to discuss monetary matters with my husband, and that his decision should be final, even though I provided half of the household income. I often found out, albeit after the fact, that my husband secretly loaned a family member money based on a verbal promise of repayment. Inevitably, this would lead to a disagreement between Joe and I, because I invariably would discover that it had not been repaid just when we needed the money most.

For a brief time, early in our marriage, my husband and I were able to forge some kind of ties with his family, or so I thought. I tried to help his younger sister with her schoolwork, for she was quite bright and had the potential to go to college. We spent some holidays together, and Joe helped his mother with the cooking. But I soon discovered from my husband that, at every available opportunity, my in-laws admonished him for not finding a Chamorro, or full-blooded Guamanian, spouse. They adamantly insisted that, as an outsider, I could not possibly understand 'their ways'. Although Joe repeatedly requested that they get to know and accept me for my individuality, they made little effort, as far as we could see. Like many culturally orthodox families, they perceived me as an intruder, and would have preferred a more 'appropriate' daughter-in-law they could hand pick from the many Guamanian families in Florida.

The constant tension between his parents and me left Joe in a precarious position. He often attempted to handle any criticism from his family alone and try and preserve some kind of relationship with them. He tried to shield me from as much of their hostility as he could. Derogatory comments made about me were often withheld. Despite Joe's refusal to discuss his parents' comments about me, I always knew when they had gone too far, for we did not speak to them for weeks after many of their more serious battles, and Joe's usually mirthful demeanor was contentious.

This is not to say that all of the tension Joe felt came from his family. It dismayed him that I did not care whether we saw his family on a regular basis or not. This bothered him because, culturally, he had been taught a form of filial piety and responsibility that should be followed even if his parents did not respect me as his wife. On the contrary, my culture had taught me to respect those who respected me, and that respect was something earned, not automatically granted. This created unnecessary tension in our marriage for several years.

Outside of the disparity about Joe's parents, our relationship flourished. We were the farthest thing imaginable from a traditional Guamanian marriage, and I venture to say that we did not represent a more conventional American marriage either. Joe worked two jobs for several years to allow me to work and attend a private college to finish my bachelor's degree. Today I work two jobs, as a high school teacher and a writer, while he works part-time and helps look after my elderly grandmother. Joe is very creative and loves to cook, decorate, and rearrange things; thus, he is the primary caretaker of our home. I am more left-brained and orderly, so I handle budgetary matters and correspondence for both of us. Joe loves to shop for clothes for me almost as much as I do. The type of relationship we have is really not indicative of either of our cultures; by combining our two heritages, we succeeded in creating something very different from both of them.

Interference from my in-laws persisted, however. Nothing Joe could say or do could convince them that he was happy with me and with our relationship as it was. His family felt they had the right to decide when we should have children, when we should buy a house, or what bills we should pay. As our marriage grew stronger, Joe voluntarily distanced himself from his family. An ultimate confrontation was imminent. After a disagreement we had with his family, all communication was severed. We learned from an uncle that the rest of the family, disillusioned with life in the States and unwilling to assimilate, returned to Guam a few months later. We have not heard from them since.

After my husband's initial dismay over his parents' behavior, I witnessed a complete transformation of character in him. It was as if the weight of expectation had been lifted off his shoulders. My husband was more relaxed than I had ever seen him. With the departure of his parents came a peace in his life that never before existed. There was no more pressure for him to report to his relatives. My family has always loved him and respected him, so in some ways they filled the void.

In modern America, Joe has found that following the values of my family is much less emotionally taxing than attempting to imitate the values of his family. However, this does not mean that he has forfeited all ties to his roots. Despite his 'Americanization', Joe retains some values that are very Guamanian.

Many of these customs concern food. We purchased a rice cooker, since almost every meal includes rice. Many meats are marinated in soy sauce before they are cooked. Our household meals include *filadeni*, a mixture of soy sauce, *jalapeno* peppers, vinegar and onions, as flavoring for many meats. We also barbecue our food often and enjoy a specialty dish called 'red rice' on holidays. Holidays such as Guamanian Liberation Day are such large celebrations that there is often food enough for a dozen families. Occasionally, Joe uses 'homemade' health remedies learned from Guamanian witch doctors, such as wearing adhesive patches on the head to relieve headaches. In addition, Joe stays in close contact with several uncles, who live in the States and are more assimilated than my in-laws. Joe's relationship with his more modernized relatives has helped him realize that he was not wrong in placing restrictions on his parents' involvement in our lives.

How can an intercultural marriage flourish? I can only respond from my own experiences these ten years. What has bonded us together for so long is a common goal: to be better off, financially and emotionally, than our parents were. This does not merely refer to material possessions, but to our souls; about being happy with our professions; about feeling satisfied with our individual educational growth; about making wise decisions based on maturity and responsibility. We also share the same philosophy when it comes to our friends. It is difficult to turn our close friends down when they need assistance, and for this reason our home has gotten the reputation for being a 'hotel' for friends in need. We enjoy quality time together, yet respect our different hobbies: if I prefer to attend a local lecture or educational event, Joe does not mind. Likewise, I do not feel slighted if he would like to go to the gym for an hour or two and work out. Our friends and my family members have seen that it is possible to have a thriving marriage with different family values as well as varied personal preferences. In fact, my sister will soon wed a man of Hispanic descent. They have been inspired by our marital success.

Are these values more American than Guamanian? Perhaps. But because we are more tolerant of each others' differences and are more communicative about our needs, they are values that inspire and fulfill us both. The only other thing that would make us both happy is his parents' acknowledgment that two dissimilar cultures can sustain a mutually satisfying relationship. We can only hope that one day they will be enlightened. ♥

Daughterly Love

by Rosi Wolf-Almanasreh

A letter to my mother:

For a long time I have been wondering how I can explain to you why I married a foreigner and that it is not really anything extraordinary or bad to do. Or is it? But because he is the reason for your disapproval — or so it seemed to me at the time — I was for years obsessed by the desire to convince you that all your ideas and fantasies about him are wrong. But what, in fact, were your ideas about him?

Do you remember? When I told you I wanted to marry an Arab, you and Papa became furious. You wrote to me, "Your children will be bastards! You're contaminating our blood!" When I called you after that hoping to dispel some of your negative ideas, the tirade of hate and contempt that came from you made me tremble. "He'll never be faithful, he'll have many wives, lock you in, squander your money and take advantage of you. People like him are swindlers, primitive, fanatics, wild . . . and people like you, our daughter, are perverse, sexually abnormal women who should be declared legally incompetent and put in a mental institution."

Oh, I'll never forget all the things you said then. Had you ever known an Arab? Had you ever been to an Arab country? Had you ever read anything about Arab countries and if so, what? What was the reason for your derogatory, racist slandering of my friend? You didn't even want to meet him. Why did you swear at me and heap dirty accusations on me?

And me? I tried to explain, to justify my views and to defend him! Why? Instead of turning around and withdrawing, I still wanted — or wanted at last? — to get you to accept and tolerate my life. Yes, above all I wanted to be loved by you. Then more than ever before. I wanted approval where none could be expected. But, I told myself that you didn't love me because of this foreigner. "He is to blame for everything," you always said. And I was only too willing to believe it, although I should have admitted to myself that your disapproval had completely different reasons. "He's to blame for it all!" Like a poisonous dart, this idea had an effect later on my attitude towards my husband, at first unconscious, unintended, later a reproach.

But who are you really, Mother, to put yourself so arrogantly and so contemptuously above others? A woman of German-Polish-Jewish-Huguenotic descent; born in 1914, a child of petty bourgeois parents from countryfied surroundings, little schooling and no profession, without much of an opportunity in your life with a husband who went his own way, whom you could only disobey secretly behind his back, whom you hated and held in contempt. Yes, Mother, and you were once an enthusiastic Hitler fan ("Like so many others," as you still emphasize apologetically to make it generally acceptable that you were a party member and an accomplice to his crimes.) You are a Puritan-Protestant, always hardworking and 'orderly'. After the war and with much effort, you managed to raise three children. They turned out fine, except, as you say, for me. You wanted them to have more from life than you had. You meant by that materially more. More money, a little house, a car, a decent living. You wanted them to be well-adjusted to society, without risks, in proper circumstances, to be like others, join the crowd and swim with the stream. And then I go and marry someone of another kind, disturb this make-believe harmony, this picture of your purity.

If only you had known how I suffered, how injured I was by your obvious rejection of me! For years I kept mulling it over in my mind, trying to figure out what I could do to make my husband more 'acceptable' to you. As if that's what it was all about!

Now, after almost two decades, I realize that I have failed in this attempt to gain your acceptance, your love and your loyalty. When the Neo-Nazis mobilized in the 80s and assaulted me because of my commitment to stand up for 'foreigners', you told me, "You've only got yourself to blame. Now you just have to cope. We don't want anything to do with it."

What is really our problem? Is it just the typical mother-daughter conflict? Many German women have married a foreigner. And I know, there are many, far too many, who, like me, have become unloved, banished daughters after marrying a foreigner or forming a partnership with one. I think we can consider the story of the conflict between you and me as part of German history and one that has to do with being a woman.

You don't like the word 'history' or reference to it. But I want to talk about this painful matter. Because I am a child not only of this age but also one of that one. A child of this country that is my homeland, even though you — and many others — have told me that I have 'forfeited' my homeland and that I should get out and go far away to hide the 'disgrace'. I no longer want to be pushed away by you or others in this country, to cover up the problems or be kept quiet, to be dragged in the mud, insulted and humiliated. I don't want to walk around with the feelings of guilt that you and so many other people constantly tried to instill into me.

I do not feel at all 'guilty'. Guilty of what? Why should I be? I'm fed up with being greeted with a pitying smile by you and so many others, as if I were dead. And all this just because his skin is a nuance darker?

Where do you get the arrogance that allows you to look down on others? Where do you get your 'information' that makes you so sure about your appraisals and perceptions of people from other cultures, especially of those from Third-World countries?

How do your own experiences in this country, your prejudices, your phobias about communism, your hatred towards foreigners, compare to our history, our colonial past, racism, colonialism and fascism that still rages like an epidemic throughout this country?

When I wanted to introduce my foreign friend to you, you refused to meet him with a bluntness I could hardly comprehend. You did not want to have the chance of becoming acquainted with something that you had classified in your imagination as strange and threatening. You were fixed to your view of the world and perhaps you suspected it might begin to waver. You preferred to cast your daughter out and lose her rather than give up your set of standards and ideas. This way foreign workers and their families have no chance but to remain the 'unknown, menacing beings who are flooding the whole place.'

You not only don't like having this 'foreigner as a son-in law', there is something else you can't stand: the fact that I cross the frontiers you consider tabu. Your petty bourgeois subservience and your forbidding yourselves to have minds of your own are closely connected to everything that effects your lives. You don't like the fact that instead of going around whispering about something with my hand in front of my mouth, I stand up for a cause as openly and as loudly as I can and don't just make a donation at Christmas once a year. You don't like the fact that instead of just paying lip service to international understanding and tolerance for all mankind, I try to live accordingly.

To you, 'a foreigner' is an artificial excuse that gives you a reason to defend the old-fashioned, fearfully-protected ideas you've hung on to your whole life. And now I come, your daughter, and don't give a damn for them and show that there are other ways. It's clear to me why you have to hate me.

Why are you — more so than my father — so unbelievably reactionary, so hard and cruel? Isn't it true that, like so many others in the world, your life has been a bad deal? Aren't you one of millions who has been cheated throughout your whole life? Cheated of the often proclaimed 'carefree childhood', lacking recognition, love, independence and self-respect? Aren't you a woman who always got trampled, who always had to make sacrifices, who was always number two, second choice? You could never make your own decisions, either about your body or about your thoughts. Why is it that recently it's mostly women who make such hateful, anonymous calls whenever my name appears in a newspaper in relation to the difficulties with foreigners in dual-national marriages?

What drives you to put yourself above others from other countries whose situation is objectively comparable to your own?

The main question is no longer why I married a foreigner and how I could do this to you and those around me but why, in this age of international relations and the opening of our country to cultures all over the world, should this present a 'question' or a 'problem'?

I am one of the harmless ones who took your teachings and your ideals literally. Yes, who took you seriously. I lived according to your declarations, spoken during festivities around the burning candles of the Christmas tree, at funerals and when you read fairy tales and stories to me.

Do you remember? One day I brought a beggar home. I wanted him to sit with us at our table and eat with us. I was shocked when you roughly ordered him to the door, gave him two slices of dry (!) bread and forbade me "once and for all" to bring "such people" into the house. It was you who had taught me I should have pity on the poor and always be helpful. When I asked you why the man couldn't at least have something on his bread, you said, "He's used to it. Besides, he should work first. Nobody ever died of hunger if they had dry bread."

I have never accepted this explanation.

Once when I was sent alone to the garden to get some parsley, I met on the street a woman from the Gypsy camp. She was very beautiful. Her aura, her clothes, her movements. I must have stared at her as she spoke to me and asked if I lived here. I explained that this was our garden and that I had to get some parsley and go home quickly . . . She laughed and said, "You don't have to be afraid of me." Then she added, "Ask your mother if we could buy some vegetables."

A few days later we went to the garden together and the Gypsy woman came again. You sold her some lettuce. Then you told her she could take some lettuce from time to time without charge. After that you told me, "You know, if I sometimes give them something then maybe they won't steal from us." In the autumn when the Gypsies came again, the friendly woman brought us a plucked chicken. She wanted to thank you for the vegetables in summer. You wouldn't accept it and told me, "It's either stolen or poisoned. But you have to admit they're a beautiful breed!"

Do you remember when, after the end of the war in 1945, the American troops moved into our town? We were all so eager to get food. We were chased out of our house so that soldiers could set up quarters there. You and Grandmother were always trying to get back into the house to retrieve things (the silverware and the crystal). I had to help you. I was sent with the excuse to get some dishes and told to act as if I were hungry. Actually, I was hungry. At any rate, I was always given something from the soldiers' field kitchen and often had to go back several times so that you adults also got something to eat. Sometimes a black soldier would take me on his arm. If I gave him a kiss on his cheek, he would give me an orange. For me that was really wonderful. But there was an unpleasant side to it. After the 'kiss' I had to be scrubbed down when I got home and you told me that the man was inferior and bad. But because of the orange which, by the way, I was not to eat but to bring to you, I should let him do it anyway. I remember how confused my feelings were. I thought the black man was really very nice and friendly and not at all 'inferior'.

Why am I telling you this? The contact we have with the people our society considers to be the 'outsiders', the strangers and the unliked plays a big role in our early childhood. The contacts I had with beggars, Gypsies, black soldiers and children's stories were always real experiences for me.

You didn't help me, not even when my husband and I had been desperately looking for an apartment for months. We were prepared to pay a normal rent, but that helped about as much as being willing to accept an awful place that had not been renovated and had coal-burning stoves. "Your husband is an Arab? Sorry" or "Arabs, for heaven's sake, they're black, aren't they?" People who were more sensitive disguised their disapproval: "Oh, you know I'd love to rent the place to you but the neighbors wouldn't approve . . ." Those who had been given the job of finding a place for us let us know it was 'already rented'. One house owner suggested I should get my father (!) to guarantee payment of the rent. I was 27 then. Besides, my father was also to guarantee that there would be no orgies and no hordes of visitors staying with us overnight. One landlady took me discreetly to one side and asked if the soles of black people's feet are white or yellow. She had always been "very interested in finding that out." Forty attempts at finding an apartment failed. I was in despair, five months pregnant with our second child. In the end, after the birth of our second child, the health authorities we had turned to arranged some sort of emergency action and we were allotted a publicly financed apartment. When we moved in, a neighbor passing by who had seven children and was on welfare said, "Look at that. Now we have the riffraff coming to live in our house. Where are we living anyway? In the bush?"

Have you ever realized how people react to women who marry foreigners and just how much I could have used your help and solidarity in those years instead of having your discredit follow me around. Do you know what everyday life is like in those circumstances? A few examples:

When Nadia was born in a small hospital in Odenwald, the nurses and doctors tried to convince me to have an emergency baptism since a 'heathen' baby could not go to heaven. She knew that my husband was Muslim. As our baby had to be sent to another hospital because she was premature, they had, without first asking me, already arranged for the pastor to come. I was in a panic. Firstly because an emergency baptism seemed to imply that my baby would soon die, and secondly because I felt I had been declared incompetent. Only after I received the help of a determined midwife, who energetically told the others off, did things turn out in my favor.

My Arab-Palestinian husband was never able to become a naturalized citizen although all formal requirements had been fulfilled. We even lost all the legal proceedings. Reason given: as a Palestinian he posed a security risk. Besides, he still had contact with people from his country and was not willing to give this up.

At the beginning of our marriage in the early 60s, my husband had only a short-term permit to stay in Germany. He was a student. I was told I was expected to return with him to his country. What this actually meant in the case of a Palestinian had to be discussed separately. I vividly recall how we lived in constant fear because we didn't know whether his permit to stay in Germany would be extended or not. We could never make plans. Buying furniture would have been stupid. What would we do with it if we had to emigrate? Basically the legal situation for dual-national couples is the same today.

When I applied for a job in a bank I was told they could use me in the backoffice but not where I would have contact "with the public. We can't have terrorists' wives sitting at sensitive working spots, you have to understand that. Of course, we don't want you to take that personally."

I could never talk to you about these problems.

After five years of our not having any contact with each other, my husband wanted me to make peace with you. His attitude towards family as an institution made it difficult for him to understand that I never spoke to you. He arranged for us to meet. From the first moment you saw him, Mother, you said, "You might as well know right away, I'll never accept you."

My husband was, as you will recall, very polite to you anyway. He smiled a bit and said, "I understand you. But I can accept you that way too." I wanted to leave right away and a fight would have started immediately if he hadn't pinched me in the arm to indicate I should control my anger.

That night I had to sleep in your bedroom in the bed next to Father. My husband had to sleep on the roofed balcony. Even today, I cannot understand why we put up with this.

Even before we married and the battles over this planned marriage were in full blaze, you told me, "If you are so perverse to need someone like that in bed, then sleep with him. But don't marry someone like that!"

When my husband received his diploma and passed his exams at the top of his class, he received a small amount of money as a prize at a special celebration. The professor congratulated him heartily and said, "Best wishes! We have a lot of respect for you. *For an Arab, this is a great achievement!*"

When my husband came home after that, he was determined to stay in Germany no longer. He was almost in tears from rage.

But after all, in your eyes my Arab husband gained 'respect' by receiving an academic degree. "With all due respect," said my father. "Never believed it'd be possible."

When I later separated from this man because we could not cope with the daily problems, Father said, "There you are! She finally found a man with a decent profession from whom she could profit a little . . . and then he's not good enough for her. He was hard-working and well-educated. But this silly woman . . .!"

Our little Nadia once spent a holiday with you. Afterwards you said to me, "Somehow I am ashamed to go shopping with her because she looks a bit darker and who knows what people might think. It's embarrassing to take her with me in town." I never sent her to you on vacation again because I did not want her to feel your contempt and hear your racist ideas. Her openness and confidence should not be destroyed by such behavior. But you are not alone in talking as you did. I can show you further examples which occurred over the years that I did not tell you about to keep you from worrying.

After I participated in a TV program and an article appeared in a magazine which, to make matters worse, had a very sexist cover page (black nude male and white nude female), I received many anonymous calls and threats which went on for days on end. They got so bad that we had to arrange for the children to stay someplace else because we had to be prepared for anything — bombs, fires, murder and kidnapping. These threats were not being made by people on the fringe of society who only let off steam. They are part of the spirit of our times and of the infested climate of a society of people who until now have not been able to get over their colonial past, their conceited feelings of superiority and their considering themselves to be the master race.

Maybe you will ask me why I still stand up for a marriage or a partnership to a person from another country if it is so difficult. You are right. I did not think that this is how my parents, my community or my country are. I only really got to know what my upbringing, what you and what my country are like once I became different from what you had expected of me, when I no longer belonged to you, had friends outside your circles and disturbed your pseudo harmony. The shock that you and others have inflicted upon me because of my relationship to my foreign husband lives deep inside me. I am so frightened and my injuries are so immeasurable that right now I am unable to come up with any positive measure that might help us reconcile our differences. My identity that bonded me to you is too torn and injured. The process of finding new solutions is too difficult. The political perspectives that white men (and white women!) still have to offer following all the destruction they have caused are too hopeless.

One thing is for sure, Mother, although you surely won't like to hear it: We are learning to live with you. Had I never taken a step over the border, of this I am sure, I would never have learned what's behind your simple-minded masks. I would never have been able to conceive how wide and how enriching the world is beyond your petty bourgeois horizon. I would never have had the many lovely, exciting and sometimes amusing experiences that go along with learning about other cultural values. These experiences have made up a hundred times for what people like you wanted to destroy because of your delusions of superiority and your ignorance.

My Arab husband and I did not succeed after all in coping with the discriminations each of us had to face daily. He went back to his home country and I stayed here. And why have I now, after several years, married a foreigner again?

It is the same question, Mother, as at the beginning of this letter. It just happened. I fell in love again. He is someone close to me. It doesn't matter what kind of passport he carries. And I didn't want to live alone but I want carry on with the experiences and dreams I've had. You won't want to understand me, Mother, because you would have to change so much in your life. Today I am able to understand you a little bit better. But I cannot forget how much you have hurt me. ♠

How Far is It to Zurich?

by Beatrice Feder

Imagine that you have just finished a family dinner — you, your husband and your two sons. Imagine that your eldest has just announced that he is going to leave the United States and move to Switzerland. What thoughts, feelings and fears would come to your mind if you were told that someone you love planned to settle far away?

When our first-born was about two years old, I complained to his pediatrician that as soon as our son had seen the doctor's office door, he had screamed non-stop and wrapped his little arms and legs around the nearest tree. The doctor said, "Yes, he is a resistant child." What should I have said to this grown-up resistant child when he told us that he was moving to Switzerland? He had never been further away from his family than the two hundred miles that took him to college, never, that is, until he spent a summer vacation in Europe!

Should we have told him that it was too far away, that he and the young Swiss woman he wanted to marry would suffer from culture shock — we would too — that his father had sworn off flying thirty-five years ago, that he didn't know the language, that we would miss him too much?

Our son had spent a summer traveling through Europe. When he came home he announced that a friend he had met at the youth hostel in Grindelwald had invited him to spend Christmas vacation in Zurich. My maternal instinct told me not to ask if the friend was male or female.

When he returned to New York, he told us that he was moving to Switzerland to be with his 'friend' — Marianne. He immediately started German lessons — he who barely squeaked through Spanish in High School — and started giving away his books and records. When the school term ended (he was a teacher in a special education department), he left his job and his apartment and he did indeed move.

When he announced his intentions at that family dinner, my first impulse was to pretend that this move would not take place. It was surely only a romantic idea.

Our son had just ended a relationship and he was looking for a change, I told myself. As soon as this thought occurred, I was stricken by another. What if he didn't go? What if this was his real chance for happiness? How could I want him to stay near us to satisfy our needs when his own were elsewhere? No one ever said that parenthood was easy, I mused. I spent the next six months hoping that he wouldn't go — hoping that he would. I recalled reading that if you had done a good parenting job, your child would be able to leave the nest.

The day that our son left was an emotional and difficult one, but it was when I finally accepted the fact that he had, indeed, already moved away. It was also the day I was convinced that the distance would not diminish our feelings for each other.

About six months after he left, he and his lovely wife came to New York for a visit and to get together with our large, boisterous family. We are all huggers and kissers — but Marianne survived.

Since then we have visited Switzerland and they have visited New York. We fell in love with Marianne and with her country, and yes, my husband **almost** enjoys flying.

Luckily, our second-born lives close by and I can use up some of my mothering skills on him — you know, 'wear your sweater, take an umbrella, eat a good breakfast'. I guess I'm doing the same thing with our 'Swiss one' long distance. ♥

Return to the Ganges

Indu Prakash Pandey

It is a glorious October morning in Hardwar at the foot of the Himalayas.
This time of year at our place in the north of India there is a wonderfully
stimulating ambience — the murderous heat of the summer is as far away as the
unpleasant biting cold of winter that comes from the mountains. With Heidi, my
wife, I stand on the balcony of our apartment and look down at the river trying to
find its way in many branching rivulets through the wide, stony river-bed. This
is where the Ganges leaves the mountains and enters the expansive flatlands of
northern India. Hardwar, 'the doorway to God' is for us Hindus a holy place to
which hundreds of thousands of pilgrims stream every year in order to bathe in
the Ganges. Every twelve years, for the *Kumbh Mela,* their numbers swell into
the millions.

Our apartment should have been finished six months ago for the last
Kumbh Mela. But even now in October there are only the naked walls of red
bricks. Between the bathroom and the bedroom there is half a wall missing and
remains of construction materials are piled up in the living room. But this
construction site is a promise: someday we will live here together — here on the
Ganges where only a few hundred kilometres downstream my home village lies
and the town where my mother, my brothers and sisters, nieces, nephews and
their children live. I've never been able to take my wife there since they do not
know and should not know that twenty years ago I married a German.

I come from a conservative family of Kanyakubja-Brahman. In our view
of the hierarchy of Brahman people, we are at the top. And it's exactly this
special status that demands that we live in strict compliance with the social
norms. Tradition and the opinion of the elders were the absolute standard of
measurement of our behaviour when we were children. Therefore I did not even
consider resisting when my family decided in 1943 to arrange my marriage — of
course to a girl from the same caste.

I was barely seventeen then and active in the Indian struggle for independence. I had even already been in prison once which had caused my family great concern. They assumed that my rebellious temperament would be soothed by the joys of marriage and that my life would fall into an 'orderly' pattern. For a long time I suffered from the contradiction that I, the young freedom fighter, could challenge the British Empire but not stand up squarely to my own family members when they forced me into a marriage I did not want.

During the entire six years of my studies at the university I was in a state of mind that is best described in Hamlet's words, "To be or not to be, that is the question." I was torn between, on one hand, learning and dealing freely and courageously with the world and, on the other hand, accepting the responsibility for my wife and children.

When in 1949 I accepted my first job at Elphinstone College in Bombay, I was already a father of two sons and had more or less come to terms with my fate. I did my best to be a good husband and father but after a while I had to realize that under the changed living circumstances in the metropolis of Bombay this was not enough for my Indian wife. She was not satisfied to be respected only as a wife and a mother. She longed to be adored as a beloved one — the way the scenes were played in numerous Hindi films that were being produced and of course also shown in Bombay. Since I could not fulfil her expectations, our relationship grew increasingly tense. But in spite of the irretrievable differences mounting up, our marriage would certainly have continued to exist — simply because under those circumstances in the 60s in India there were no alternatives; escape was impossible.

Then came the year that changed everything. In 1962 I was invited by the South Asian Institute in Heidelberg to teach Hindi. I left India, my wife, our three sons and my whole big family. For the first time in my life I was free from family clans. I told my best friend that I did not consider returning just to get stuck in the same dilemma again.

But strangely enough, far from helping me stabilize my emotions, the unexpected liberation threw me into a deep crisis. In our traditional society with its many restrictions, I had been protected and emotionally sure of myself. The forced marriage had been, in retrospect, not without its pleasures and the newly won freedom was not without pain. In India I had never been alone and I had no idea what loneliness was. But in Heidelberg I learned what it means to be lonely, and above all what it means to be homesick. I could not separate myself from my past nor could I react appropriately to the challenges of my new surroundings.

With mixed feelings, I realized that everything in Germany functioned properly, even the people. In India one can only dream of such things since every water tap drips and daily life is mastered according to the principle of *Chalta hai* which could be translated as "It doesn't matter anyway." I liked the persistent and thorough manner applied in Germany to every task but I was horrified that human beings behaved like machines — as it appeared to me — and that they could be so insensitive to the concerns and needs of their fellow human beings.

Men seemed to be worse in this regard than women. Women were more open, more curious about the unfamiliar and more willing to take time for others and deal with strange customs and ideas. But I was thrown into another conflict when I realized they often had no second thoughts about changing their sexual relationships and demonstrating them by kissing and embracing in public. For me, the man from the morally strict Indian middle-class, this confrontation with sexuality produced a kind of forbidden fascination. It attracted and repulsed me at the same time. This becomes clear in a few lines translated from a poem I wrote then in Hindi, my mother-tongue. The poem refers to the flowing together of the Danube with the Ilch and the Inn in Passau:

At this joining of rivers
that Germans refer to as 'Mündung',
what I saw there —
how should I say it
how should I describe it to you?
New partners were formed
every night at this 'Mündung'.
On benches along the promenade
one played in the summer nights
the game of 'love' . . .
The black cover of the night,
like a curtain
hiding them
their play with nakedness.
Foolish people!
Every evening —
but with what kind of hope? —
do they lie in the arms
of strangers . . .

My feelings of insecurity were so deep that for many years I could find no peace. It suited my state of mind that for years I moved from one country to another — from Germany to the U.S.A., back to India, from there to Rumania and back again to Germany.

During these years of searching and emotional insecurity, I was divorced from my first wife. Of course it was my wish, not hers, to be divorced. Divorced women have had and still have a very difficult position in Indian society. And almost thirty years ago this was even more the case. Hindu girls are brought up to do anything for their husbands, even the unthinkable. And so, after much inner struggling, my wife was able to bring herself to file for the divorce in order to fulfil my wish. For this I am deeply indebted to her for if I had filed for the divorce, no Indian court would, in those circumstances, have granted it to me.

Therefore I feel obliged to accept the conditions my wife attached to her consent to divorce, among other things that I am to keep her informed about my life and my well-being and that I make sure that she does not have to suffer from material needs. Besides this, it was her wish that the family should not learn about our divorce. As a divorced woman she would have been treated as an outsider and would no longer have been able to participate in religious or family ceremonies. So she did everything she could to keep up the impression that she was still married to me. Her moving several years after our divorce to America to live with our eldest son made it easier to conceal the truth of the matter.

Admittedly, this arrangement also has advantages for me. Since our divorce involves a taboo, there was no reason for confrontation with my family. When I visit my over 90-year-old mother and my brother about once a year, we can be together as if nothing had happened. Of course they suspect something's not in order but they stick to the motto 'nothing can be what is not allowed to be'. If I told them openly that I am divorced from my Indian wife and that I've been married over twenty years to a *Mlecha*, someone 'impure', how would we all be able to cope?

On the other hand, my German wife, whom I met several years after my divorce, and I have been suffering now for twenty-five years from this uncanny situation. In India the places where my family and relatives live are 'forbidden territory' for Heidi. For twenty-five years she has been visiting this country regularly. But when I go to see my family, she has to stay with friends or acquaintances in another town. Of course she gets the feeling then of being shut out and shoved away. Heidi has grown to know India well enough in the meantime to know that with us a person is not regarded only as an individual but always seen in context with his or her family.

My two sons lived with us for many years in Germany. My wife took care of them. Like every family, we had our ups and downs. In the meantime, one son married an American and the other a German. Both 'foreign' daughters-in-law have visited my family in India which shows how times have changed after all. That young people who are living abroad also get married abroad does not mean they will automatically be excluded from the community. But for someone who gets divorced and then re-marries, and that the re-marriage is with a 'foreigner' — no, that's something else for my generation. And so my German wife can only look on while the daughters-in-law are accepted by the family while she can never let herself be seen there. The fact that she will never be able to meet my mother hurts her deeply.

Perhaps it's better that way. Maybe the injuries on all sides would be even greater. We agree that after all these years it is too late to confront my family with my divorce and re-marriage to a German. After all the years we have been together, Heidi has become accustomed to my culture and has, remarkably, learned my language. Her fluency in Hindi enables her to speak to women of my generation who usually do not speak English.

In India, parents still arrange the marriages of their sons and daughters. Almost all women still consider their husbands and children as the most important aspects of their lives. Obligations to the family still take precedence over one's own desires. There are many codes of behaviour, customs and rituals that express and preserve all this. Now, my German wife can look at all these restrictions with new and different eyes. There are many things she doesn't like — also many I don't like either — but she would never be as presumptuous or thoughtless as to put down or insult Indian people. That way she has made many friends in India who are replacements for family. And soon she will have her own four walls there where she will not only be a guest.

This home is also important to me. It connects the first half of my life spent in India and the second that I spent abroad. Even if it is always only for a few months, I'll always return to the Ganges. ♥

Coping with

Crisis

Caress

by Nicole Oundjian

When I was a little girl in Cincinnati, Ohio, my second grade teacher, Mrs. Nixon, slapped her large, liver-spotted hands on each of my knees and crashed them together. The inside of my knees were bruised for a week, but I never again sat with my legs spread apart.

I still say thank-you, I still don't point and I still press my knees together. I tell my boyfriend that the sum is greater than the parts, but he just says I'm old-fashioned.

I'll tell you the story, then you can tell me.

I had a tough day yesterday. I'm a photographer, and my shoot hadn't gone as I had planned — my Hasselblad broke down and a model never showed up. Then an older guy at the Chinese grocery was flipping through an erotic magazine, and pointing out particular shots to me. I did my best to ignore him, but that type always seems to come after me. The funny thing is that there was a girl behind the counter who was wearing a white sweater and obviously no bra. What do I do to attract them?

When I finally arrived home, Erik, my boyfriend, announced we had a party to go to. I dreaded this party so much I had made a point of forgetting about it. Of course, he reminded me.

"It's been planned for months, even before you got to Denmark," he said. "It begins at five, and they start eating at five fifteen. Please get ready."

"Fine," I sighed. "But I'm taking a shower first." I stormed into the bathroom — one of the tiny European kind, with the shower almost directly over the toilet — and let the hot water numb my back. I squeegeed the place, put on my robe and began to get ready.

I guess Erik felt guilty about rushing me and offered to brush my hair. That's how we met, you know. Two years ago, he reached out and grabbed a handful of my black curls at an art opening. I screamed, but a friend of mine introduced him as a Danish furniture architect given to unusual behavior. I don't know if that justified or nullified his behavior, but eighteen months later, he told me his visa had expired and now, here I am in Aarhus, Denmark. Everything seems different to me now, but he still loves to brush my hair.

"I think you'll know everyone," he said as he dried my hair, "but I want you to know that these things can get a little wild sometimes."

"What do you mean? Are you going to get smashed?" He doesn't get drunk very often, but sometimes, when he's with his friends, things get too out-of-hand for me.

"That's not what I mean. It's just that sometimes these parties can get a little wilder than what you're used to in Ohio. People don't talk about work, and sometimes, they let loose completely. You know, they express their selves."

"It's themselves Eric, not their selves," I said. I was getting irritated at his diction and his insinuation that I was somehow being puritanical. I tried to put myself in a better mood, but I felt plain and weirdly American. I wanted to call Donna Turtil, my best friend in Cincinnati, go to Barleycorn's for a drink, and not feel like my every word, every movement was being scrutinized. Maybe I did it on purpose, but I automatically put on a plain white t-shirt, a pair of Levi's and a black sweater. I looked so American, as if every drop of my ethnic background had been wrung out and homogenized into middle-class Ohio. I felt victorious, as if I had scored for my side.

When we pulled up into Henrik's house just on the outskirts of Aarhus, I felt hot and cold. We could hear laughter and shouting, and in the background, an old David Bowie album.

"Hey, *Glædde Jul*! We thought you'd never get here. Come in," Henrik bounded into the kitchen to get us two beers. "You're on time. All the food is ready, and everybody is hungry. Sit down." I felt as if I had personally held up dinner.

I was already uncomfortable when I was reintroduced.

"Naw! Er du Jody? Undskyld, taler du dansk?"

"Sorry, I've only been here a month, but nice to meet you."

An ample fellow with a thick accent stood up from the table.

"I'm Søren, and I happen to be one of your old man's bestest friends, and very good at stealing his women."

I thought about the last time I had heard of the term 'old man' and 'bestest' in my circle of friends. "Oh, you guys go back a long ways?"

"You better be careful Erik, I can already tell she likes me." Søren cackled, and lit a cigarette just as Henrik began serving huge platters of roasted pork and cracklings, tiny boiled potatoes, fried eel, smoked, marinated and pickled her-ring, raw eggs, warm patés, meatballs, baskets of rough black bread and bowls of butter and bacon-topped fat. Several cases of strong Christmas beer lined the wall nearby.

I'm vegetarian and ended up spending most of the meal pushing the food around my plate, and averting my eyes from those of the Danes. Occasionally, a conversation, obviously meant to include me, would begin, but once it became interesting, the Danes would switch to Danish. Natural of course, but I ended up feeling very alone and lonely in a very close-knit group. To make things even more uncomfortable, Erik would begin translating. I concentrated on folding my napkin into precise angles and brushing the crumbs from my plastic place mat. I began chewing my food forty times, and making sure my mouth was always too full for conversation.

"So, do you like Denmark Jody?" A redheaded woman I recognized as Lene pointed a fork at me.

"Well, so far. I've only been here a month, and I've been working most of that time."

"*Naw*! she exclaimed in Danish. "You already have work? That's fast. But you Americans are like that. Work, work, work."

"Yea, I guess so. What do you do?" I felt like I was asking the wrong question, but I had to start somewhere.

"Oh, I'm in school, studying political science. Do you know about employee-owned companies? I just finished a paper on them."

"No, I don't, but I'm sure they are interesting."

Without saying a word, Lene put her head into the crook of her boyfriend's neck, and licked it from base to the ear. She straddled one of his legs, and still looked at me.

"Do you know Arne? He's an accountant, and great with numbers, especially my numbers," Lene laughed. I guess I must have blushed.

"You Americans don't like this, do you? I noticed it before, when I spent two weeks in Michigan. I was with a family — and the two boys wore suits all the time and prayed. They told me I looked cheap since I didn't wear a bra. Ha! Just say no! But don't mean it."

I couldn't believe this was happening to me. I felt hot and cold and sick. I looked at Erik, but he was oblivious to my situation, and deep in conversation. My belly filled with pressure that rose from my throat. I excused myself, got up, and went to the bathroom. I had eaten and drank too much — the heavy, nutty taste of the Akvavit, and the smell of the fat on my fingers, and worst of all Lene's high-pitched voice. I scrubbed my hands, splashed water on my face, and returned to the table.

By that time the guests had begun to clear the table. I was collecting my plate, when Erik leaned over, kissed me and touched my breast.

"What the hell are you doing? Don't you ever, ever do that in front of other people." Even though he is my boyfriend, I felt invaded and exposed.

"Oh, for Chrise sake, relax. This isn't America. The police aren't going to break down the doors because we're having a little fun."

"Look, I don't care if these people sit on each others' faces. I just can't do that."

"Oh, sometimes you are such a tight-ass. Danes are just normal people feeling normal, natural things. All you Americans have to figure it out with a shrink — and then you still don't admit it — even to yourselves. You've always had this attitude about sex, that it's dirty or embarrassing. Why can't you just relax and enjoy it?"

"I can't believe we are having this conversation. I like sex, but not in front of other people. Shit. How many beers have you had?"

I got up, and put my dishes in the kitchen. By this time, everyone had migrated to the living room to dance frantically to the Rolling Stones.

"Look, I am sorry. I just don't feel comfortable doing that kind of thing. Erik? Can't you understand that? Look, can we have this conversation outside? I don't feel so good."

As we were going into the yard, I saw one of Erik's friends lying on the floor, his wife, I assume it was his wife, sitting on top of him, gyrating to the music.

"Doesn't she work at the Ministry of Culture? Geez, Erik, I mean, why do this in front of each other?"

"Why the hell not? What difference does it make? Do you have to be behind a door to express your love?"

"That's not what I said."

"Yea it is. What are you afraid of? Afraid somebody might see you? Might see your body? Your feelings? Might see you out of control?" He licked his lips and laughed at me.

"I can't believe this. You never talked this way in the U.S."

"Well, now I'm home and this is the way I feel at home. Don't you think I can feel this way? Don't you think I just want to feel you sometimes in front of my friends? Don't you think I can do things I can't always explain?"

We slowly walked around the parking lot, and as we approached Henrik's house, we passed a row of parked cars. I tried to support Erik, and keep him from slumping against them. In one swift movement, he swung up one arm and let it fall like a dead weight onto a windshield. I screamed, but the windshield didn't break. I didn't make a sound the second time when his hand broke the glass. ≈

Dream 1002

by Monica B. Suroosh

I am a third generation American, of German descent. My husband is Persian. He left Iran eleven years ago and came to America, after two years in Germany. It would seem to take an extraordinary love to bring two such different cultures together. With us, that has not exactly been the case.

American and European cultures teach that marriage comes after you have dated for awhile and fallen in love with a special person. In the Iranian culture, dating is not allowed. A man decides when it is time to get a wife. He may see a girl that he likes, learns that her family's values are basically the same as his; then his family approaches her family and an engagement is arranged.

This is what happened to me, only I was too high on romance to see it. My husband had learned to use the best of both cultures to get what he wanted. He treated me like a princess, kissing my hand, bringing me and even my Mom, roses. He treated me to the best restaurants, talked intensely to me for hours. He carried me in his arms to a beach hideaway, then sang to me in his native language. I was securely in his trap. My prince had come. After only two dates, we were engaged.

My parents planned an intimate wedding for us, complete with harps and violins. I had my dream wedding gown and I felt like I had just stepped out of the pages of BRIDES magazine. A little girls' (American media-made) fantasy was fulfilled.

But I was not being realistic. Only a few days after our wedding my husband gave me a huge dose of reality. He told me, honestly and politely, that he was not in love with me. He respected me. I had all the right ingredients to be a good wife. I had the values he thought were important. I was a good cook and I came from a good family. I also had the right hips for bearing children. He knew that I was the type of person that he could love, someday.

Someday . . . what a shock that was. I felt myself fall off the pedestal I thought he had put me on. I would never have the romantic adoration of a special man, like I'd watched longingly on television.

He told me all this with no reservations about how it would affect me.

His attitude was that once we were married, he did not have to try to communicate. Romance was not what he expected in marriage. We were married and that was the end of it. Even sex was mechanical. In his view, girlfriends and wives are two different things. A girlfriend you can romance. You want to be with her and talk to her. As his wife, I am more of a business partner. Everything is very practical. We both have an obligation to uphold our commitment to each other. He said the love that I was expecting comes through years of building a family together. All he wanted from me was patience to let the love grow. I had never experienced this level of commitment before. Having to learn to love your spouse was new to me.

Along with having to go through all the normal adjustments that a couple usually has while dating, I had to live with the idea that my new husband did not love me. I couldn't acknowledge the respect, promise of future love and solid commitment he had given me.

I was insecure every minute. I was extra jealous. Why would he stay with me if he did not love me? I removed the threat of past girlfriends' interferences. I convinced him we should move across country. Within two months of our wedding, we had.

Then the jealousy and insecurity also cost me a well-paying managerial position. I could not work the extra hours it required. I needed to be with him every second. I was half-scared he would find someone else while I was working. He might think I was not a good wife if I were not there to wait on him.

My attitude and his unwillingness to talk caused many problems for at least the first three years. I was a walking pressure cooker, afraid that every move I made would be something he could not stand. I felt I had to make him love me.

I set out to be the perfect wife, Persian style. I got a cook book from the library and learned to cook all his favorite dishes. I would wake up with him at 4 a.m. and lay out all his clothes. I learned and practiced his traditions and gave up mine. I tried never to need anything, even to go to the doctor or dentist. I waited until I could hardly see before I finally asked for new contact lenses. I never gave an opinion on anything until I knew what his was so that I could be sure to repeat it. I did projects and papers for his college classes. All the friends we made were Persian. I tried to be a copy of his mother. I was off balance and running in circles. And all that time, he never expected any of this. He was a devoted, committed husband. I just couldn't let go of my concept of marriage and love. It was constantly fueled by the mass media that had made me feel like I was missing something.

I began to put myself down every way that I could. I was trying to get positive comments from my husband. But it was only driving him away from me. My self-esteem was at its lowest point.

I could have ended the marriage at any time and recovered myself, but I was too proud and didn't want to lose face with my family.

Holidays were especially hard. I'd see couples everywhere sharing the day in some special way. Valentine's Day and our first three anniversaries went by like any other days. My birthday too. But the holiday that he made the most of was Mother's Day. This told me that I was doing a good job as wife but he still didn't think of me romantically.

The birth of our first child was also full of hurt. He was with me to see the birth but not to hold or comfort me. He did not bring flowers or do anything special. It was just another of my duties, done. I went home the next day, which was a Sunday and our first anniversary. He went to work that day, even after his boss had said the extra hours were not necessary. Again, my expectations of a couple's most intimate moments were shattered.

With children entering into this relationship, I had no choice but to change. I could no longer keep up the exhausting pace of looking after my husband's every need. I had to think of the children first. It was an adjustment for both of us.

I have learned to try every day just to be myself and be confident that I do have his love. Most of the time it seems everything is going smoothly except when I get sick, have a problem I need to talk about, or have extra stress. Then he is the last person I can go to and count on being on my side. I still wonder at times if he is only in love with the way that I take care of him and the life we have made with the kids. If I became handicapped, would he still want me?

I have never allowed myself to be a challenge to my husband. I think that explains some of his arrogance. Now he has to do extra special things at times to get my attention from the kids. He will surprise me and do the dishes once in a while and he gives me time away from the kids on some weekends. After the birth of our second child, he did bring me flowers and let me rest a few hours afterwards. I see a new admiration for me developing in him. This gives me more confidence in myself.

It helps that the emphasis is not on our relationship so much anymore; but rather it is on the family as a whole. We are focused on the children now. We have put our differences into perspective because we don't want to threaten the children's security.

I know many other couples who are very close. One of the factors that keeps them close is that they share a common activity. Our common interest is to bring our children up the best we know how. He sees how much they need him and is actively involved with them. He takes time to play with them and change or feed them. He is very good at disciplining when I need the extra support.

We try to run our family as one team. We came together to start this family and achieve the same goals. I know we have taught each other a lot. I have learned not to put so many expectations on others. When romance happens, it is extra special. Now it is genuine. He has learned that romance has its place in a marriage too. It wasn't just a tool for dating. And most importantly, he tries to talk to me more.

In the beginning of our relationship I was confusing my infatuation with him for love. Things can change about a person, like gaining a lot of weight with pregnancy. Infatuation can't always hold up under those changes. What we have now is a contented love. We try to understand, trust and respect each other's differences. I do miss romance and am very envious for a few days after being with a couple that shares that romantic love. But I try to look at the nice family life we have built and not worry so much about fantasies. It is nice to feel content, but it was 'hell' getting to this point.

Sometimes I still feel resentful about losing my career. My husband is very supportive of my working on a home-based career. It has always been a goal of mine to write, and now I am working on my writing career between diapers and bottles. My husband purchased the best equipment and supplies for me to pursue my goal. He pouts though when he is home and I want to lock myself away to write. So I know I am always free to pursue any goals I want as long as it does not disturb him or the children.

Ironically, a few months ago I was at a party with mostly Persian people. I was trying to talk a girl into marrying my brother-in-law. I feel that for him this is the best way because he is not used to dating and gets hurt very easily. For my son though, I would like to see him develop a friendship with someone he has a common interest with and build a love through this friendship. For my daughter, I would like her to have fairy tale dreams, but I know this is not realistic. She will need someone who will understand her and be there when the going gets tough, but I will not let her settle for just security. I want someone for her who will adore her. I want both of my children to understand that a person does not need to be married to be a success in life. ♥

Fences

by Susan K. Perry

My husband was backing our bulky camper into its parking spot. To accomplish this he needed to maneuver it between two brick fence posts. I signaled him to stop. He misread the meaning of my hand motion, and later, as we surveyed the minor damage to the fender and the fence post, it became clear to me that our crossed signals were one more symbol of the difficulties of intercultural marriage.

John, from whom I am now divorced, is originally from Lebanon. But even if he hadn't been raised in another country, ours would STILL have qualified as a mixed marriage. Over the years I discovered that, beyond the usual male-female barriers and the obvious cultural differences, we were entirely dissimilar — and, as it turned out, incompatible — people in a number of other ways.

For a while we managed to laugh about the more trivial of these dissonances, as all couples must. Just because he does long division in a different way doesn't mean you can't get along. Up to a point, it was an enriching experience attempting to join forces with someone who often seemed not merely foreign-born, but downright alien. Yet eventually, we lost our sense of humor. The struggle to understand each other simply became too exhausting.

Once, to make sense of my life when it was in the throes of transition, I found it helpful to list the ways we differed. Perhaps if other couples considered the following variables before committing themselves to marriage, much pain could be forestalled.

<u>Small town versus big city background:</u>

John was born and raised in Lebanon, in a village of 3000 inhabitants, where he knew every person and nearly everyone was a relative to some degree. I was born and spent my earliest years in New York City, the largest city in the U.S., where I knew well only my nearest relatives and a few people in my apartment building. John spent the first 24 years of his life in the same stone house. For one reason or another, I moved with my parents every three years or so throughout my youth.

Every few months during our marriage, John would receive a call from one of his old friends who was in town for a few days, and he treated each like visiting royalty. Hospitality to one and all is a paramount virtue in small towns. It meant more work for me to entertain all these 'strangers', and sometimes I complained.

When John first came to the U.S., he used to stop his car to help any stranger in need. I thought, with my big city cynicism, that he was being foolish. It took a few years of reading American newspapers and of needing help himself and not always receiving it before he began to adopt a more cautious attitude.

Big family versus only child:

John is one of eight children. I am an only child. I was used to getting nearly everything I wanted, while he knew there wouldn't always be enough of everything to go around. When I complained of the work it took to raise two children, John was impatient and unsympathetic.

It's hard for me to tune out distractions, possibly because there were so few in the house in which I grew up. On the other hand, John could be sitting inches from a typical stormy quarrel between our two sons and not notice it.

Night person versus day person:

John used to have to get up very early to go to work. I'd get up even earlier to prepare his breakfast. It became a habit, and it wasn't that much of a hardship for me, since once I get out of bed, I'm awake. John, on the other hand, used to dress, shave, eat, drive 23 miles to his office and sit at his desk for an hour before fully awakening (at least, so he said).

Then when my eyelids would close for the night, John would stay awake another hour and a half watching the late news on TV. Occasionally he'd try to go to bed earlier, but he couldn't sleep. I finally learned not to talk to him too early in the morning, and he caught on that if he asked me to iron his shirts past nine at night, I'd grumble loudly.

Smoker versus non-smoker:

I was never able to adjust to John's smoking. When our first son was six, he asked me, "But Mommy, why does Daddy want to die?" Now, it appears, John does want to live, since he managed to quit smoking after our divorce.

Another point of contention: salt. I refused to cook with much of it, since my body doesn't handle it well. John said nothing tasted as good if you added the salt later (his family owned a salt works and he grew up enjoying very salty dishes).

Engineer versus social worker:

John was an engineer when we were together, and I was a social worker who went back to school and became a nursery school teacher and director. Engineer-types tend to have very practical world views. Personally, I think people who consider the human consequences of their actions are actually more practical. And of the two of us, I may be the more detail-oriented. We debated often over who was the most logical and rational.

I do not believe the world can be divided into left-brain and right-brain types, nor do I feel that the terms male and female define who we are, except in the obvious biological ways. John and I certainly have different aptitudes, though. He can fix anything, or at least is unafraid to try. Hammering a nail into a wall makes me nervous. My strengths are more word-related.

I have since realized that both John and I have critical streaks, neither of us seeing what a child, for example, has done right as quickly as what he has done imperfectly. But that's not a trait that strengthens a relationship.

Extrovert versus introvert, or water-skier versus reader:

When I first met him, John was fairly gregarious. I used to be uncomfortably shy in all new situations, especially social ones. Later, he learned to enjoy spending much of his free time at home, either working on a car or watching TV. His favorite leisure pastimes became camping and water-skiing, while mine have remained reading and talking about people and ideas. John's interests appear to be mostly external and related to things, while mine are more interior and mental.

I don't swim, and I was always miserable going out on the boat — a necessity to arrive at the perfect water-skiing spot. John once told someone I didn't have any hobbies, that reading doesn't count. While many couples manage to pursue different interests and come back to each other refreshed and ready to share, our discrepancies were too great.

Were we from very different cultures? Yes, and that certainly contributed to our relationship difficulties. But it doesn't, in the final analysis, explain anything. We have each remarried, John to another American, I to an American also. We are both far happier now. ♥

Nights of Wine and Roses

by Margaret Ellen Jones

Final exams ended at the University of Arkansas, and Elsa and I went to the Rosewood Rendezvous to listen to the band, drink wine coolers and dance. Divorced and with two sons in high school, I wanted an advanced teaching degree that would allow me to support my family more easily. We talked about our favorite topic: life in Latin America. Elsa told me, "I'm so envious that you lived in Mexico two years!"

"It can be a wonderful life. For about what an average American earns, you can afford maids, a chauffeur and a gardener. But Latin America's not always a bed of roses. You have to watch out for those 'Latin lovers', you know. Just kidding, of course."

"Do Latin American men run around on their wives a lot?"

"It depends on social class. Poor men don't make enough money to have affairs, but well-to-do ones almost consider it a sign of manhood to have a few *'chiquitas'* on the side. I knew a couple of Mexican men like that. And yet they put their wives on pedestals. One of these men had six children at home and three more by his long-time mistress. She lived from what he gave her, and the wife even knew about her."

"I'd divorce my husband if I found out he was keeping another woman."

"Yes, Elsa, but you're a college graduate with lots of options Latin American women, even rich ones, don't always have. Because of their religion, they don't even consider divorce."

"So the 'other woman' has no chance of the man divorcing his wife and marrying her?"

"Right, even though he supports them both. And these men, unfaithful as they are, sometimes put their illegitimate sons through college. Remember, upward mobility is not the reality in Latin America that it is here in the States. The gap between the rich and the poor there is so wide that this is about the only way poor women can better themselves. Rich men don't marry poor women. And even though they're often smart and pretty, these women are still poor. And of course they want their children to have a better life than they have, which is what we all live for, isn't it?"

We were finishing our first drink, when a couple of Hispanic men who were friends of Elsa's sat down at the next table. Elsa introduced everyone, and the men joined us.

One of them was Ramón. He smiled, shook my hand and sat down. Several years younger than me, he had thick black hair, warm eyes and bronze skin. He ordered me another wine cooler, and we began to talk.

"Where are you from, Ramón?"

"Venezuela."

"No kidding! I spent two weeks there last year. How long have you been in the States?"

"Only one year. I spend most of it studying the English."

"I understand. I'm studying Spanish."

"No kidding! *Entonces, ¿por qué no hablamos en español?*"

"*Está bien.*"

We spent the rest of the evening together. When he said, "*Tú bailas como una mariposa,*" I was flattered. If an American had told me I danced like a butterfly, I'd have laughed in his face. When the bar closed, Ramón asked for my phone number and I thanked him for a wonderful evening.

The next weekend, Elsa and I were getting ready to go to the swimming pool when Ramón called. I accepted his invitation to go dancing.

"I'll pick you up tonight, okay?"

"I'll be ready."

Elsa and I lay by the pool talking about my plans for the evening. "He's probably one of those hot-blooded Latin lovers. Don't fall for him until you get to know him, because you could get hurt."

I didn't answer.

That night I put on a new dress, then sat down to watch TV while waiting for Ramón, but I wasn't interested. It grew later and later, and I had to remind myself that Hispanics were always running late; it was nothing to be upset about. When the doorbell rang at eleven, I opened the door with a forced smile.

Without apologizing about the late hour, Ramón grinned and walked in. I made some *sangría* and handed him an atlas so he could show me his hometown. He talked on and on about the beautiful Venezuelan countryside. Around midnight he asked if I still wanted to go dancing.

"*Claro, Ramón. Vámonos.*"

We sat at a small table by the dance floor and ordered drinks, then danced until the bar closed. Ramon took me out for breakfast, and we sat long after the meal was over, drinking coffee, telling bilingual jokes and laughing so hard I was afraid we were disturbing the other diners. It was daylight when he took me home. He walked me to the door and kissed me good night but seemed unwilling to leave. Against my better judgement, I invited him in for coffee.

He eagerly agreed, though all he drank was a sip; he was much more interested in my lips.

I stood up. "Look, Ramón, I've had a wonderful evening, but it's time for you to go now."

"I'll never understand you *norteamericanas*; a person from my country would never tell a man to go home; it would not be polite." Although he wasn't smiling, he hadn't been offended, for he called again the following week.

We continued to date, and it turned into a memorable summer. Ramón knew how to dance, how to talk, and he lavished me with compliments about how beautiful I was, how well I spoke Spanish, whatever came into his head. He called me "*mi amor*", "*querida*", "*vida mía*", all the love words I'd read but never heard.

As time passed, our romance deepened and we became lovers. Ramón asked me not to tell anyone I was going out with him, and I complied, without understanding why. Elsa suspected we were dating, but I refused to discuss it.

Though it was awkward, I respected Ramón's wishes because I didn't want to lose him. I was insecure and thought he might be ashamed of me. After all, he was handsome and friendly, and he had his choice of many women prettier than me. I wasn't sure how much he cared for me, even though he spoke of undying love in romantic phrases.

From what he said, his parents were well-established, so he didn't have to worry about money. He took me to elegant restaurants and gave me expensive presents. Because I loved flowers, he often brought me a dozen roses.

In September the boys came back home after spending the summer with their father, and I introduced them to Ramon. Jason and Scotty were open and friendly; Ramón was only twelve years older than Jason. They would play soccer together on weekends.

In time, their affections cooled, and by Christmas, conversation among the four of us had become strained. The boys managed to have something else to do whenever Ramón and I invited them out for dinner or a movie. I sensed they didn't like Ramón, so we stopped talking about him.

After the boys came back, I never spent the night again with Ramón. Regardless of how much I wanted my relationship with Ramón to continue unchanged, it was more important to me to preserve the image of a chaste mother to my sons. This new situation was hard on Ramón because I insisted on being home by midnight, regardless of where we went.

Frustrated, he said with large, sad eyes, "Sometimes I think you love your boys more than you love me."

"Of course I love them, but comparing my love for them to my love for you is like comparing hamburgers to hot dogs."

"You are so logical! I have never met a woman as logical as you are — not even in the United States of America."

After Ramón got used to the new rules, his attitude softened. "Darling, that's one of the reasons I love you. I think much more of you as a person and especially as a mother because of your love for your children. There are depths to your character I never realized before." He was becoming quite articulate in English.

Tears came to my eyes. He did understand! The values that were important to me were also important to him. Despite the time we spent apart, I began to think maybe there could be a permanent future for the two of us.

One night Elsa called and invited me out. I hadn't heard from Ramón for a few days, which wasn't unusual, so I accepted.

When my eyes became accustomed to the dark, I saw a man who looked a lot like Ramon sitting at a table with an attractive young blonde. I couldn't see through the smoke, but when they stood up, it was definitely Ramón! The woman kept putting her hand on his arm as they sat, and they danced close in an intimate way. A knot came into my stomach and I wanted to rush onto the dance floor and pull Ramón away from her.

Trying to enjoy myself, I ordered another glass of wine, but couldn't swallow it for the lump in my throat. A man I'd known since before meeting Ramón invited me to dance, and I talked him into driving me home. I had to get out of there! He took me straight to the apartment, then I told him good night and went inside, not caring what his opinion of my brusqueness might be.

I tried to go to sleep but was still awake at three when the doorbell rang. I went to the door in my robe. "Who is it?"

"*Margarita, mi amor, déjame entrar.*" I opened the door and let Ramón in.

"What are you doing here at this time of night?"

"I came to see if you are okay."

"Of course I'm okay; why wouldn't I be?"

"I saw you with that other man, and I thought, I thought, well . . ." He couldn't finish. "*Ay, mi amor . . .*"

I tried to act more curious than jealous. "Who was your friend?"

"Oh, she's just the sister of Emilio." He flopped his arms about in the *Latino* way, designating a matter of no importance. "Emilio had a date tonight, and he asked me if I would take her out. I was really just baby-sitting." He giggled, a little too obviously.

"Oh, come now, surely you can do better than that!" I waited, but he didn't answer. "Does she have a name?"

"Of course, *querida*; don't be silly." He laughed nervously but remained evasive.

I yawned.

Ramón tiptoed to the bathroom and bedrooms and looked in. "Well, I just came to see if you and the boys are all right. I can see you're sleepy and I should not have come. I'll call you tomorrow, okay?"

"I'd rather you never called me again, Ramón." I crossed my arms to hide my shaking hands.

He looked at me. "I'm sorry you feel that way."

I returned his look with no emotion whatsoever.

"What can I say?" He stood very still.

This time I was the one who didn't answer.

He shrugged his shoulders. "If that's the way you want it." Then he left.

I locked the door and leaned against it with weak knees. So Ramón was jealous too! It was all right for him to be out with another woman, but when he saw me with another man, he had to come and check on me. He apparently had one set of rules for himself and quite another for me. Talk about the double standard!

The magic was gone. Catching him with another woman brought reality into the open at last. I felt a headache coming on, so I took an aspirin and a sleeping pill and went back to bed.

At ten the next morning the doorbell rang, and I dragged myself out of bed to find Elsa outside.

"I thought you might need someone to talk to."

I squinted at the light while consciousness returned. Wordless but full of gratitude, I threw my arms around her.

We went into the kitchen where I made a pot of coffee. The boys had left a note saying they'd gone to play tennis.

"I guess you knew I was dating Ramón, didn't you?"

"I figured he was the one. Did you know before last night he was dating other women?"

I stared, not believing her.

"I've seen him with that blonde before. And she's not the only one. I wanted to tell you but hated to spoil your fun. After last night though, I knew it was time to talk."

"He tried to tell me she was Emilio's sister! Long blonde hair, and she's supposed to be a *latina*!" I paused to steady my voice. "It was bound to happen sooner or later, Elsa. But it's over now. And I'm glad. I really am." The necessity of convincing myself forced me to repeat a little.

"There's something suspicious about a man who wants to keep a relationship secret," said Elsa. "You know what I mean — as if he were married or something."

"You're right. I tried to ignore all that, but now it's finally explained, it's a relief. I jumped over a big hurdle last night. And now I feel better; I really do." But I had to fight to hold back the tears.

"I'm turning my life back over to Scotty and Jason, who are going to need me during the next few years. And God knows, I'm going to need them!" Tears finally broke through. "I had feelings for Ramón I never had for any other man, . . . but it was the love of the poet, the romantic, . . . and I'm basically a realist. I guess I should feel bitter toward him. But I don't. Hurt, but not bitter. He reacted the way he was brought up, and I understand."

"Margaret, men are not brought up to act the way Ramón did last night. There's no excuse for that!"

I decided to tell her. "Ramón never talked much about his mother except to shake his head and say, '*Es una santa.*' Then one day I made him explain. Did you know she raised one of her husband's illegitimate children by a mistress he had for years? Ramón's mother raised that child right there in the house with Ramon and her own children."

Elsa stared at me.

"Don't you dare tell anybody."

"Don't worry; nobody would believe it." She sat thinking a moment. "I wouldn't let the little bastard in the door. I couldn't stand a constant reminder of my husband's infidelity."

"Yes, but don't you see, the little boy's not to blame. Ramón's mother did the loving thing, the Christian thing. Instead of allowing an innocent child to grow up in ignorance and poverty, she opened her heart and her home and took him in. Ramón wasn't exaggerating, she is a saint.

"I believe Ramón really loved me, in his own way. But his way is not my way. He'll make some nice girl a good husband some day, but I could never be that girl. If I were ten years younger and didn't have two teenage sons, I'd fight that blonde for him. But I've got too much to overcome.

"And besides, I'd have to lay down some ground rules about honesty between a man and a woman. I've already learned Ramón's not the type to follow rules. He's too much of a free spirit. Oh, I'd love the roses, all right, but I'm afraid the thorns that come with them would break my heart." ℵ

The Door

by Jo Ann Hansen Rasch

"My god, I'm sick of Mexico. It's worse than visiting your parents in Ireland," exclaimed my husband, shaking the handle of the heavy carved door. "Nothing works in this country."

"Darling, don't fuss. It only takes a little understanding."

I took the key from André and placed it in the lock. Carefully I unblocked the mechanism and the door opened. André stalked into the room. He marched over to the window and with an impatient toss of his arms pulled the sliding glass shut. Then he turned around and said accusingly, "I'm going to spend another night being bitten to death." Uninterested in any reply, André went into the bathroom and shut himself in.

Two minutes later he was back again.

"I don't know why we've come for Anita's wedding. She's already been married once before. I thought you Catholics couldn't do it twice."

"You know how close we are and I enjoy seeing my friends. Oh, why do I try to explain? You're so self-sufficient."

Already, too many years had gone by since Anita and I had shared a train compartment and discovered that we were both going to Geneva. We had been in contact ever since. I sighed. The holiday was turning into a nightmare. I knew André loathed traveling, but he had come, wanting to please me.

"My dear, being self-sufficient is a compliment for a Swiss. Please, where did you put the insect repellent?"

I withdrew a bottle from my suitcase and handed it to André. Now he was going to spray the room purple, so I seized my nightgown and took shelter in the bathroom.

After undressing I started to brush my hair. It was electric and stood out, making my face look full and vital. I was stimulated. New places did that to me, but André only felt comfortable in Geneva. His town had everything a person could ever want, he always said, and I almost agreed. Geneva WAS a lovely place to live in: safe, clean, but . . . shaking my head, my thoughts returned to the present.

At that moment André came into the bathroom. He was wearing pajamas that made him look vulnerable. I knew that he was miserable but I didn't feel like helping him. He quickly brushed his teeth, then left me alone.

I turned away from the mirror, put my lingerie in the wash basin and ran the water. I would do some minor chore to keep my hands busy and my mind fixed before going to bed. It would be a shame to start worrying about our different backgrounds; I was too happy for that. A fountain of emotion surged up inside me. Tonight I felt that my senses were inebriated. Mexico made me drunk. There was so much colour, odour and sound. At the Plaza under the spell of the *mariachi* I had danced until my legs gave way. And the singing . . . just like in the Dublin pubs. I had learnt long ago that it was possible to climb over the language barrier if I really wanted to.

I finished my washing, hung it up to dry, then went back into the bedroom where André was absorbed in a book. I glanced at the title, THE MIDAS TOUCH, printed across the cover in gold letters, as I sat down on my side of the bed and picked up my own book. It seemed that that D.H. Lawrence's American novel was situated in the area where we were staying.

"What did you say dear?" murmured André.

"I was saying that Lawrence's quest for an ideal community became a devastating experience."

"I'm not surprised. The price this place costs and even the telephones don't function."

I tried again. "The weather is going to be glorious for the wedding," I said but André had returned to the charms of money and power. I gave up. What did the weather really matter? It was strange how one could fuss about rain on a wedding day.

A mosquito buzzed near my head. André lifted one hand and caught it.

"That's the fifteenth," he said with satisfaction and laid the bloody corpse on the sheet next to all the others. I slammed my book shut and got out of bed.

"I'm not tired and this room is suffocating. I'm going downstairs for a drink."

"There's some bottled water in the bathroom," André reminded me.

"No, I'd like a real drink."

I threw off my nightgown, pulled on a dress and tightened the belt about my waist. André turned a page, unaware or uninterested in my sudden agitation. I knew that it was useless to provoke a discussion.

After all, what did I really want? André loved and protected me the way Swiss men had been protecting their women for centuries. I understood that, but if only I could live freely without always making justifications for him. It would be so much easier if André metamorphosed into the sixteenth dead insect. At that moment he looked up from his book.

"Well?" he asked.

Without warning that single word submerged me with fear. White. Terrifying. Unknown. My skin tightened, as if to keep my body from falling apart. I had to act, do draw myself together.

One step, then another, I approached André. I would try to communicate one more time.

"We exist in two different worlds, and I'm going to live in mine as I want," I said, looking him straight in the eyes.

André stared back, waiting to hear the reason for my outburst. Like a thick rope, silence knotted us together.

"Let's talk about it tomorrow," he said, before reopening his book and starting to read.

I turned abruptly, and lifting up my chin, walked over to the door and pulled on the handle. But the door was stuck. I jerked the knob and struggled to adjust the key. What a fool I was. I should have remembered that the bloody thing needed mending. Now what was I going to do? Should I turn around and fall into André's arms and cry my heart out? Or maybe I could just laugh off our differences or pray to the Virgin of Guadalupe for patience.

Slowly I got down on my knees, but instead of invoking the patroness of Mexico, I set to work to open the door. ¤

Common Ground

by Lila Bartsch

I am in front of the mirror, getting ready to go out, taking extra care to look my best. But it is late and I should hurry up.

"Mary, Honey, it's almost quarter of," John shouts across the barrier of bedroom walls and the evening newspaper.

Mary is the westernized version of my Iranian name, 'Mehri' — a slight modification, but one that, nonetheless, has made my life in America much less complicated.

"Coming," I say, feeling guilty about not being punctual. 'Honey' summons my American sensibilities, punctuality being one of them. It addresses that part of my character formed after coming to America, leaving out the inner core which precedes John. It leaves out the shy school girl who grew up in a brick house just three blocks from the mosques. But 'three blocks' is an American yardstick. There is no such expression in Farsi, my native language. It seems the American part of me is taking over. No matter how hard I try now, I find it difficult to revert to my old self again. That part only comes to me in momentary flashes before the tide of the present washes it away like a picture drawn in sand. I am back in the room staring at the mirror. The clarity of my reflection wins over the blur in my mind.

* * * * *

The French windows of the air-conditioned restaurant are sealed tight but through the glass panes a spectacular view of the Potomac at dusk stretches out in front of me. We spot our friends right away. Hussein and Ferdouse are facing the entrance. They wave. Jimmy and Louise have their backs to the door. Hussein and Ferdouse are both Iranian. Jimmy is also Iranian — his real name is Jamshid. His wife, Louise is American, a Californian, to be exact. A chorus of protest and laughter greets us as we sit down. Ferdouse taps her plate with her fork. Mockingly, she announces the arrival of 'Madame' and 'Monsieur'.

Gradually, we all settle down around the table, three childless couples about to have one of our regular, monthly dinners. We are in an Italian restaurant 'with three tablecloths' as Ferdouse puts it, using her own privately-invented grading system for the equivalent of a three-star restaurant.

Her husband, Hussein, extends a ceremonial welcome in Farsi.

I mutter something appropriate in return but my eyes are on Jimmy who is, unfortunately, on the far side of the table from me. He looks handsome in his navy suit and his pastel blue shirt. A strand of his dark, curly hair hangs over his high forehead. His eyes are a deep brown, like two cups of coffee. I suppress a strong urge to tell him how good he looks. I don't think the comment would be appropriate. In the country where we both were raised, a compliment from a woman to a man, and a married man too, can be misinterpreted. Instead, I turn my attention to his wife, Louise. She is tall and very fair. Her hair is newly cut and carefully coiffed. She is wearing a blue silk dress.

"I love your dress, Louise."

"Liz Clairebrone, who else? I'll wear whatever she designs, even if it's a *chador*."

Everyone laughs.

Jimmy and Louise look a perfect couple. Jimmy is the one with the charm, of course. But Louise is the efficient, practical half — the wife who would push her husband forward until he went very far. Louise gives perfectly orchestrated dinners for Jimmy's business associates. Her parties are so smooth, one wonders if they have been rehearsed, like wedding ceremonies.

Ferdouse and Hussein are even more of a couple. They have their roots in the same soil. They are like two branches of the same tree. It doesn't take a lot of effort for them to reach out and touch each other. All they have to do is to lean slightly in the other's direction. Their closeness is a kind of oneness so rare in a mixed marriage. It shows in the way they talk together, the way they look at each other. I doubt if John and I will ever have those telegraphic conversations, those exchanges of looks, or if we ever will be capable of communicating so many words in the course of a simple look, a twist of a smile, a brush of a hand. But things cannot be perfect between Ferdouse and Hussein either.

Ferdouse complains from time to time of Hussein's 'possessiveness' or of his 'male chauvinism'. But as far as I know, this is true of all the men of my childhood — my father, my uncles and my male cousins. Is that perhaps the reason I, myself, am married to an American? But there is another side to an Eastern man's possessiveness. A positive side. When I compare Hussein with

John, Hussein is the warmer, more protective type. He is the one who calls Ferdouse from wherever he is to make sure that no burglar has broken into their house, that Ferdouse hasn't had a car accident.

As a child, I had resented this protectiveness that rendered me a sheltered existence and restricted my freedom. But now that I don't have it, I miss it. I even need it. John takes it for granted that I am capable of looking after myself. He hardly ever worries for me. Or if he does, he does not show it. There are times when I long for that secure feeling I experienced as a child — that someone stronger than myself is watching over me.

My thoughts are interrupted by Ferdouse saying, "I ran into Samie yesterday." Samie is an American woman who lived in Iran for many years. She is also married to an Iranian and speaks fluent Farsi. "I almost asked her and her husband to join us," Ferdouse continues. She is looking at Louise. Everyone smiles knowingly. Louise doesn't like Samie and she makes no secret of it. John touches Louise's arm lightly as if to soothe her and half-seriously asks her, "Okay, Louise, tell us why you don't like Samie."

"Oh, I don't know. I suppose she's just too good at being Iranian. I don't trust people who are so at ease in another culture. They can't be real."

"Like Mary and Jimmy, you mean," Ferdouse cuts in mischievously, looking at me. The others laugh. Louise has a hurt look.

"Not really. Mary and Jimmy don't act as if they were Americans, I mean born Americans. You know what I mean . . ."

"Oh, I don't know," John says, "Just listen to Jimmy when he orders dinner for us all. You can't get to be more American than that." Everyone laughs, Louise included.

"Why did Samie and her husband come back anyway? Why didn't they stay in Iran?" Louise asks, not letting the subject of Samie go.

"They left during the hostage crisis, like a lot of other people." Hussein says.

We are quiet. The subject of Samie comes to rest. Sounds of conversation from other tables drift onto ours filling the temporary vacuum. John is the first to break the silence.

"By the way, where were you all during the hostage crisis?" John asks, "I know where Mary and I were."

"We were in Tehran waiting for things to ease up, then we gave up." Hussein says.

"Well, Mary and I were dating. Then all of a sudden I'm like a sore thumb because I'm going out with an Iranian girl."

"Louise and I didn't even know each other then, lucky for Louise." Jimmy says.

"I think Iranians are still a little unpopular with some Americans," Louise says, "so when I meet new people, I tell them right away that my husband is Iranian. I say, 'We've been married for five years and I've been a hostage ever since!' That breaks the tension right away."

We all laugh again.

We order food. From my end of the table, I see John's face in full, his narrow bones, his pale forehead topped with a fine layer of blond hair. Everyone else is seen only in profile. I put the faces together, in my mind, the six of us into three pairs. Why John and I? Why Jimmy and Louise? Why this pairing of the opposites, of strangers. Why not Jamshid and Mehri? How could the two of us, being born in the same town, have missed each other's paths and travelled thousands of miles to a faraway land and teamed up with strangers? Perhaps, I have yet to get over the reality of my mixed marriage and my leaving home. There are still those odd nights when, waking up next to John, I panic from being so far away from home. In the darkness of our bedroom, I feel like a child who has wandered away and gotten lost in the woods. Woods that stretch on forever.

"I think I'll have the same thing as Mary," Jimmy says ordering the chicken dish that I chose. Somehow this makes me happy, confirming our similarities. Jimmy is one Iranian man who makes me feel totally at ease. With him, somehow the male-female gap, so prevalent in my country, seems narrower. Perhaps that gap drove me away from the familiar world of my childhood — the faces, the streets, the bazaars, and the minarets — and made me adopt another language, another culture. Luckily, I was young and not yet set in my ways. I learned whatever I could, first at college and then, from John. I convinced myself that I was happier with an American than I could ever be with an Iranian. And now, after all these years, I have come across someone like Jimmy. What I sought years ago in vain has turned up here, unexpectedly. Why is it that when Jimmy is present, John seems to recede into the background? Only his foreignness stands out. There are just a few years of my past that I can share with John. But with Jimmy, I can share my whole life. I can restore the real me and fuse my past and my present together. With Jimmy, there is no end to reminiscence and laughter.

Once, when the six of us were having a *sushi* dinner, Jimmy and I discovered we had both known the same primary-school math teacher. Jimmy imitated the teacher, reciting multiplication tables in exactly the same voice. I laughed until my eyes watered. Hussein and Ferdouse laughed too. Then Jimmy tried to explain the joke to Louise and John, but they didn't catch on. Somehow the humor got lost in translation.

After coffee, we walk along the river. The summer evening is warm and humid. A threat of rain emanates from the partially covered sky. Dark waters lap the shore. Hussein points at a circular building on the opposite side. It is lit up by hundreds of lights.

"That's the Watergate Building." We look where his finger is pointing. We all know about Watergate like we know about Samie and the hostages — more common ground for us to share. In the diversity that separates us all, these common grounds strengthen and nourish our relationships. There are innumerable things that the six of us cannot talk about together. Experiences we have not shared. We only have America of the eighties in common, and a fraction of the seventies.

For a while we are silent. I have fallen into step with Jimmy. I feel content. The humid warmth of the evening wraps itself around my shoulders like a velvet shawl. I wonder who will talk first and in what language. Jimmy speaks first, and to my surprise, in Farsi.

"When you were a child, did you ever go on river picnics on moonlit nights?"

His question opens long-forgotten vistas in my mind, a panorama of water, light and darkness. I see another river, the river of my childhood thousands of miles away from the Potomac . . . the ancient bridge with the many arches, faded and crumbling in appearance but strong as steel at its core, standing there hundreds of years. I see the picnickers, each family nested in one of the arches, sitting on mats around their samovars and pots of food. And I see the full moon, shining high above the curves of each arch. As children we ran past the arches of the bridge, watching the moon duplicate itself under each arch, as if there were many moons.

"Did you?" Jimmy repeats when I don't answer.

"Yes, almost every month. They were our favorite outings. We had to have long naps in order to be allowed to go on the picnics."

"I remember how excited we were too. We would wait until after the sunset before loading up the cars, then we'd be off."

I look up at the sky to search the moon. It is not a full moon. It is a new moon, thin and brittle like tinted glass, not at all like the moon of the ancient bridge they played hide and seek with. By its position, at the zenith of the sky, I can tell that it is very late. I can tell the evening is over. That night I sleep peacefully. My dreams are colorful and reassuring.

* * * * *

The next day I gather all my courage and call Jimmy in his office. I want to see him outside the matrix of our monthly dinners. I say I want to give him a copy of my resume. When I put the receiver down, I have the impression that he has expected my call. In the afternoon he meets me in the lobby of his office and takes me to the cafeteria.

"I was going to break for coffee anyhow."

The cafeteria is large, bare-looking and self-service. Jimmy picks up a tray and joins the small line of employees taking their coffee breaks. I stand there awkwardly until Jimmy pays for the coffee and we sit down. I can't help thinking that the cafeteria is the wrong setting for our first meeting together. Quite a contrast to the three-tablecloth restaurant in Georgetown. There are no tablecloths at all on the hard, shiny surfaces of the tables.

We talk about the night before which somehow seems far away now. We discuss the meal we had and the quality of the service. We begin in Farsi but gradually drift into English. Both of us seem tongue-tied in Farsi. For some reason English feels equally unsuitable. It is different when our American spouses are present and we have the excuse of speaking English for their sakes. But now that the two of us are alone, it does not seem right to speak a foreign language. The conversation remains constrained. Even my body feels stiff. I try to relax in my chair.

Jimmy slides the sugar bowl and the Coffeemate sprinkler across the table to me and I busy myself with my coffee. But the magic of the night before evades me, as if it evaporated with daybreak. I list the missing elements in my mind — the Potomac, the three-tablecloth restaurant, the wine and most of all, John, Louise, Hussein and Ferdouse. I begin by missing John and then the others one by one, including Louise. As if each and everyone of them were needed to create the bond that ties Jimmy and I together. As if Jimmy and I could enjoy each other's company only within that matrix of monthly dinners.

I look at Jimmy. He too, looks pensive as if about to disclose a secret. Finally, he leans forward and rests his elbow on the table next to his empty coffee cup.

"Louise is very envious of you."

"Envious?"

"Of your job-search. I told her you'd be coming to the office today with your resumé."

I feel surprised. A little betrayed even. I have not mentioned our meeting to John. Again, I busy myself with my coffee, tilting the cup to drink the last drops of the tepid, milky liquid. I don't want Jimmy to see my face. But he pauses to catch my full attention.

"Can you keep a secret?"

I feel the fast beat of my heart.

"Louise is expecting a baby. She mustn't know I've told you. She's planning to announce it herself to you and Ferdouse at some kind of luncheon. So you see, jobs are out for her, for a while anyhow."

It takes me a few seconds to recover. Then I congratulate him.

"Thanks Mary. I can't believe I'm going to be a father."

For the first time I'm conscious of Jimmy's and my own foreign lilt and the way we both stumble over the pronunciation of certain English letters. It is like music in need of a fine tuning. This is an odd meeting. Two Iranians in their American cloaks. I see the two of us as we really are, thousands of miles away from our hometown on the other side of the world. Two Americanized Iranians. I see the extent to which we embody our American spouses. There is as much of Louise in Jimmy as there is of John in me. There is so much of America in both of us. I miss John again. He is my link, my umbilical cord to this culture in the same way that Louise is for Jimmy.

"Louise is desperate to have a girl but pretends to prefer a boy for my sake. She's heard all those stories about Eastern men wanting a son. To be honest, I'd rather have a girl too." Jimmy goes on.

We've finished our coffee. He looks at his watch, says something about a meeting. He accompanies me to the lobby where we say goodbye. He turns toward the elevator and I head for the door. Then I hear him running after me. I stop.

"The resumé, you forgot to give me the resumé."

I fumble in my pocketbook and give him the sheets. We wave and I step onto the sidewalk where the brightness of the afternoon engulfs me. ¤

Somebody Else's Life

by Susan Tuttle-Laube

Today it was especially bad. The tight feeling in her chest had gone up into her throat, almost strangling her. It was an effort to swallow. If she thought about the feeling too much she'd start to have trouble breathing. Like last time. And then the panic would set in.

"Can't let it get that far again," Lynne told herself and slowly breathed out, gazing out the apartment window as she did. Another gray, overcast day. Nearly three weeks straight of dull, damp weather. She allowed a tear to trickle down the side of her nose before angrily wiping it away with the back of her hand. A very small sob escaped her. She sniffed hard, turned away from the window and headed for the kitchen.

An empty coffee cup sat on the counter and, although it wasn't quite 7 a.m., her husband Uli had been gone for over an hour. He claimed that he got his best work done at the office early, before the other engineers came in. But it didn't mean he came home any earlier in the evening. In the beginning Lynne had tried to get up with him so that they could at least have coffee together, but she was just too tired. And Uli had casually mentioned that he rather liked the silence of the apartment in the early morning hours. It gave him time to gather his thoughts before leaving.

Lynne swallowed hard again. She took a deep breath as she angrily knocked the coffee grounds from the filter of the espresso machine they had gotten as a wedding present. "This is ridiculous," she mumbled to herself. "I can't start the day this way." Tears welled up without warning as she packed fresh coffee into the filter and turned on the machine. It made its familiar humming sound as it forced water through the tightly packed grains of coffee while Lynne waited, the "on" light swimming before her tear filled eyes.

Uli had suggested that Lynne see a doctor about the breathing problems and the tightness in her chest when she first mentioned them. Maybe it was asthma or an allergy, or even a strained muscle. She found a doctor who spoke some English and made an appointment. But the doctor hadn't been too helpful. He did some poking around, listened to her chest and asked her how long she had been in the country. He then asked her if she was homesick. She left his office frustrated and angry. At home in the U.S. the doctor would have been much more thorough, there would have been tests and maybe even an X-ray and less talk about countries and homesickness. As if homesickness were something to go to the doctor about. The tightness and the difficulty breathing were real. They sometimes woke her up at night. And they were there every morning when she got up to the empty, dark apartment.

Lynne came back from her thoughts to see the coffee just as it swelled over the edge of the cup. She switched off the machine in time but spilled the over-filled cup as she lifted it. "Damn," she whispered and reached for a dishrag. She squatted down to sop up the coffee from the floor, and saw with dismay that the floor was in need of a real cleaning. She wondered if Uli had noticed. He was critical of her housekeeping, noticing things like a dusty shelf or a basket of unfolded laundry in the hall. Sometimes he'd make comments or ask her what she did with her time. She felt obligated to keep a clean house for him since the truth was she didn't have anything else to do all day. She didn't work, knew very few people and couldn't communicate with the neighbors. But on some days she felt so depressed that she could hardly manage to get herself up, let alone make the bed.

But there were other days when she felt a bit spiteful. As if an untidy house could be her means of revenge. On those days it was all Uli's fault for bringing her to this foreign country, making her give up her job, her family and her friends. Then she would leave the bed unmade, dishes unwashed and forget to clean the hair from the bathroom sink. She'd leave drawers half open and the blinds closed. If she was in one of these moods on her wash day, she'd skip it, meaning Uli probably would bring an armload of his shirts to his mother to do up. The odd thing about these "spiteful" days, as she came to think of them, was that she was free of the tightness in her chest then and could breathe easier. But there was a down side. When Uli would come home he'd look around and become more silent than usual. He'd be polite, ask her if she was feeling all right and then ask her if she minded if he went out for a while. She never asked where but after he'd leave the tightness would return. She'd pick up a little around the house, swallowing back tears, aware of each breath. Then she'd go to bed, waiting for him to return. He'd usually come in around 11, quietly undress and neatly fold his clothes over the back of a chair. He'd noiselessly slip in beside her, unaware that she was awake. And within minutes his regular breathing told her he was asleep and she was alone again.

When she met Uli two years ago in the States, things were different. He was on a six-month project with a Swiss engineering company. They met at a party and it was easy for Lynne to fall for him. Uli was very charming and his accent really won her over. He'd say funny, original things, like once, when his hand brushed against her thigh he told her she had 'beautiful shanks'. She adored the way he said 'somesing' for 'something' and she was especially fond of the way he unconsciously lapsed into Swiss dialect during their most intimate moments together. For him, she was everything the girls he had known in his country weren't — spontaneous, fun and flirty. They had some great times together. Then things became more romantic and serious. When his project ended and he had to return, they continued the romance via long, daily letters and expensive phone calls. He invited her to come visit and meet his family. She saved up her money and vacation time and flew over.

The visit was fantastic. It was her first time to Europe and Lynne embraced it all with enthusiasm. Uli introduced her to his friends and family. They went out of their way to speak English with her and seemed very interested in everything she had to say. There were endless introductions, lunches, dinners, bottles of wine and romantic walks through cobblestoned streets. She felt special. The whole experience had a dreamlike quality to it. She felt as if it were almost somebody else's life.

The time together went by too quickly. But it ended with a proposal. Lynne felt sure and ready and she couldn't bear to be separated from Uli again. The idea of moving to a foreign country and being married to Uli was nearly too good to be true and everyone told her so. When she got back to the U.S. she gave notice at her job, sold her car and furniture, and moved back to her parents' home. Uli came over and they had a big wedding in the U.S. with her family. It was a tearful goodbye, but all her friends were envious at the glamorous new life she'd be living in Switzerland.

The glamor lasted about two months. Uli had a lot of time back then. They had long weekends, sometimes taking off for the mountains or Paris on the spur of the moment. They were always together. Uli was patient and considerate, careful to include her in conversations at parties, translating when he had to. Lynne called him at work at least three times a day to ask how to do things and how to get places. And he'd call her just to see how she was doing. He'd often surprise her by coming home early. It was a time of dinners out and breakfast in bed.

All too soon, things began to pick up at work. A new project was started and Uli became busier. He had less time for Lynne. He surprised her by asking his mother, who spoke little English, to come over to their apartment and help Lynne get things settled and to keep her company. These days were awkward for Lynne, who wanted to please but was frustrated when her mother-in-law would rearrange a shelf Lynne had just organized, or wipe down a counter she had just cleaned. They couldn't communicate and Lynne frequently felt that she wasn't doing things quite right. Uli acted hurt when Lynne asked him to ask his mother to come by a little less often.

He also suggested she start language lessons, and she did, but she didn't do well. She felt inept at languages and bored by the class. And she was frustrated by the fact that the high German she was learning was not helping her understand the rapid Swiss dialect she heard around her. Uli seemed disappointed when she announced that she was going to quit. But he couldn't understand what it was like for her. After all, languages came easily to him. She assured him she'd probably pick it up again. But secretly she wasn't too sure.

Secretly she wasn't sure of a lot of things, she thought as she finished cleaning up the spilled coffee. She sighed and carried her coffee into the dining area. A basket full of ironing sat next to the chair on the floor. Yesterday had been one of her "spiteful" days. Uli had seemed annoyed when he came in last night to the mess. He said something about "everyone having their job to do" before going out. She knew he had gone to his mother's because there were six freshly ironed shirts on hangers hanging on the back of a chair. Lynne felt a twang of guilt which was quickly replaced by anger. "He should have married his mother" she murmured, lightly kicking at the shirts with her toes.

Uli expected a lot from her. When she agreed to move here and give up her job, just ten months ago, they had talked about her getting work here. But it didn't happen. Her lack of language skills kept her back, and her options were limited. She didn't mind keeping house, but suddenly the rules and expectations were different. When Uli had sort of "moved-in" to her apartment in the States for the time that he was there, he ironed his own shirts. He never said a word about dishes in the sink or dust on the leaves of a houseplant. He helped around the house. But things here were a lot different. And Uli was different too. There was a pressure to keep things neat and orderly, up to some invisible code (which became visible whenever her mother-in-law came by). At first she tried hard to keep up. But as the days dragged on, and Uli became busier with work, it became a struggle for her to keep up with even the minor tasks.

Even the parties and dinners had changed. Their Swiss friends seemed to speak English less and less, lapsing into dialect and leaving Lynne out in the cold. Uli didn't bother to translate everything for her anymore. Last weekend at a party Lynne felt the first pangs of jealousy since meeting Uli as he relaxed and laughed with a Swiss woman, sharing some private joke which she was not part of. Sometimes she couldn't help thinking that they were laughing at her, talking about her, secure behind the wall of language which excluded Lynne.

Lynne kicked at the shirts a little more actively. One fell down in a crumpled heap. The same shirt he had worn to the party last weekend. The party where she sat silent most of the time, drinking more wine than she usually did, sinking into her chair. SHE'D probably have his shirts ironed perfectly, dinner on the table and a floor so clean you could eat off it. SHE'D also love doing it and they could joke in Swiss all day and call each other '*Schatzli*'. And in bed together SHE could be sure it was her he was talking to.

Lynne felt her chest tightening again. Tears welled and she tried to will them away. She became aware of her breathing, each breath consciously drawn in and out. She thought that if she didn't think about the next breath, it wouldn't come. She started to feel a little light-headed. Her only thought now was, "don't panic, breath slowly, don't panic." But her heart pounded and waves of cold and heat poured over her. Her hands began to tingle and then her feet. She gripped the table. It had never been this bad before. She thought she might pass out. And then the phone rang.

Lynne reached for the phone and answered it, whispery and breathless. It was Uli. Tears streamed down her face. She sat down on the floor.

"Uli," she cried, "please come home right now. Something is terribly wrong." She then hung up the phone, wrapped her arms around herself and sat rocking on the floor, waiting. ¨ •

Author's note: 'Somebody Else's Life' is not a true story. I don't know Lynne, nor is this story based on my own experience. But I have known 'Lynnes' and 'Ulis', I have known culture shock, and I have known loneliness. It is a fictional story, based in reality.

Dilemma

by Kate Mühlethaler

Tears welled up in my eyes as I replaced the receiver. I couldn't understand it. Hans had been so unlike himself, evasive even, when I'd mentioned his Christmas Party. For the first time he hadn't even seemed glad that I'd phoned. I felt the distance between us acutely. I was at home in England and he far away in Switzerland.

I looked out onto the busy street below. The ordinary, everyday scene of busy people passing by failed to calm me, a child was screaming his head off. I felt strangely restless. The pale winter sun disappeared behind a dark menacing cloud. I shuddered and attempted to gather my thoughts. I tried to comfort myself that he'd promised to tell me all about the party when I went over for skiing in a week's time. There was something odd about his voice, not just his accent this time.

What a pity I had to miss his party celebrating his thirtieth birthday. I'd been determined to make Hans something he could enjoy with his friends. After racking my brains for weeks, I'd decided to send him a large jar of homemade mincemeat, a recipe my friends adore. Perhaps my mincemeat would help destroy the myth that British food was uneatable, I had thought wryly. How many times had I longed for lemon and meringue pie, trifle, fruit crumble with custard, or even bread and butter pudding, while perusing an unexciting Swiss dessert menu, which usually consisted solely of various kinds of ice cream.

I'd taken extra care with the mincemeat for Hans, wrapped the jar in shiny paper and tied a red ribbon around it. The old-fashioned label proudly proclaimed 'Kate's Mincemeat'. Before mailing it to him, I'd enclosed an explanatory note, telling him the mincemeat could either be used for small individual pies or one large one.

Suddenly I knew what had happened and why I felt so unhappy. Obviously, he'd met Someone Else at his party. Someone ravishingly beautiful, clever, witty and a brilliant skier — in short everything I'm not. This meant the end of our relationship. As he'd said, he would explain it to me in person when I arrived. He was too soft-hearted to break it to me on the telephone, I decided, as I reached for another tissue.

A week later I was staring out of a large window in the Whisper Jet as the familiar barracks of Berne's Airport came into view. Would this perhaps be my last visit? I tried to spot Hans waiting behind the wire fence — and was he ALONE? I told myself to stop jumping to conclusions and give the poor fellow a chance. Yes, I must be positive, I decided. The plane was dead on time. My stomach lurched as I gathered my things and prepared to leave the plane. How often I'd laughed with my friends over letters to Agony Aunts in magazines, at titles like 'He's found another, what shall I do?' So many people got into messes with their love-lives, but I never had, not until then anyway. It wasn't amusing anymore. I attempted to 'pull myself together'.

"Hello, Darling, did you have a good fly?"

That's polite, meaningless small-talk, I thought as I pecked his cheek. "It was okay," I blurted out. "Listen, if it's awkward having me here, under the circumstances, I can go and stay with Heidi in Zurich."

"Whatever do you mean?" asked Hans, bewildered.

I looked up into his face and noticed that his hair was short. SHE probably hadn't liked it long and so he'd had it cut. Was anything else different? I couldn't be sure. We climbed into Hans' ancient Renault in a tense, unusual silence. He took my hand. I was again touched by the natural kindness that had first attracted me to him and I began to sniff.

"Look, what's the matter? Don't you feel good?"

"I'm okay. I just want to know what happened at your party. You were so strange about it on the phone." The words came out in a rush.

Hans looked disturbed. He took a deep breath.

This is it, I thought. I'd been able to think of nothing else for days. A sense of unreality overcame me. I felt like the heroine in a third-rate play.

"Well, I don't know quite how to tell you this . . ."

Here it comes, just like I'd heard in umpteen films and plays. I braced myself.

"I don't want to hurt you, but . . ."

Oh, for God's sake, get it over with, I pleaded silently.

"Well, you know that present you sent me?"

What an odd beginning, certainly not the standard one, I thought. I nodded miserably.

"And you know my English isn't very good?"

I was becoming curious, in spite of myself.

"Well, I read the label and your note and just to be sure, *ja*, what it is, I look up 'Mincemeat' in this pocket dictionary you give me last year. It says *Hackfleisch*, so I think it some kind of pickled meat, as it smells funny, see, and then I look for word 'pie' and find it is *Pastete*. Well, I was too lazy to make some dough for pies for the party, I decided to have spaghetti."

I was beginning to wonder when he would ever get to the point.

He continued, unable to look at me, "Spaghetti is so easy when cooking for many guests, you know," he explained hastily. "So I just chop up some onions and garlic, throwed in the mincemeat and then added much *pelati* and tomato purée. As usual, I was in a wery big rush. I was a terrible cold, you know, bad nose and I didn't vant to infect the sauce by tasting it. I ask young Peter from upstairs to have a quick try. I tell him it is a special dish from England."

I suddenly realized he had used my mincemeat as spaghetti sauce. How ghastly! But what about HER?

"Peter make a rather bad face when he taste it. He advise me to add a lot more spices and I did."

I was spellbound. "What happened next?"

"Well, I cooked the spaghettis . . . "

"Spaghetti," I corrected him automatically.

"And make a salad and then we all sit down to eat . . . it was terrible. One after the other, they all put forks down and there was awful silence. I tried some, honestly Kate, you know, it was . . . UGH! I explain to guests that you make it just for this party and it's an English specialty for Christmas. I even pass empty jar around with that lovely label you make. Someone saw it was already made in October, it must be *kaputt*. Then Bernie go in hurry to bathroom . . ." His voice trailed off dismally. "I couldn't say it on the phone."

I threw back my head and laughed. Tears began to stream down my cheeks. I grappled for a tissue. I laughed until I choked.

Hans couldn't have known how relieved I was, but joined in my laughter. Soon we were both bent over convulsing in mirth and I had a sudden picture of the birthday crowd, also choking over their plates of spaghetti. Hans took me into his arms, probably thinking he would never understand women, especially the English-speaking variety. At that moment, it did not seem to matter.

The next present I gave him was a better dictionary. ♥

Identities

Banana Peel Bridges

by Bill Kirkpatrick-Tanner

When speaking with my Yankee family and friends, I occasionally refer to my wife as 'the OREO cookie of my existence'. Very cute, isn't it? But when speaking with the Swiss, she's 'the BASLER LECKERLI of my existence'. The practical reason for the difference is clear: Americans are without a clue as to BASLER LECKERLIS and the Swiss have been deprived the divers joys of the OREO. The world is not a perfect place. But although the point is clear in both cases, the discrepancy demands addressing: which is she, an OREO or a LECKERLI?

The problem of identity, of course, is a psycho-philosophical banana peel. Brilliant minds have ruminated about the issue at least since Aristotle guessed, wrongly, that A = A, and I don't expect us to resolve its complexities by bedtime. It boils down to the questions "Who am I" and "Who are you?"

Dogs don't have this problem, but as human beings, from the time when, as children, we realize we can lie, we grapple with the difficulty of knowing (like, really **knowing**) the people around us. Love may be nature's way of paring it down to a manageable size for us. But today we're not interested in paring it down, we're interested in cranking it up, specifically: how do you get to know someone from a different culture? Identity is tricky enough in one culture; in two cultures it's a banana peel on an oil slick.

By way of example, let me tell you how adorable my wife is, starting with the obvious, her Swiss accent. Some day a great theorist will turn his musings to the phenomenology of accents and explain why foreign intonations possess such sexual allure, why it was so important that Garbo talked, why my heart started slam-dancing with my sternum when I first heard my wife speak. Her English is excellent, but who, tell me, **who** could resist the lilt in her pronunciation of my favorite baseball team, the "Sheecago Cubs," or the fact that she comes from a "wery, wery small willage?" It was love at first sound.

There's one snag, however: that's not how she really talks. She occasionally garbles an English word, but — get ready to be impressed — she's **fluent** in German (or as close as a German-speaking Swiss can get). I plummeted in love with the way she talks only because my own monolinguality prevented her from talking the way she usually does — in German.

In other words, an accent is the linguistic equivalent of red skies at dawn. Beautiful but symptomatic. Cross-cultural lovers should realize that in most cases, one partner is attempting to communicate in a foreign language. Obvious enough, I know, but remember what even the best translation can do to a poem; now think what it can do to a human being. (The caveat applies, by the way, to gestures, too.)

Although I immediately started learning German after I met my wife, and was doubtless just as irresistibly adorable with my own accent, I couldn't carry a conversation in German for the first year. So English was the operative language in our relationship. And this was at that most critical stage, while we were getting to '**know**' each other. Luckily, I've since discovered that she has scads of ways of making herself understood in any language, and that, as recompense for my grammar lessons, she has more than a few things to teach me; nonetheless I had to learn that language-based first impressions are to the personality as mascara is to eyelashes.

But although language tyrannizes, it represents merely one of the major obstacles to discovering your partner's identity. Not only are the impediments to getting to know each other numerous, they are also elusive, exotic, enraging, staggering and stupid.

Take intercultural gift-giving, which between two consumer societies should be easy enough. But nothing is simple, like when I was living in New York and my LECKERLI sent me a new CD from Switzerland as a three-and-a-half-month-since-our-first-kiss anniversary or some such. Now, in Switzerland the CDs are sold freely naked, unencumbered by the tonnage of cardboard and plastic that shrouds a CD in America. This I did not know. So when I received the unpackaged CD, I naturally assumed that my adorable little OREO cookie, the skinflint, had opened the CD, listened to it, probably even **taped** it, the miser, and then tossed it off to me as a gift! Months later, when I first was in Zurich, I learned of her innocence. But who's to say what lingering impressions the incident has left behind, perhaps when I occasionally interpret her native thrift as cheapness, like when she won't let me blow our tax reserves on a Porsche.

Okay, that's true. I may have a latent touch of cheapness lying around somewhere myself, perhaps even equal to my improvidence, who knows? But the core of the identity problem lies in the fact that a person's individuality can't be summarized by a simple list of apposite adjectives: to say that someone is cheap or cute or smart just doesn't do justice to his or her complexities. As the Taoists point out, "Thirty spokes share one hub," and so it may be with identity: at the middle of our personality is a dominant disposition, out of which radiate a host of peculiarities that continually change with our moods, growth and external influences.

Readers who, like me, were silly enough to leave their homeland for mere undying love will understand this, since new cultures are good at coaxing out new aspects of our personalities. For example, since my wife and I moved to Switzerland, I haven't changed all that much, fundamentally, and yet my new surroundings have awakened some new qualities in me. Superficially, what started out in my case as your classic happy-go-lucky easy-going fellow has metastasized before my very peepers into that fastidious subspecies of marble known as the Swiss. Unexpected traits, like the ability to get myself organized (long dormant, presumed extinct), have lurched to the surface of my personality, displacing my characteristic procrastination. So while my American friends remember me as a slothful, lumpish do-nothing (to know me is to love me), my new Swiss friends think I'm some kind of upstart Bartleby the Scrivner. These new friendships get very restricting, since only my old friends let me get away with the nonsense of being the person I was ten years ago — and actually still am. A leopard **can** change his spots, and it doesn't make him a tiger.

These superficial cultural changes carry, of course, the danger of a banana peel buttered. My wife and I met in one country and then moved to another, and these changes seem to mean the dreaded: **I'm not the same man my wife fell in love with.** And might that not cause problems in the long run? What if she fell in love with me precisely because of that very happy-go-lucky attitude, now snowed under by the Swiss avalanche?

No matter.

Because now we get to the secret that should give hope to cross-cultural lovers everywhere. We may be influenced by the culture we're living in, but we can, ultimately, transcend it — a few adjustments here, hold your fork differently there, and you've got it sussed. You can still 'be yourself' in another culture, because culture is nothing but a product of a prevailing mentality, and like all products can be freely purchased, enjoyed — and discarded.

Cross-cultural partners are specialists at this: each is at times forced to put up the cultural 'cash', as well as lower their own trade barriers. Intercultural relationships form the GATT negotiations of love. Each partner is forced to penetrate the other's cultural shell, transcend it, pull back the shell to reveal the tender meat of identity, climb the spokes to reach the hub.

That's where we cross-cultural lovers have the advantage in the identity dodge. Persons from the same culture can go through life never pulling back that shell, never realizing they should. But we confront and overcome the cultural barrier every day, without even considering that by doing so we build a bridge over that impotent banana peel and get to know (like, really **know**) our partners. ♥

Mistaken Identity

by Floramor Kjær

"Congratulations! You have taken the first step towards discovering an eternal treasure! This will happen when you find your number one Asian lady whose main objective in life is to please her husband. The enthusiasm shown and the pleasure they derive in accomplishing this goal is almost embarrassing! The beauty in this unique kind of treasure search lies in the reality that somewhere on the vast Asian continent, a compatible lady is waiting for you and we intend to do everything within our power to help you find her!"

The above text is taken from a pamphlet of a mail-order bride business, an agency that sponsors women, the majority from Asia. Of these, more than fifty percent of the women are from the Philippines. Their addresses are sold to men who mostly come from western Europe, the U.S.A. and Australia. Some people call this business 'citizenship through marriage' because the objective of both parties is a permanent relationship via letter writing.

For example, a woman from Thailand pays the agency for advertisements of her personal ad, and a man pays the agency for the addresses of the women. The man eventually becomes attracted to a woman, then he flies to her country, marries her and then brings her back to his country where she eventually becomes a citizen.

I am a first-generation Filipino-American woman who was born in the U.S. I am an American citizen and I consider the San Francisco Bay Area my home. I am not a mail-order bride and I had never met any mail-order brides when I lived in California. I did not even know about the mail-order bride business until I came to Denmark to visit my Danish boyfriend, who has since become my husband. We met while he was an exchange student in California. We are the same age.

One rainy summer day in Roskilde, Denmark, I learned more about how others might perceive me. I was staying in my Danish boyfriend's house. One night we went to a party and I met some of his former schoolmates. Many could not imagine that I came from the U.S. I did not know Danish then but I did recognize some words that sounded like English and heard the word 'Philippine' when they spoke. Other than this, I noticed that there was a lot of drinking of Danish beer.

The following day I asked my boyfriend if I was paranoid to think that his friends were talking about me in a negative way.

"Many Danish people think that Asian women are exotic, but . . . not 'pure'. Some of my friends were surprised that you didn't smile as much as the other Asian women who are brought to Denmark. They joked that it didn't seem like you would do my laundry."

"Well no wonder I felt like I was being talked about, especially with my long, dark hair."

"When a Danish man is with an Asian woman, people think that he brought her here," he continued.

"Bought or brought?" I asked.

He grabbed a local newspaper and opened it to the back pages. In it we found an ad of Filipino women seeking citizenship through marriage. After reading it, I realized that throughout that party, many of his classmates might have perceived me as a 'buyable' object. It was upsetting to be considered a whore just because I am Filipino. I became angry. This anger and my curiosity triggered me to learn more about the mail-order bride business.

I wondered what Filipino traits these men sought and why they would consider acquiring a woman in this way. I wondered why the women do this and what can be done about it.

Asian women are projected as 'untouched' by western civilization, as smiling rice-peasants and persistent hard-working housewives who do anything to please, and as oriental prostitutes. These projections are seen in television commercials in the U.S. showing flight attendants or also in advertisements in weekly news magazines showing cute, happy and giving women.

In a 'How to Find a Date' book, some men who choose this service say:

"American women have lost their femininity and are just as callous as men. They don't wish to be submissive at all."

"I don't want a wife who is career-minded, I want someone who doesn't care about the outside world, someone who will make her life around me. She must be a virgin."

"With oriental women, family comes first. They make faithful wives who are family-oriented."

One journalist from a daily newspaper wrote that apparently many men who use these marriage services are middle-aged or older, disillusioned and divorced. The man needs to have enough money for the membership fee, plus extra capital for transportation, his traveling expenses, wedding fees and more. Another journalist from a monthly magazine stated that statistics indicate that the average age at marriage for the husband is 52, for the wives, 32. The Asian bride trade is tailor-made for those men who feel they will be young by having a young wife. Divorced men and elderly widowers may have more modest goals of wanting a cheap housekeeper or a live-in nurse.

It is difficult for me to believe that some men would pursue such a type of relationship and yet I keep finding many advertisements by numerous businesses thriving on selling brides.

Why do the women do it? A spokesperson for the Immigration and Naturalization Service in Washington, D.C., stated that apparently, they want to go to another country. Once they reach their new country, however, their stories do not always end happily. It is a situation that is rife with the potential for fraud and for people getting hurt. Most of the Filipino women speak English. Many of them who get involved in this business live in poverty and hope that marriage to an American or European will bring them wealth and happiness.

What really happens in the modern mail-order bride business? In a typical situation, the man is between 45 and 50 years old and the woman or girl is between 19 and 25 years-old. The man is usually well-off or economically secure. He has to be to pay for all the expenses. The woman has only a little education and must have enough money to pay the agency for the advertisements. The man expects her to be the Asian stereotype. When she does not live up to that role, he often abuses her. She may be a modern Asian woman and may not be submissive. Most countries expect her to stay married to her American or European partner for at least two years to become a citizen of his country and for her to be able to bring her family from her country to her new country. Officials do not support her if she gets abused. Sometimes abused women are able to stay temporarily in shelters for battered women, but at most only six weeks at a time. Before the two years are over, her husband can send her back to her country or, if she does not live in the same household as his, the immigration department may eventually do this. She may end up staying with the man because she would feel like a failure to her parents if she returned home again. The mail-order bride business is another form of slavery.

Many say that it is a 'marriage of convenience'. Most of the mail-order brides that I have met in Denmark would not like to admit that they went through this experience to live in Denmark. There are some mail-order-bride couples who end up happy together. It would be hard to judge who has more of the advantage.

This does happen in Denmark, so there have been people who will first ask me, "How old is your Danish husband?" A few times when I was walking on Stroget in Copenhagen at night from my fitness club to my apartment, Danish men have asked me, "How much tonight?" No, I was not wearing revealing clothes. They approached me only because I am a Filipino woman. There are a few bars that employ women from Thailand, Brazil and the Philippines as dancers or escorts here in Denmark, especially in the capital, Copenhagen.

I have not been able to come up with a solution to this overwhelming problem of the mail-order-bride business. It is actually outlawed in the Philippines and illegal in Denmark but there are four of these agencies in Copenhagen alone and I have seen ads for agencies in Sweden too. Some are advertised openly in international newspapers in Europe.

What I have found is that as a Filipino woman, I can bear witness that not all Asian women who live in the West, and are married to non-Asian men, are mail-order-brides. People who do meet me can hear that I'm American when I speak Danish, Spanish or English. When I speak English, many can understand that I'm from the U.S.

In a Danish newspaper article, a Filipino nun was interviewed about the problems with mail-order-brides from the Philippines. She answered that this business is not original. For example, Swedish men would buy women from Holland or Poland. The reason why it is more concentrated in Asia, in particular the Philippines, is because the Asian countries are not doing well economically. To stop this business, it is not enough just to warn the women who are willing to accept marriage this way, but we have to help their countries do better financially.

It still upsets me and I wish that I could do something more about it. ♣

My Family and Other Foreigners

by Terri Knudsen

I'm an American, my husband is a Dane. The first years of our relationship were spent on 'neutral' ground — in South America, where I was teaching and my husband was working for a Danish firm. We lived in three different countries before moving to Denmark. Moving around the world is something I personally found exciting. But our move to Denmark was different. I was suddenly in my husband's country, surrounded by his family and friends, language and culture. I felt very dependent on him and developed an even closer relationship to our children because they were also foreigners in Denmark.

After a short time, my children became 'Danes'. Instead of English, Danish became the language they felt most comfortable speaking. As time went by, I became assimilated and integrated into Danish society. I have always wanted my life to be basically the same living abroad as it would be living in the States. That is the main reason I'm not just a spectator. I believe in actively participating in the community.

I am active in the children's school, participate on the parent-teacher committee in their classes, am on the board of the tennis club and coordinator for the junior tournaments, have been active in the local scout group and became a basketball referee. After learning Danish, I got a job teaching English to adults and children. My husband, his family, our Danish and my American friends living in Denmark tell me how well I've 'adjusted' and 'adapted'.

But for some reason, those words bother me. Maybe it's because adapting always involves changing and conforming to be accepted by others and possibly losing my identity in the process. This could happen in a country like Denmark, where more importance is put on the group than on the individual.

Identity has a lot to do with individuality — an important part of this being my nationality and background. I find it more and more difficult to hold on to my identity. I feel like a different person depending on the situation I'm in.

Danes expect me to be 'Danish', because I look like them and have lived here so many years — a Dane with an accent. Americans expect me still to be 'American' and don't understand the changes one goes through living abroad. Our family life is not the same as theirs because of cultural differences and other expectations of society.

I am trying to raise my sons in a bilingual and bicultural home. It sounds good in theory, however, in practice it has been one of those experiences I hope I can look back on in years to come and be able to laugh! The result of my efforts is that suddenly I found myself to be the foreigner in our family. I am Lars and Bo's American mother, my husband's American wife and the American on the block. I have had to learn to accept that my children are now Danes, and they have also reminded me of this from time to time. I'll never forget the day my youngest son turned to me when we were discussing vacation plans and said, "We should decide because we're all Danes and you're an American. It's three against one!"

During a language course four years ago, we had to draw a picture of our families. My family was in a circle and I was on the outside looking in. I feel that my assimilation and adjustment to the Danish culture has made me feel more a part of my family, but I have also made sure, for my benefit as well as theirs, that my children also become a bit 'Americanized'.

Activities, people, traditions and experiences, however, such as the four seasons, American sports, songs and books that were once a part of my childhood and life are almost forgotten or replaced with the Danish equivalent. I have taught my children 'The Itsy-bitzy Spider', read Dr. Seuss to them and played softball with them. We celebrate Thanksgiving, the 4th of July and Christmas. Christmas, which is celebrated on the 24th in Denmark, is given a new dimension by continuing the 'stocking' tradition.

My children's upbringing includes a part of my culture, but it's still a foreign culture to them even though they are U.S. citizens by birth. At times I feel like I'm teaching an American Studies class! Their participation in certain activities seems to be based on trying to please me. My husband is supportive and understands the importance of our children learning about their American heritage but leaves the teaching up to me. It is not a mutual effort. As a family, we seem to move in two different directions.

I recently had a visit from an American friend's son who was traveling through Europe. I had a wonderful time talking to him about the States — politics, music, university life, etc. When he left, it hit me that I'll never be able to talk about the same topics to my children unless they decide to live in the States someday. Of course we'll be able to talk about other things but that closeness that comes from growing up with the same language and culture will never be there. Sometimes I feel a resentment towards my husband, which I realize is based on envy, because he shares the same language and culture with our children.

When we were in the States as a family two years ago, I had a hard time accepting the fact that my children are also 'Danes' in America. I had hoped for a magic transformation when we landed in New York. They had a wonderful time, but I found myself making excuses for them, explaining why they spoke English with an accent, why they weren't familiar with certain foods, toys, TV programs and athletes and why they seemed to be more reserved than their cousins and my friend's children. It's hard for my family and friends who have never raised children abroad to understand why our children didn't feel comfortable speaking English or feel 'at home' in the States.

When living in South America, I remember talking to a British woman who was married to a Paraguayan. I asked her if she had any advice to give me on intercultural marriages. She told me, "Think twice before marrying a foreigner." I was young, in love with a wonderful Dane and felt that love would conquer all! Now, after thirteen years of marriage, eight of them in Denmark, I feel that so much time and energy has been put into adjusting and learning the language, that not much time has been left for our relationship. I don't feel that the adjustment process has been a sharing experience and something that we have gone through together that has strengthened our relationship.

I'm sure that many misunderstandings and marital problems are based on cultural differences. I prefer to make spontaneous decisions and express my feelings. My husband prefers to avoid direct confrontation and is a bit reserved. Like most Danes, he has the sometimes admirable, but mostly irritating trait of being stubborn and not giving an inch. These could, of course, be due to our personalities, but the differences seem more apparent since we moved to 'his' country.

We have a good life together and two well-adjusted, happy children. I should be content, but every time I see a film or program depicting American family life, I start comparing it to ours. I can't help but think how it would be to have a mutual language and the same cultural and traditional background. Boring? Maybe, but the grass always seems greener on the other side.

The truth is, despite the difficulties living in a foreign country and speculating on how it would be if I were raising my children in the States, I could never live in the States again — not with my family — and that's what we are, a family.

Our children are not just Americans or Danes, but members of a larger, international community. I hope they will become more interesting, tolerant human beings because of their background. Someday, maybe they will carry on the tradition of teaching their children English songs, reading Dr. Seuss and celebrating American holidays.

Living in Denmark and raising a family in a bicultural home is a balancing act. If an American woman came to me today, very much in love and asking my advice, I would say, after years of experience and even momentary regrets, that you should try not to dwell on what life might have been like in the States, or as time goes by, worry and contemplate the future in a foreign country. My advice would be to learn to do as other women do in intercultural marriages; hold on to your identity and take one day at a time. ♥

Some Roots Start in Pockets

by Heidrun West

The rose bushes have never been as opulent as this year. The branches arch under the weight of blooms, spilling their beauty into this fragrant morning of our twenty-sixth year of marriage. We have all grown. The weeding, watering, feeding and pruning have turned this dull patch into a garden.

I have not always been a gardener, and when I look back at the beginnings of our married life, I see a few potted purple and white petunias in a window box on a balcony in Geneva, nothing more. I understood so little then — about petunias and about partnership. Marriage was just a shift of roles from being a daughter to being a wife, a transfer of allegiance. I was not aware then I needed more than a partner, that I was desperate for an identity I could be comfortable with. But first I had to learn about seedlings and their need for consistent care before I understood that only plants with a strong root system survive transplant- ing.

My roots, however, did not have favourable conditions for growth. I was born in Sudetenland, in the northern corner of what now is the Czech Republic. As Sudetenland has been eradicated from the map, my existence is founded on the void that it left. And yet I want to claim a piece of ground, a cultural heritage for myself.

The border regions of Czechoslovakia were first settled by German-speak- ing tribes in the 12th century, and remained Germanic until they were forcibly integrated into Czechoslovakia in 1918. These German-speaking people were part of Hitler's Germany from the time of the Munich convention until 1945. This annexation meant my father had to fight in Hitler's army. At the end of the war, my family was expelled from Sudetenland to Germany together with three million refugees of German origin.

In 1946 — I was just over a year old — we were ordered to leave. Being allowed to take only what we could carry, my mother had piled everything she could into the stroller with me. It was February, and the roads to the station were thick with slush and ice. The stroller was hopelessly overloaded, the axle soon broke. I still wonder what kept my mother from breaking. Like cattle, we were boarded up in wagons bound for an unknown existence.

My father had just been released from an American prisoner-of-war camp and was working on a farm in Germany. With luck, stubbornness, diligence and bribery, he had been able to find out about our transport and was waiting for us when we reached Southern Germany after our seven-day odyssey.

At first we shared one large room with twenty-five people at a refugee centre, but then we were allocated two rooms in a farmhouse. Formerly storage rooms for grain, they were one floor above the pigsty — rooms befitting our status as refugees. The connecting door to the farmhouse was bricked up and a wooden staircase built along the outside, so we would not dirty the house with our presence. The stairs led past the open window of the pigsty, where in winter the warm air would condense and freeze on the wood turning the whole staircase into a treacherous path to the outhouse next to the manure heap. That degradation may sear my skin now, but as a child, one is spared the pain of deeper reflection.

I was four years old when my baby brother contracted diarrhea. As 'pigs from Sudetenland', we were sent away from the doctor's door. My father 'organized' a five-ton truck to take him to the nearest hospital, an hour's drive away. My brother died of dehydration as my mother placed him in the nurse's arms.

By the time I was school-age, I understood that *Fluechtling* (refugee) was not a nice word. I became adept at adapting. I learnt to be unobtrusive, to make other people's behaviour my own, to speak their dialect — anything not to be noticed. But I did not learn to identify with my passport that declared me as German.

I was eleven when my father found a job in Switzerland. I clearly remember the joy and delight I felt: there are no wars in Switzerland! I could barely believe my good fortune. We had a real apartment with central heating, a bathroom and a toilet all to ourselves! What luxury, what paradise! But then came the first day at school. I had no idea how different Swiss German was from Schwaebisch. The teacher made a joke, the whole class laughed, except me — I had not understood a word. I felt forlorn, cut off. And I sat alone, because "Germans stank." Suddenly it was wrong to be German, when in Germany it had been wrong NOT to be German. In history class we drew the battle field of Morgarten in 1315, but there were no safe versions of the war that had just happened. When I asked my parents, I could feel their scars tearing. I did not want to see my mother cry.

At seventeen I left home to go as far as my savings would take me, which was to Edinburgh. There I soon learnt that doors would open more readily if I said I came from Switzerland — which, after all, was geographically true — than if I referred to my German passport. And my English was too limited to explain my personal history. Then I found a job in Geneva and met 'my Englishman'. I fell in love with him because he had a gentleness I had never experienced. He brought me orange juice when the other young men were trying to seduce me with wine. In Scotland I had met people with some of his traits, but I had never seen them wrapped in such a pleasant package. I was hooked. Life without each other became increasingly meaningless, and we started thinking about marriage. It was time I was introduced to his parents.

We squeezed into his red Mini and drove to Coventry for 'inspection'. I knew his parents had lived through the blitz. I had heard how his father had dug through the shattered bricks with his bare hands to rescue the baby whose faint whimper he could hear somewhere in the rubble. The baby died in his arms.

And there I sat on their sofa — a young woman whose father had fought in the army that had poured destruction over Coventry. The words in their last letter to my fiancee, "your plans to marry Heidrun have come as a real blow to us," stood in the room. I hardly opened my mouth, afraid I might hurt them with my German accent.

I drank tea when I would have preferred coffee. I ate the sandwiches and the cake that were offered to me, although I could still feel the waves of the Channel churning in my stomach. Exhausted from the long journey and the effort of making a good impression, I was glad when we headed for bed. As a guest I had the privilege of using the bathroom first. What a relief to wash off 700 miles of dirt! But when I wanted to unlock the door, try as I might, the key would not budge. Should I sleep in the bathtub or call for help? I certainly did not want to make any 'fuss' — a crime I knew the English abhorred. My future in-law's bedroom was next to the bathroom, my fiancee's further along the corridor. I tried to call him without his parents hearing me. To no avail. Soon they all stood outside the door. I could hear my father-in-law say, "we'll just have to break down the door. The lock must have rusted through, we haven't used it in years." As feet and fists hit the wood, the door opened with a crash. I could not believe my eyes: Laughing faces met me.

Yet painfully aware of the trouble I had caused, I could not share their laughter. I only wanted to shrink back across the Channel. My fiancee's dry comment "can't take you anywhere!" did not help either. British humour was not something I had taken in with the rules of English grammar. Everybody — except me — thought the whole situation was terribly funny. Being conditioned to locking doors, I had come to a home where locks were not needed. But in the end, my turning the key in the lock had the unexpected effect of unlocking the door between us.

Shame and guilt throbbed through me the next few days as I walked past remnants of the war, visited the old cathedral that bombs had reduced to a mere shell and the new one commemorating the many dead. Just being born in Sudetenland, a part of Hitler's empire, made me feel I was somehow responsible for that devastation.

Our visit to Coventry had appeased my future in-laws, but soon our wedding arrangements suffered another setback — this time from my parents. They were delighted with my fiancee; it did not matter the slightest that my father had once been indoctrinated to see the English as enemies. No, it was not prejudice, simply fear of not fitting in at their daughter's wedding. Everybody would be conversing in a language my mother neither spoke nor understood. My father refused to participate because he had seen an English film in which the father of the bride led his daughter to the altar in some peculiar step. No, my father was adamant, he was not going to make a fool of himself. After much panic and pleading on my part, they did come. With friends and family, we counted ten different nationalities at the ceremony — a truly multicultural wedding.

With my marriage licence, I acquired the right to apply for a British passport. I swore allegiance to the Queen and Her Heirs, making sure not to pronounce the 'h' in heirs, as our Danish friend had done to everybody's amusement. The blue passport made me a member of the United Kingdom and its colonies. Yet, my husband was quick to point out, "British you are, English you will never be." I am still ONLY British, but it is a joke — not a threat. Our second son, Michael, who was born in Zurich, has a British passport too, but does not identify with his heritage: "I was born in Switzerland, this is my home, my friends are here." He intends to apply for Swiss citizenship, even if it means doing Swiss military duty. Anthony, our first son, was born in Philadelphia. Like Michael, he never lived in England, but the five years in the US left such a positive impression on him that he applied for an American passport, which he now holds in addition to his British one.

Acquiring British citizenship, in my case, meant losing my German national-ity. But I went further, also denying my German mother-tongue and letting English become the language of our everyday talks, our arguments, our intimate moments. Not that I was aware of this denial of my past. That understanding came much later.

I remember that precious moment when I was first alone with my newly born son. With motherhood, my own mother-tongue was forcing itself back into my consciousness. I felt this chain of women behind me: my mother, my grandmother — and I had become a link in that chain of German-speaking women. English suddenly did not seem natural. To coo in English was like hearing someone else coo. But German sounded just as odd, like an unfamiliar echo from deep inside me. During the four years in Philadelphia, I had hardly spoken German. When speak-ing it to my baby, was I taking him away from my husband? My maternal instincts won. I sang the songs my mother had sung to me, because they felt right. And my husband sang the nursery rhymes from his childhood.

I learnt about Humpty Dumpty and Jack Sprat who ate no fat, about Rupert and Noddy. I went on to study the Victorians, their social history and love-lives. I even acquired a fair knowledge of modern British poetry, but I have never learnt English humor. My husband claims this is due to one of my legs being longer which makes pulling it so easy. I have, as yet, not been able to pick up a warning cue in his deadpan voice. He gets me hopping mad before I notice he's joking. I am what Piaget calls 'a concrete thinker', stuck in the footprints of my ancestors. I am not sure how much of my German-ness has rubbed off on my husband, certainly not my self-discipline (which he calls 'pig-headedness') nor my orderliness. Every morning we go hunting for his car keys, office keys, magnetic card and wallet. If anything, his easygoingness has rubbed off on me. My handbag now also occasionally features on the 'officially lost' list.

What has changed, of that I am certain, is his way of handling disagree-ments. In his family, fights never happened. So when our first quarrel took shape, my husband coolly picked up the newspaper and started to read. I stood in front of him, letting loose a diatribe of accusations. No response. The only sound coming from him was the rustle of the GUARDIAN as he turned the pages. I fetched my coat and dramatically made my exit, slamming the door behind me. Out in the cold, dark street, my anger drove my steps, but I kept listening for his footsteps. He must be sorry by now, he must be coming to get me back, I thought. No steps. No place to go. Slowly, I walked back. Softly, I opened the door. He was still READING!

When we quarrel now, he booms his "you always do" at me before I have a chance of lancing my "you did it again" bit at him. When I tell him I am not deaf, he screams back, "I never scream." But he does.

Over the years, my parents-in-law have accepted me as their daughter. In turn, they have become my 'parents-in-love', the misnomer my students frequently pronounce. In my in-law's house I met a cheerful thoughtfulness and kindness I did not know existed. My father-in-law shared his love for gardening with me. We were never happier than when we walked through a public garden together, our pockets bulging with seeds and bits of plants we had snipped off with our fingers. My husband always walked a long distance away from us, too embarrassed to be associated with 'thieves'. "Imagine, if everybody did that!" he would complain. But his words could not stop us. WE knew it was good for the plants! I still have many flowers in my garden that started as seeds in our pockets. Now that my father-in-law is dead, I carry on his tradition as a gardener. I try to use the same care with which he handled a fragile seedling. I prune the roses, divide the perennials, plant daffodils under trees and crocuses in the lawn, and sometimes I even remember to clean the tools. The day my father-in-law died, I went into the garden, took a number of rose cuttings and planted them close to the flowering cherry that was already in bloom. An uncommonly large fraction took root, and every year more buds appear. They vary in colour from delicate pink to dark red, from ivory to amber, but they all bear the same name: 'Grandad Roses'.

My husband, unfortunately, did not inherit his father's talent. As a scientist, he has developed his own binary method, distinguishing between plants that can be cut (or killed) with the electric lawn mower and those that are halved with the hedge cutter. He considers this not only a highly efficient and effective method, it also grants him the time to pursue, as he says, more scientifically challenging tasks. Certainly, as far as gardening is concerned, I am the one to keep the English flag flying.

I have learnt more than nursery rhymes from my husband, more than gardening from my father-in-law, and more than positive thinking from my mother-in-law. They have taught me to appreciate a sense of fun and jolliness and to enjoy making a fool of myself at times. I've put it all in that bag marked 'identity', the bag I am still filling at forty-seven.

I will probably never have an irrefutable sense of 'this is my home, this is my city, this is my country'. But I will certainly have a nice garden — wherever we are. ♥

Black and Gold

by Latease Copeland

I remember being told about this Danish 'Law of Jante' almost before I got off the boat — figuratively speaking. "In Denmark we don't wear gold and fancy furs and silk dresses to show off who we are. We don't try to be like the cinema stars from Hollywood." The hostess had said this to me openly, in front of all the other guests at what supposedly was a welcome to Denmark dinner party given in my honor. That bit of advice, if you will, came from someone who had really mattered to me then, someone whose respect I'd really wanted.

Even now, years later, especially with my eyes closed and my mind in reverse, I can still feel the pain and humiliation of that evening. I try desperately to change gears but once my mind starts rolling, that is next to impossible — it is downhill all the way.

At that party years ago, I had wanted to call out to him, my husband, for help. He was sitting right there across the table from me. But I couldn't. At least three of my five senses no longer functioned properly. He didn't offer a comment, not even a gesture. I knew right then and there, for the very first time since we'd met — for the very first time since we'd loved — that I was on my own.

My ears were so clogged at that point I could barely decipher the rest of the conversation, or more accurately, the monologue. The hostess was going on and on about being reminded of how, after the war, people — touristy, show-off types — were flocking into Denmark flaunting furs, gold, diamonds, all sorts of jewels and other assets they had obtained through the ill-fate of others. They were the nouveau riche, the pretenders. People without taste or class or conscience. People who had simply taken what they wanted or paid next to nothing for articles of great value because they thought possessions made them noticed, gave them importance. They thought things made them somebody.

I couldn't understand all that was being said. My head was spinning and the hostess would revert to Danish from time to time — partly in search of the right English word and also, I felt, to slight me. Still, I knew the entire long, piercingly painful monologue was aimed at me.

"Danes don't like show-off pretentious people," the hostess reiterated. Then she continued lecturing, "We have something called the 'Jante Law' which means we are very careful and don't think much of people who think too much of themselves."

Knowing now what I didn't know then doesn't make the memory any less painful. The 'Jante Law' encourages deceitfulness and jealousy, not to mention hypocrisy.

My husband has told me time after time, "You must learn to forgive and forget."

I tell him, "You can't unring a bell."

This whole 'Jante Law' business, I later discovered, comes complete with its own ten commandments. It is a literary metaphor for a group mentality as old as sin which stifles individualism, creativity, personal achievement and so forth and so on. Incredibly enough, this 'law', with its almost legal status, promotes mediocrity, one of the things I'd always feared most. In other words, Danes shun those who dare to be different. The things that I, as an American, had been taught to strive for are the very things that Danes find repulsive and hold most in disdain.

Why hadn't he told me about the law of Jante? I felt he should have at least warned me. He hadn't. If anything, he encouraged me. He reveled in my flamboyancy. From day one he became my magic mirror, constantly assuring me that I was indeed the most ravishing of them all. We'd met in Manhattan. I lived there. It was my city, my turf. I loved it and so did he, the young Danish student on summer holiday. I was a fashion model. I looked it. I dressed it. I lived it. I loved it and so did he when he was my boyfriend. Or so he said at the time.

We fell deeper and more passionately in love than either of us had ever been before. "In love," I often told him, "is such a safe, comfortable, secure place to be 'in' if you're not there all by yourself." He agreed. I told him a lot about life and love and things. I, being ten years older, naturally felt wiser about life and love and things.

The seasons came and went. He stayed. We were inseparable, joined at the hip, siamese lovers, if you will. School, country, family, friends be damned. We were in love. We married.

I considered fashion my forte. Nevertheless I had felt awfully apprehensive about that first and fateful social outing in Copenhagen. I wore a basic black silk dress — à la New York. When in doubt, black will always do. To me, silk was as basic as black. I didn't care for or own a string of pearls. I preferred gold. That's what I wore. One chain, not my usual three. I did, however, have lots of tiny gold rings on my fingers; all small bands, some were bamboo, some braided, some with teeny tiny little stones or diamonds. Nothing ostentatious. Or so I thought.

It was he, my husband, who had encouraged me. He said, "Wear your fox." It was a great, big, oversized, ankle-length Canadian blue fox. I had other coats, of course, but he liked the look of me in the fox. I thought maybe it was too much for the occasion. It was, without doubt, an attention getter. I wore it well. It made me look like somebody. It made him feel important. Besides, it was winter, very cold. Most of all I trusted him. As a matter of fact, in route that very evening he had exaggerated, "WOW! You look like a million dollars! Way to go babe!" He enjoyed all his newly acquired American expressions. I sometimes wished we could leave home without them.

The looks from the hostess had made my fun mood burst. I wanted to slide under the table, or better yet, just leave. But I didn't. I sat there through the whole miserable evening having to 'grin and bear it' in silence. Later, after the fact of course, I thought of all the sharp witty things I should have, could have, ought to have said. But how could I with my senses all out of sync? I sat there wondering if there was something in the water here or in the air perhaps that causes acceptance, passivity, complacency? Something that turns people into wood, mere pieces of furniture? I distinctly remember looking over at him, my husband, with pleading eyes. He looked at his plate. The others, like lame, mute cheerleaders, sat silent and motionless but nonetheless obviously supportive of the hostess. I knew in my heart of hearts that this was going to be a full-fledged battle if not an out-and-out war, and since I had no bombs to drop, I certainly could use a foot soldier or two. Husbands are automatically drafted — or so I had believed.

What keeps bringing that first 'welcoming party' of years ago back to my mind? How on earth have I managed to open that old can of worms again now? I thought I had put all that to rest and was no longer haunted by that particular part of my past. Well, I'm wrong. All it takes is something so simple as attempting to read Aksel Sandemose's A FUGITIVE CROSSES HIS TRACKS in which the term 'Jante Law' was coined, and BOOM! I'm fuming. Suddenly I feel as though someone has ripped open an old wound right above my heart and dumped a whole mess-load of salt in it. It hurts.

I throw the book across the living-room floor and surprisingly enough, realize that outburst of emotions actually makes me feel a little better. So I jump up from the sofa, run to the book and kick it once, twice, thrice down the hallway. But that only makes me feel silly. And rightfully so.

I can't help recalling how flippant my husband had been at that dinner party when I'd finally gotten him alone and asked all the whys, how-comes, and what-fors. He simply shrugged and said, "You'll get used to them and they'll get used to you. Just don't take them too seriously, especially that Jante Law stuff. It's overrated and it's preached far more than it's practiced."

"Well, it's certainly been preached here tonight. How can I not take it seriously. I feel as though I've been ostracized before I ever get 'in' so to speak," I stated, trying to appear calm and collected.

"Personally I think it's more of the old sour grape syndrome than anything else. It's definitely not worth a confrontation. Just say '*ja, ja*' — the Danish equivalent of that patronizing 'yeah, sure' that's so American — and let it go at that. It's really no big deal," he had said as he rejoined the party, offering no apologies for himself or anyone else.

"Huh, no big deal my foot," I whispered as if it were a secret I didn't want anyone else to hear. Had he, my would-be rabble-rouser come home to his clan to conform? To be a head nodding *ja, ja*, man? Well I knew one thing for sure — our record breaking honeymoon was over.

What had happened to my innate (anti-Jante Law) spontaneity? It was one of the very things I felt had attracted him. I should have taken off my gold and my dress right then and there and placed them on that hostess' plate and sat bare-breasted at the table. That would not have been more rude than I felt they had been to me. I could have said calmly, "Oh well, when in Rome, do as the Romans do." But I couldn't. Spontaneity was all well and good but rudeness . . . no. I wasn't raised that way.

Romans . . . I wished. When in Rome, they'd called me '*bella*' while making wild gestures of friendship and affection. Parisians would raise a glass of wine in my direction and simply say '*la femme noire*' and throw in an 'oh la la' here and there for good measure in that special way that only the French could. However, in Copenhapen I'm called by my name and that is that — cut and dried.

Finally I hear the apartment door opening. I start for the door, stop, then turn to look for the book. It is half way down the hallway — exactly where it landed after my last kick. I go back for it then hurry to meet him.

"Hello," he yells as always, "I'm home."

I hate it when he announces his arrival that way. It sort of makes me feel like an antiquated housewife. As if he expects me to come running with slippers and pipe! Some sort of June Cleaver in black face!

"No kidding," I retort, standing in the foyer watching him take off his jacket, with both hands on my hips and my head bobbing, still holding the book and wanting desperately to pick a fight.

"Uh, oh," he says, "what's wrong now? When you stand like that I know I'm in trouble. What's up? Come on, talk to me. What did I do this time?"

"Nothing," I say flatly. "It's more like . . . well . . . what you didn't do." It isn't easy for me to hold my anger when he so easily surrenders before the battle even starts.

"Okay, I give up," he teases. "What didn't I do? Flush the toilet? Take out the garbage? Walk the dog?"

"No, come on, give me a break," I plead, realizing he isn't going to oblige me and getting even more annoyed by his humor. "It's this book," I say as I wave it in front of him like a fly swatter.

"Didn't read it," he says solemnly while holding his right hand up in the gesture of swearing or making an oath. "What's the matter with it? Somebody broke the binding? Dog-eared the pages? Spilled red wine on it? Wasn't me."

"It wasn't I," I correct him as always, hoping he'd do the same with my Danish. He seldom does. However, he reminds me often enough that he has picked up his American phrasing and choppiness from me. It isn't a compliment.

"I or me, that's debatable," he challenges. "I looked that one up last time. Well, whatever," he says in final resignation, not really wanting to play that game any longer. "I'm tired and I'm hungry. I just want to sit and relax a bit before dinner. If that's all right with you!"

As a matter of fact it isn't. Even after four years of playing the housewife, I still haven't got the routine together. Contrary to the female norm, I have no genetic aptitude towards 'wifing', not in the homemaking sense of the word at any rate. I haven't even thought about dinner and am not the least bit sorry. When we first met I had said straight out, point blank, "I eat out. I don't cook."

He had replied, just as straight and to the point, "No problem. I do." And so he did. In Manhattan.

I feel like kicking myself. If only I hadn't started reading that book. Seeing those commandments, all those 'Thou shalt not believe thou art something,' etc., etc., etc., in black and white had triggered such a negative emotion in me, leaving me with a desperate desire to yell, to have a screaming fit. And yet, I know it has absolutely nothing whatsoever to do with any of that old Jante mumbo jumbo per se. I've lost that battle a long time ago. I *ja, ja*'d my way through one social gathering after another. I've often felt I am *ja, ja*-ing my way through my life. I've been plucked like a chicken of all my frills and fineries, brought down to size, put in my proper place. I concede. Follow all the rituals. Behave according to the norm as best I can. But still, there are a few sparks left unignited within my soul. The war to retrieve some portion of my identity isn't over, of that I am sure.

No, it has nothing to do with anything that I can in all honesty single out and attack, not even the natives. I've been confronted with clans before and remained undaunted. So I may as well blame it on the rain, or the dark, gray winters, or on the direction the wind blows on any given day, or on him, my husband.

I still have great difficulty making my tongue say all those funny sounds. Languages have never been one of my strong capablities. This I attribute, and rightly so, to my tone deafness. Contrary to the stereotype, I can't carry a tune from one note to the next. No latent career opportunity there. I've been unable to find a job in Copenhagen mainly because the job hasn't found me. I retired from modeling when we made the move. It was time. I can't return to it now even if I want to. I feel I've been stripped of that certain something that made me the model — special, interesting and exciting. So here I am, taking my frustrations out on him, the scapegoat . . . But then again, not really.

It's a game we play. A game of life. A game of love. In his heart of hearts he knows how much I love Manhattan. How much he too had loved it in his own way. He had been wild and savagely wonderful there; known on occasion to howl at the moon. There had been no one to answer to, no one questioned. He said we'd go back. No, much more than that, he had promised. Yet, this is his turf. In Denmark he is many things that matter to many people: friend, brother, husband, son, worker, countryman, a native. It is all indigenous. He feels safe and secure here. He is in control. Isn't that the way it's supposed to be? Of course, he feels it is.

I start to follow him to the couch, then think better of it.

"What's the point?" I ask myself. He's heard it all before. Most importantly, no one makes me stay; no one ever suggests I leave. That isn't an issue. Walking away from love is like walking away from life. Sane, sensible people just don't do that. Or do they?

I go instead into the kitchen and take from the freezer one of only three dishes I've perfected — some leftover chile con carne. I make it by the gallons. He never complains. Too bad. I still feel fussy. I just can't seem to change gears; to get my mind rolling in the right direction. I've burned a lot of bridges bidding good riddance to bad rubbish. Still, deep within the recess of my soul, I know the past will remain present as long as there are wounds to be healed. ♥

German Love

by Rosi Wolf-Almanasreh

Protocol of a consultation:

"I need your advice," said the young woman. "That's why I brought HIM along." With her thumb she pointed to her husband on her right. She is from Friedberg. He comes from a small town in the eastern part of Turkey.

"Have you already been to a marriage counsellor?" I asked him.

He nods. "Yes, the wife always takes me along. But it doesn't help."

"You see," the young woman interjects, "see how he's always against everything. That's how it always is. He doesn't understand anything, that is, he doesn't **want** to understand anything! He just wants to do what he wants. He thinks we're in Turkey. There men do what they want, you know how it is . . . But we live here in Germany. Here women aren't treated like that. Here a man loves his wife. I tell him that again and again. You understand? You do understand, don't you?"

"Shut up! Oh, how you talk. Shut up!" says the man. He looks grimly at the floor as she snaps at him.

"I'll talk as much as I want and say what I like! We have free speech here, you know, not like it is where you come from . . ."

She leans on the little round table between us and starts to cry. Her face quickly gets red and swollen. I can tell that she had been crying before her arrival at our counselling offices. Her husband is embarrassed and looks at the floor.

I sit there in front of this couple feeling irritated and angry. On one hand, I'm furious at this woman's way of speaking to her partner, the way she haughtily refers to HIM and bad-mouths everything about his countrymen. It bothers me how she describes how things are done here and tries to glorify her problem into a cultural one. On the other hand, I know how difficult it is for a woman in central Europe to deal with his ways and especially with the some-times aggressive simplicity of his words.

255

What do they expect? What does she want? Is it really the cultural difference that set off this confrontation or is she subconsciously using his 'culture' to win a power struggle?

While I'm considering whether to interrupt this woman's uncontrolled outburst of crying or whether to just let her cry, the man gets up and looks around. He goes to a washbasin, takes an empty glass nearby, rinses it out and fills it with fresh water. He comes back and, by dipping his finger in the glass, rubs drops of water on her forehead, on her neck and back again on her forehead. Gently, lovingly, almost tenderly. That's something, I think, he has done often. He wants to comfort her. But her face remains tense. She continues her sobbing and cannot accept this comforting.

"Stop using that dirty water," she says loudly and aggressively. "You think you can solve everything with water where you come from. But here it doesn't work, here it won't help at all. You just want to make a good impression, don't you?"

She straightens up, pushes him away and looks at him angrily. The water mixes with her tears, runs down her face, over her collar and down her blouse.

The man sits down silently at her side and looks again at the floor. I can see that he's gritting his teeth.

"How long have you been married?" I ask him.

"Eight years," he says without looking at me. I can tell that he'd like to leave. He's furious. I can tell that he is also ashamed, ashamed of the whole situation. It bothers him that a stranger is being informed about his private problems.

"And how long have you been in Germany?"

"Since I was thirteen. Now I 've been here sixteen years."

"Are your parents, brothers and sisters here?" I asked, hoping that the situation would first cool down a bit. I know that immigrants in Germany are used to hearing such questions. Where they come from. How long they've been here. Whether they like living here. It's small-talk, like about the weather, just to carry on a conversation, not because the person asking such questions is really interested in the answers.

"Parents in Turkey. Brother here," says the man briefly. He sits with his side to the table, slightly away from me and ill at ease, and he keeps turning the wet tissue back and forth between his strong hands.

I know he finds it very strange to have to talk to me, a stranger, about his marriage. But the fact that he came along for this appointment shows he must be really interested in finding a solution to this conflict. I also know that it might help if I give them both a few tips so that they can learn how to get along better with their different feelings. But I have to be careful not to react like most people from my country usually do. I can easily put myself in his situation but I know that he also has to learn to understand his wife's feelings. I have the impression that he wants to keep the relationship with his wife and improve it.

"Do you love your wife?" I begin with a frontal attack, knowing that this question is very intimate and for him very embarrassing. But I am confident that he knows my country and our way of answering.

"Love?" He looks at me for the first time briefly and with lack of understanding. I know that he considers such a question as almost impertinent. "What does that mean? She is my wife, I have to live with her. That's the way it is with us! Love comes and goes and depends on a lot of things. In spite of that, we stay together."

I nod and look at her. She sits with her head bowed, resigned to the circumstances.

"What do you think about what your husband says?" I ask her, hoping that somehow we'll find a way to talk together. "It surely hurts you to hear your husband say something like that, doesn't it? — But you want to find a solution. You want him to show his feelings, to show you in your way that he loves you, don't you?"

"I don't know what I want," she says, continuing to cry but more softly. "I'm so confused. You know, everybody was against it, against our marriage. My parents, my brothers and sisters, friends. Everybody is against the Turks. I don't have anything against foreigners. I used to get along well with him. I liked it that he didn't talk so much and was so quiet. You know, a calmness radiated from him. Not like the other men. Maybe they were right. Maybe we are, after all, too different." She sobs.

"He does everything," she continues. "He always comes home after work. He helps with the cooking. But his friends, they bother me when they sit around for hours at our place. Talking, drinking tea. I don't understand them. I don't exist for them. But he gives me all his money. Not like the others who send all their money to Turkey. He doesn't drink. But on Sundays, he always sleeps almost all day. I'm fed up with that! Nobody can be that tired. He probably sleeps so he doesn't have to have anything to do with me. His friends work in shifts. I wish, for instance, that he'd sometimes go for a walk with me the way

German men do with their wives. In a park, in the forest or for window-shopping." She looks at me desperately. "And I wish he would tell me at least once that he loves me." She throws her arms on the table, buries her head in them and sobs.

"That's the way it always goes," he says. "I just don't understand. Eight years like that. How am I different from a German husband? He goes out, drinks beer in the beer joint. I don't do that."

"Are all Turks like that?" she asked me in despair. "All of them? Can't any of them say they love their wives? Some nice words? Or go for walks like everybody else?"

"I do everything," he says. "Really. I bought everything for her. Washing machine, dishwasher, leather coat, living room — I don't know why this woman is so unhappy and so mean!" The man looks at me challengingly. "I'm supposed to treat her like they do in films. That's not decent with one's own wife." He shakes his head in refusal.

"I couldn't care less about the washing machine," she cries out. "Do you understand? I couldn't care less!" — The tears run further down her cheeks. "That's the worst part of it. I know that he loves me," she carries on, "but I can't stand this kind of love anymore! I can't stand the Turk part of him. The peasant part of him. And always this devoted look and this saying nothing! He should love me in German, German . . . oh, I don't know how I should explain it. I'm so ashamed!"

"She wants love. But she doesn't respect me. I respect her, and her family even though they don't want to set eyes on me. Her mother, it's horrible, the things she says about Turks. What is love? Something I whisper into some-body's ear? That's nothing!"

The husband had turned to me. I nodded. The older I get, the more I feel like he does. He continues, "I already do everything German, everything. From morning to night. Eat German, speak German, greet in German, sleep in a German bed, wear German clothes and watch German TV. I can't stand doing more German things than that. She is a good wife but she only wants words. Empty words. For me, what I do for her, how I live with her, that's love."

"Do you love him then?" I ask the woman, "and do you tell him so?"

"That doesn't matter," she throws back. "It's not me that's the trouble but him, you know, how he acts. He has to learn what it means to be emancipated, that's what he needs. He should finally adapt to life here!"

The husband keeps looking down, playing with the tissue. ≈

Advice from

the Clever

and the Wise

Heavy Matters

by Donna Schaper

He weighed around 300 pounds and she weighed around 300 pounds. They arrived right on time for their premarital appointment, sat down together on my couch, and broke it. If this was the most expensive appointment I have ever had as a parish pastor, it was not without rivals. Some costs were more spiritual; I have had to pay for them longer.

The risk in conducting a marriage service is that the vows might not last. Clergy people may not be responsible for making the vows last but we are not innocent bystanders either. We see the chances a marriage has, usually within the first few minutes. We see the body language. We see who does the most talking. We see who is in charge. And we see the history of the family and of the culture. We see the realities they face in their cultural, racial and religious background, in their relative ages, their economic backgrounds. We see the things the couple bring to the marriage that they cannot change. These histories help a marriage last the more similar they are, and they provide obstacles the more different they are. Homogeneity helps marriage last. That doesn't mean that we should only marry our own kind but it does mean that marrying other than our own kind will involve us in some interesting challenges.

I first learned of the challenge of diversity to marital covenant when I worked as a chaplain at Yale University. Because of the large number of internationals at Yale, many people married across cultural lines. Many people fell in love with the kinds of people that their family of origin would prefer they not have fallen for. Jews and Catholics, blacks and whites, rich and poor, French and Mexican, all these weddings caused more than a small stir. Often premarital work involved keeping the mothers of bride and groom a few inches away from total hysteria.

In the beginning I sided with the couple against the cultures of their diverse origins. Your love, I thought, is beautiful enough to manage these diversities; in fact, it is made more beautiful by your diversity. I learned eventually, after performing hundreds of marriages, to see more than one beauty. Culture advises caution; love invites risk. Both have many good points. But when culture says that Protestants and Jews have difficulty being married, when culture warns a French woman and a Mexican man that their love will have to survive their different nationalities, culture is right. Often couples do not see the difficulties in the beginning. Love is working its magic and smoothing off the rough edges. But when their child is born and she assumes Baptism and he assumes Bris, get ready for an interesting conversation. When it is time to buy furniture, and she assumes credit and he assumes cash, watch the sparks fly. When his idea of the holidays is two weeks with his mother, and hers is a beach, take cover. The costs may be greater than those of airline tickets.

Love has a right to be blind to these difficulties; the officiating minister does not. It is his or her responsibility to point them out, to prepare the couple for diversity, to create a fertile ground in which marriage vows may grow and last.

Romantic love loses its capacity over time to enjoy differences; other skills have to take its place if vows are to last. One therapist told me that he did not like to work with patients who are in love because romantic love is all about mystery and therapy is all about understanding mystery. I love to work with people who are in love; I also like to work with people who have a sense of their future and know the transformations that their love may go through. Couples need mystery and control. They need to master their own mystery. If the couple does have unalterable differences, it is my job to help them to adore those differences. Without teaching people to adore their differences, my participation in their relationship has a hypocrisy to it.

I learned this the hard way. I also married a man who was different from me and I too assumed that these differences didn't matter. My own marriage convinced me that differences do matter. My husband is Jewish and I am an ordained Protestant clergywoman. He comes from the American upper middle class and I come from the American working class. While we share educational and national and racial backgrounds, religious differences alone are enough to keep us talking. I make all sorts of assumptions that he does not make or understand. I think we should practice our religious faith in worship regularly and frequently. I think that holidays have a religious aspect and that, for example, Thanksgiving means going to church. He does not assume the regularity of worship nor the holiday connection to worship. I think that 'things are going to work out' if the matter is spiritual or psychological. He thinks they won't. He thinks that 'things are going to work out' if the matter is financial. I do not. Although we have agreed to instruct our children 'both' ways in terms of religion, the number of disagreements that result from that agreement are amazing. It is not always clear whose world view is making decisions. The issues are not only matters of our personality but also matters of our class and religious values. Learning to spot and enjoy these differences and values as they show up in our arguments is crucial to the survival of our relationship. This is also crucial for intercultural couples.

For example, we make sure to celebrate both Christmas and Hanukkah so as not to confuse our children any more than is necessary. We teach our children to be proud that they are 'both'. Not all children will grow up adoring their own difference.

There was the couple who already had four children. She was 23 and white; he was 20 and black. There was every reason to believe that the children were the product of their union. They were dragged to me by an uncle, visiting from Liberia. The bride was six months pregnant. "This time, he is going to marry her," proclaimed the disgruntled uncle. The husband abandoned the family three months after the marriage for what was the last time. I wish this couple had broken my couch instead of my heart.

He was short, rich and Paraguayan: she was American suburban, Jewish and had learned just enough Spanish to communicate with him. We did the service in Spanish and English. Everything was fine until it became clear he had not actually divorced his Paraguayan wife.

He was Muslim and she Catholic. Readings from the Koran and the New Testament were used. They had not decided on a country where they both would live: both told me it didn't matter. It did, but they were still being carried by love to residence in that place where it doesn't matter. The longer they can live there, the better. Yes, I warned them that three years was close to the maximum.

My sister married a Korean man. Things went well until his family showed up, all sixteen of them. These two have lived happily in Minneapolis with what my sister describes as 'half of Korea'. My brother-in-law still plans to go 'home' someday.

Most of the couples I marry don't have this much spice. More often than not as pastor, I am item number seven on a list where six is flowers and eight is invitations. The couple has already booked the caterer and they dropped by to make sure I was available the hour before the restaurant was.

Few of the people I marry actually belong to my congregation. Perhaps one or two a year. There was a time all weddings were 'inside' the family. Those days are long gone and couples from almost every country are nostalgic about the old days when cultures did not blend the way they do now. We may have lost some depth and familiarity and simplicity. But we have also gained freedom from an oppressive uniformity.

In my community I am one of a few clergy who is counted on to perform the unusual services. I perform sacred unions between homosexuals. I marry people of all faiths to each other and do so gladly. I realized in my own marriage that there was a bond beneath our differences and that it is an important one. We both were alienated from our past to similar degrees. The kinds of homogeneous, 'old world' weddings that my congregation would prefer are between people who are not alienated from their past. This alienation from the past is painful for people over time. It makes us spiritual refugees, exiles. It also opens us to delight in differences and to new, if more shallow, unions, the depths of which we will have to forge ourselves. We have our alienation in common and our sociology as differentiating. I perform these 'different' weddings gladly because I believe more in the future than I do in the past. So do the people who marry across 'lines'.

Many people I marry are Catholics, once divorced, who have been rejected by their own parishes. The pain is visible on their faces. Because they have already been rejected by one church, I usually refuse to reject them again, no matter how flippant their reasons are for showing up at our door.

I have learned to bring up the matter of birth control, particularly when different cultures are involved. In an intercultural situation, I rarely know what the norms are from the culture of origin. I like to find out.

In the first interview I ask them to prophesy what the difficulties of their marriage might be. I always tell the couple that I will be there for them, no matter where they move or live, if they have marital problems. Sometimes I get phone calls three, five, seven years after the marriage. "Do you remember what I said I thought would be the problem in our marriage? Well, guess what? I was right . . ."

Once the groom came drunk to the wedding. I stopped it and made the guests sit for two hours while he sobered up. I have always felt disturbed by this particular experience. It was probably a no-win situation.

If this was my worst experience, surely having young women come in on the arm of older men is the second worst. I probably have more prejudice against these kinds of weddings than against intercultural or interfaith ones. The worst of both genders is expressed, masculine youth lust and feminine dependency on Daddy. Usually I find myself saying something about this stereotype and asking the couple if they have evidence to show that they do not have this problem. Again romantic love covers up sociological differences: people of different ages, like people of different national backgrounds, have differences that they may not always fully understand. My job is to highlight these differences. Awareness is crucial.

We are all being prepared for marriage by what we see on television, by what we see at parties, by what we hear over the back fence and chiefly by what we remember of our parents. Our memory is not accurate (we saw our parents as their children!) but it is the strongest indicator of our own marital expectations. Intercultural relationships, as much as any other kind, need to understand their psychological foundation in their parents' behavior. Again the clergy person should watch for love's blindness. A bride may promise a groom that her behavior is nothing like her mother's. Don't believe her for a second. Likewise grooms and their fathers. Couples sometimes need help to understand their own origins. The pattern of our parents' life and marriage is our psychological homeland in the way that our native land is our cultural homeland. Interestingly, many intercultural couples I have married come from intercultural families.

If the parents are divorced, that will matter to the couple as they marry. If close friends are divorced, that will also matter. Those preparing to marry need to be instructed in marriage's failure and what to do when covenant fails. I have learned never, never to side in a divorce. Even if the man is an abuser, and the wife severely abused, it does seem to take two to tango. By not taking sides in a divorce situation, we can show a lot about forgiveness and what our expectations are for resolution of the conflict. We can also prepare people for the interactive nature of marriage. A healthy individual will not be blaming mother and siding with father at the age of their own marriage. They will see the systemic nature of the trouble.

I asked one couple after they had been married for five years how their 'intercultural' marriage was going. Their response was beautiful. "Now we are married, no less Jewish, no less Armenian . . ." The goal is not to lose our cultural background but to enhance and enrich it.

I cry a lot at weddings because a little community is made and the way is prepared for love to be sustained. I probably enjoy the complex love of intercultural couples even more than I enjoy the simpler loves of those with similar backgrounds. I remember in college the night Martin Luther King was killed. My roommate and I stayed up talking all night. We agreed that the end to racism was interracial marriages and children. I still believe that. No doubt I have some high hopes for peace through intercultural marriages as well. But I don't think that couples can bear the weight of keeping their relationship alive while making world peace! Keeping love alive is a matter of exquisite delicacy and deserves all the attention it can get and all the preparation it can get.

I have watched furniture and hearts break under the load of covenant. I have watched the magnificence of marriage turn into the distress of divorce. Fortunately we are all strong enough for these difficulties because people keep getting married, showing that strangers can become intimate and that some can even stay intimate over time.

I have learned that each partner of every couple coming to my office weighs at least three hundred pounds. Some of the pounds may be in tradition and history, others may be in flesh. Both require scrutiny and care. Both are worth adoring. ∞

The Two Stones

by Stanley Mason

When I am asked how I coped with the problems of an intercultural marriage, I find myself strangely at a loss. Admittedly the culture clash (if such it was) lies many years back, so that memory may have mellowed its outlines; and it is true that there were attendant circumstances that pushed it somewhat into the background. All the same, it isn't every day that a boy from a mining village in the English Midlands marries a girl from a fishing village on the Lago Maggiore that spans the frontier between Italy and Switzerland.

The attendant circumstances just mentioned were, in brief, that we were both living in a third cultural area, that of German-speaking Switzerland, and that before long it was war-time. We were thus in a common predicament. We also had other things in common: we both knew what it was to be poor, and we were both in one of the lower echelons of the underprivileged. This doesn't mean that we were not very much aware of our cultural differences. At that time, neither of us even knew the other's language. Our love letters had to be written in French.

Yet I would be inclined to say that our different cultural backgrounds added spice to our relationship rather than confronting us with insuperable problems. There were snags and minor emergencies, of course. My girl-friend's parents were not at all keen on having an Englishman in the family, and my prospective father-in-law threatened to shoot me on sight. When the first hostility had been assuaged, there was the question of a Roman Catholic marriage, which in the eyes of my future mother-in-law was the only kind of marriage there was.

On this point I exercised something you can't do without if you want to surmount cultural barriers: tolerance. I agreed to go through a Roman Catholic wedding ceremony. There was no question in those days, however, of village Roman Catholics letting anything so outlandish as a United Methodist into their church. The bond was forged in the priest's house, and I remember being aware, as I murmured my "*sì*", of a large soup carton on top of a dusty cupboard.

I can better illustrate the virtues of tolerance with a practical example drawn from everyday life. There were a lot of Italian pupils in the boarding school at which I was then teaching. For this reason we were occasionally served at mealtimes with bowls of large beans, neither broad nor runners, but of a kind unknown to me hitherto, on which the Italians proceeded to douse lashings of olive oil before scoffing them. Fresh from England, I watched them with discreet disgust. Though not a chauvinist by nature, I had been brought up in the belief that British is best, and that Britons were for some reason a nobler race than the others, including of course the Italians. (Today this attitude, which still seems to prevail in some quarters of my island home, strikes me as pretty grotesque; but we are all, at least to begin with, the products of our environment.) So for a time I contemplated this bean-eating with a measure of revulsion. But I was never a die-hard; my attitude changed as I adapted to influences from outside my own culture. One day when I was particularly hungry — the beans were served as an entrée before the main course — I plucked up courage and decided to try a few. I found them unexpectedly tasty. The next time I took more. The day even came when I sprinkled them with olive oil. In the end I was taking more beans and anointing them with more oil than the Italians themselves. Culturally speaking, I had shown myself capable of salvation.

But to return to marital matters. I have always claimed that marriage is rather like dropping two rough, irregularly shaped stones into a leather sack and then shaking them up interminably till their bumps and corners are worn off and they roll smoothly against each other. I need not emphasize the fact that you have to do a lot of shaking. Cultural divergences are of course among the factors that make the two stones initially rough and incompatible.

I can quite credit that such divergences may even seriously jeopardize a partnership if they are particularly crass. Any Westerner who marries a Japanese, or an Arab, or even a Turk, may have difficulty in finding a comfortable compromise when exposed to the strict domestic traditions and family hierarchies that prevail in the East. I felt real compassion for a young lady who married a Muslim, a man who was urbane and charming as long as they lived in the West, but as soon as he set foot on North African soil exchanged his trilby for a fez and slipped into the role of a pasha. Such people have real problems; but when the cultural backgrounds involved are those of the Western world, from Seattle to Salzburg or even to Smolensk, I believe that they can be blended without all that much heartburn, provided of course that a modicum of goodwill is forthcoming from both sides.

For my own part, coming from a rather puritanical society and a raw northern village, I found it wonderful to have a second family into which I was eventually accepted as one of their own, and a second home among sweet chestnuts, figs and pomegranates on the sun-drenched shores of a southern lake. Nor need anyone go entirely without the creature comforts of his own origins. A Mediterranean girl can in the end make just as delicious mince pies as a lass from Pontefract. I remember well the first time my wife made a few jars of my favourite jam. I walked into the kitchen and found them there on the table, each with a neat label bearing the inscription: Black currents.

Put in brief, there are two things I should like to say about intercultural marriages. The first is that having two backgrounds, while it will obviously cause occasional friction, may also be a genuine enrichment of one's life. The second is that the cultural discrepancies are in most cases less troublesome than the purely personal dissonances.

To go back to our stones in the leather sack: the two cultures may be thought of as affecting the general shape of the stones, making them more squarish or more oval, but the really ugly asperities on them are due to individual character traits. And here there is no alternative but to wear them down little by little by dint of resolute and protracted agitation. So all I can say to young intercultural couples is: be tolerant, show goodwill, make allowances. And above all: keep shaking! ∞

Oral Affairs

by Deborah L. Thomas

You can tell many things about a man by the way he takes care of his mouth. I've had a lot to do with men and their most intimate body part — no not that — I mean their mouths, of course. Seriously, your mouth is a very private part of your body and unlike your other private parts, it is exposed. You can see and touch it. Everything that goes into that mouth, affects every part of the body. No wonder then that people, especially men, are so self-conscious about their mouths and who and what goes into them!

I've been in many mouths. As a dental hygienist who lives and works in Switzerland, I've had the opportunity to clean the teeth of many nationalities. Professionally speaking, I've learned the language of 'reading mouths' over the many years I've been gum gardening.

I think Europeans in general have rampant gum disease and smoke too much. Probably a lot of this is due to lack of education about dental hygiene. From what I've seen of their mouths, I'd think twice before marrying a European.

Take the Swiss men, for instance. They come to their appointments on time and pay their bills on time — that's the Swiss way. The Swiss way also includes cleanliness and beauty but their mouths are far from it. Germans have extreme periodontal problems and definitely have the worst breath, probably due to the poor dentistry they've had in a country with socialized medicine. French men appear suave and debonair on the exterior but wait until they open their mouths. I'm sure they only brush once a week and think that rinsing their mouths everyday with good, expensive wine cures cavities. Eastern Europeans, if they own a toothbrush at all, probably use it for something else. I'm convinced they think dental floss is for sewing buttons on their clothes.

Turks tend to have lots of gold teeth — right in the front. Yuk! Southeast Asians may eat healthier and live longer than most but their teeth die younger. I once had a Vietnamese man who wanted to sue me for removing all the black stains from his teeth. The black stain was due to his diet of betel nuts, which he considered to be some sort of status symbol. Imagine that!

The British tend to have good teeth but lots of plaque — a sure sign of laziness. However, the Italians for me are the most typical. If they're lucky enough to have posterior teeth, they are probably loose from gum disease. They only take care of the front teeth, for appearance sake. It doesn't matter that they can't speak or eat. The Italians are noted for being so romantic, but if you knew what I know, you'd pass on their advances and recommend a good dentist!

Americans tend to take the best care of their teeth. Of course, it is a large country of people from many cultural backgrounds but wherever they come from, they tend to brush, floss and get root-canal treatments instead of extractions. They certainly have more fillings than people of other countries because they consume lots of sweets and junk food. Americans are very smile conscious, much more so than other nationalities. But if you think I'm recommending American men on the quality of their mouths, you're mistaken. They may look and act tough in films and on TV around the world, but once they get into a dental chair, they are the world's biggest babies! Their moaning and groaning make them some of the worst patients I've ever had.

Let's face it, of the millions of mouths from all over the world that I've cleaned, I've yet to find a dental love match. All I'm looking for is a nice smile and a healthy mouth. It should be so simple. Would a dermatologist marry someone with acne? Or a hairdresser someone who's bald?

So I'll keep scraping tartar. Maybe one day, somewhere, a tall, dark, handsome man with a beautiful smile and a rich, disease-free body will sit down in my chair, open his mouth and have nice teeth and no plaque or tartar. Possible? Yeah, but not likely. I'm 36 and still single.

Before you marry a foreigner, have a good look in his or her mouth. That mouth says a lot before it utters a word in any language. That's the tooth, the whole tooth and nothing but the tooth. •

Whose Rules to Live and Love By?

by Jane Christ and Jacob Christ

The mobility of people since World War II has caused frequent contact among people of different cultures. Multinational companies move executives and scientists from country to country. Students from the Third World visit in the West and Westerners take up assignments in the Third World. Many 'guest workers' or foreign workers are spreading new cultural elements from their faraway countries. Thousands of asylum seekers have landed everywhere in Europe, and streams of immigrants from Latin America are trying to find a place in the United States and Canada. Is it then surprising that there are many more intercultural and interracial marriages than ever before?

Understanding people who live in a different culture has become necessary for world trade and world peace. For those married to someone from a different culture, this understanding is a necessity. Culture prescribes the way relationships between people should be. In matters of family life, different cultures have different outlooks and different 'rules'. Sociologists and cultural anthropologists have provided some knowledge to psychiatrists, psychologists and other helpers to improve their ability to deal with people from different cultures.

Relationship problems in an intercultural marriage are not limited only to a period of adaptation, as happens with culture shock. The couple is obliged to live with their cultural differences for a lifetime. There is also no return to their former life. One of the two partners is always living in a foreign country or culture; sometimes both are, as when they are living as foreigners in a third country.

If you are about to be a participant in an intercultural marriage, it is necessary you realize that you marry not only an individual, but also your spouse's culture and often your spouse's family adhering to that culture. This fact is sometimes not apparent at first, especially when you fall in love with a foreigner and contemplate your marriage in a country other than the one where you will live permanently.

Many people are able to adapt quite well to another culture as individuals on a temporary assignment and seem to make excellent marriage partners outside their own culture. But this lasts only as long as they are temporarily in the country of the spouse-to-be and they have short-term personal or vocation goals to be realized. When they return with their foreign partner to their own families and culture, they adapt again, this time automatically, to the demands of their home culture. They seem, to the surprised partner, to fall back into a stereotype of that culture.

Some typical conflicts are, for example:
- the strong formal obligations to the family of origin in Asiatic people,
- the strong male dominance in African or Islamic people
- the need for social equality in North American and some European marriages as well as the expectation of closeness (even 'romantic' closeness) as promised in popular magazines and marriage 'manuals'.

In the last example, the marriage relationship is valued as an island of intimacy, separate from family. Conflict will occur when someone from a 'progressive', psychologically sophisticated, Western or North-American culture marries someone from a more traditional culture. A 'liberated' and independent woman who gets married to a man with traditional values and family ties will find herself alternatively oppressed and fenced in or abandoned and left out by her spouse's family. Conflicts like this occur also in marriages of people from the same nationality. For instance, there are Turkish couples living in Western Europe who need help because the wives want the freedom Western women have. They come into severe conflict with their traditional-minded husbands, sometimes with disastrous results.

What makes an intercultural marriage succeed or fail? To answer this, we have to consider the importance of each spouse's 'value system'. Our values come from our ideas and assumptions we picked up as children and take for granted. They are the 'rules of the game' we follow when dealing with people around us. We do not usually think about them any more than we consciously think of the motions necessary to walk. We assume that everybody else accepts these 'rules' since they were commonly shared in our home culture.

Cultural differences in values have, until recently, received little attention from psychotherapists. They focus on problems of individuals which can, of course, be discovered in an intercultural marriage as well. Sensitivity to intercultural issues leads to a better understanding of both partners and to helping them with their relationship.

Intercultural marital partners inflict suffering on each other unwittingly and without bad intent. They do not recognize the intercultural component in their conflicts and confuse value conflicts with personal issues. Each partner attributes ill will, stubbornness, outright aggression or general 'character problems' to the other partner. Each cannot understand that their own cultural rules taken for granted, approved and validated by their own society can cause suffering to their partner. Accusations fly back and forth. Alienation, separation and divorce may follow. Value conflicts are not personality disorders. They come from the differing values of each partner's home culture.

To solve these problems, it helps if both partners become aware of their own individual values, ideas, opinions and prejudices. Unexamined prejudices cannot remain sacred. They must be brought out in the open and made subject to negotiation.

Is it surprising that intercultural marriages have a greater potential for conflict than marriages from the same culture? Respect for your partner's values is necessary for a successful marriage. When one or both partners signal that the limit of tolerance has been overstepped and compromise or collaboration is impossible, divorce may be the only solution.

What factors are important to consider before entering an intercultural marriage? The list of considerations is more complicated than it would be for marrying someone from your own culture. Your future partner's culture may not be familiar to you. You may not even have a clear idea of your own culture. You may not have had an opportunity to try out your ideas, opinions and prejudices on people who don't share your own culture. You may want to consider the following questions:

- What is it like to live in my partner's country?

- How would I tolerate the absence of my home culture and the new demands of my partner's culture?

- Do I know my partner's language well enough to make myself understood in my partner's country?

- Will it be possible for both of us to keep our privacy and the primacy of our marriage or will other family responsibilities and loyalties intrude at every step?

- Does my partner belong more to the family or to the community than to me?

- Why is a person of another culture so attractive to me and why am I also attractive to my partner?

- What are the personal reasons for my choice of this partner and how will this choice influence my relationship to my own culture?

Answers to these questions may be obtained by talking to other intercultural couples and encouraging them to share their experiences of coping with cultural differences. You may be advised to visit your future in-laws in your spouse's country. A visit is better than no visit and may make some things clearer. But it may not be enough. People often behave differently while having visitors than they do in daily life.

An example is the marriage of Fritz and Sally, a couple living in Europe. Sally is the American partner. Fritz went to America as a young man to work on a two years' assignment for a Swiss company. In America he was able to adapt very well. He changed his Germanic first name to Fred and he was well-liked and at ease with American customs and culture. He knew that his stay was limited to the duration of his assignment. He met Sally there who was an ambitious, up-and-coming career woman with many interests. The easy-going young man from Switzerland fascinated her and Fred was attracted to Sally's initiative and her complete self-reliance in everything she did. Both enjoyed stepping out of their own cultural context and wanted a partner who was 'someone special'. Neither had any idea that 'being someone special' could become a problem. At first Fred and Sally had everything going for them. They were married in Sally's hometown, with family members from Switzerland present.

They got along well for the next year while they were still living in the U.S. Sally was looking forward to the move to Switzerland at the end of that year. She was eager to get to know her husband's country. Shortly after their arrival there, things became different for both of them.

Fred became Fritz again. His family, to which he was very close, made many demands on him. Sally often felt left out as she did not understand the language Fritz and his relatives spoke. Only as an afterthought did Fritz some-times translate parts of what was said to Sally. She had enrolled in an intensive course in German, but her knowledge of that language seemed far from sufficient to help her understand her new relatives. They did not speak the German she was learning but spoke a dialect she could not comprehend.

Sally became unhappy. She felt utterly superfluous with Fritz being so well taken care of by his family and numerous friends. She feared she had lost the Fred she had married and loved. She had become dependent on him emotionally, and she was no longer self-assured. She did not have a job to give her a minimum of self-esteem.

Fritz was happy to be home again and was not paying much attention to Sally. He gradually became impatient because of her lost self-assurance and her increased dependency, not to mention her many complaints about everything. She was no longer that special woman he had loved.

Sally needed time and help to see that her difficulties were not caused by depression nor any peculiar mental disorders. She could not just blame Fritz for being inconsiderate and insensitive.

Fritz took it for granted that he could visit his family and his numerous friends and girlfriends from the past at will, and by himself, without including Sally. Sally had not expected and could not accept being left alone so much. She no longer felt very 'special' to Fritz and felt she had to fight for time with him. She was determined to remain close to him and to keep time free for the two of them alone. This was a value she brought from her culture. She also demanded an equal say in major decisions for their partnership, something Fritz was reluctant to consider. Each one had to evaluate the other's expectations of the marriage. Coming from different backgrounds, they had not realized the consequences of cultural differences and had not reckoned with this kind of difficulty. As their case shows, the very traits that attract intercultural couples to each other in the first place often become the main problems in their relationship later.

Value conflicts have two extremes. On one hand, adaptation to the new culture can be total, even to the point of over-adaptation. One spouse (often the wife) gives in to all the other's wishes and melts into the culture around her. Such an extreme has its dangers. The whole over-adaptation can collapse and unforeseen hostility becomes suddenly apparent. One woman got along exceptionally well in her spouse's country until a miscarriage set off a depressive reaction in her. She experienced an upsurge of anger against her husband. She felt he was imprisoning her and that she had lost all her freedom. She quickly arranged for a transatlantic ticket to fly home to her mother and sister, leaving it unknown whether she would return or not. After her over-adaptation, this move was quite a shock for everyone.

The other extreme is the total refusal to acculturate. Your own cultural identity is rigorously preserved; nothing but your own language is spoken and contact with the new culture is left to a minimum. If this happens in an intercultural marriage, considerable problems, arguments, mutual devaluation and alienation will occur, particularly if, as in many European countries, society exerts considerable pressure for adaptation.

Problems occur when people who cross cultures over-adapt to the point of endangering their feelings of identity. But problems also occur for those who overdo their efforts to preserve their identity at all costs by refusing adaptation. The challenge lies in finding the proper balance between these two extremes.

Intercultural marriage provides longer-lasting and deeper value incongruities than marriage within one culture. It demands hard work in mutual understanding. When successful, an intercultural marriage can have exceptional rewards for being interesting, exciting and indeed very special. It offers an invaluable opportunity for widening your personal horizon and for seeing yourself and your native culture more objectively. It enables you to see beyond your own neighborhood, hometown and country. The creative potential is substantial and as significant as the much more talked-about hazards you may have to overcome. א

Thy Country 'tis of Me

by Gay Scott O'Connor

Love makes the world go round, and marrying a foreigner makes the world smaller and more familiar.

In my family, we make a habit of marrying foreigners, and my relations have wed themselves all over the globe. Although this may cause travel problems, there are great advantages too. Forget hotel bills: the family network would put Sheraton to shame.

I have three nationalities — Jamaican, British and Swiss — and had hoped to pass them all on to my children. I hadn't reckoned with the bureaucratic mind. South African super-athlete Zola Budd apparently snaffled a British passport on the strength of a British-born grandfather and ran for Britain in the Olympic Games. My kids have a British-born grandfather too, but no-one is throwing British passports at them. I admit they're lousy athletes, but is fleetfootedness the only spirit that won the empire? The trouble is that the grandfather in question is my father, and as far as Her Majesty's officials are concerned, maternal grandfathers are thoroughly inferior, and no use at all. Only paternal grandfathers, it seems, carry the mystic genes necessary to transmit nationality.

The Jamaican position is even more baffling. My daughters were born in Kingston and are automatically Jamaican, but my son made the mistake of being born in Zurich. I once telephoned the Jamaica Mission in Geneva to see if I could wangle him a passport.

"Was the boy born in wedlock?" warbled a carefree voice on the telephone. I admitted he was.

"Then," giggled the voice with apparent satisfaction, "he has no chance at all."

"I'm getting a divorce," I said. "Can't we make it retroactive?"

"No," chortled the voice. "Children may only inherit Jamaican nationality through the mother if they were not born in wedlock. Did you ever hear anything so silly?"

No, I never did. But I think I've figured out why so many canny Jamaicans are born triumphantly illegitimate.

You can marry the boy next door and still find yourself marrying a foreigner if you're Arab, he's Jewish, and your address is Jerusalem. Ulster's Catholics and Protestants know the same plate-glass frontiers. But there are islands of sanity everywhere. My Catholic nephew recently married a delightful Jewish girl, and they had a whale of a wedding, with a priest and a rabbi performing the smoothest double act since Ginger Rogers and Fred Astaire.

You probably know the bore, some of whose best friends are Jewish / Black / Hindu / Turkish, until his daughter becomes engaged to one, and he turns into old man Capulet, forbidding banns left, right and centre. The business world can be just as blinkered. The wedding of a well-known English chocolate firm to a huge Swiss-based multinational firm left the English howling that their national heritage — SMARTIES — was now in the clutches of devious Zurich gnomes. The Swiss were not a little supercilious about all this Anglo-Saxon breast beating, and charged the English with xenophobia. Not long after, the Americans took over a famous Swiss chocolate firm and the Swiss promptly went into culture shock. When will the world grow up?

The best thing about intercultural marriages is that they build bridges, turning 'them' into 'us'. There will be bumps and shocks aplenty, but it is more than worth it. Family fights, however messy, rarely lead to war and mayhem as international conflicts do. No matter how infuriating one's in-laws may be, one quarrels with them as individuals, and not as faceless wogs, wops, yanks or krauts. My mother-in-law and I had rows galore, but we never hurled Scuds at each other. We didn't even toss rolling pins.

The heritage of multicultural families is immeasurably rich. In every field, from cooking to religion, race and language, horizons stretch wide. Some of us may go through a phase of rootlessness, a feeling of belonging nowhere. But if we live through it, we come to realise that we belong everywhere, and that the world's our oyster.

"*E pluribus unum!*" cries America's eagle, and Jamaica chimes in proudly, "Out of many, one people." How long before the world as a whole can say the same? Let's all marry foreigners! The uniting of nations is too important to leave to the politicians.

♥ ♥

AFTERWORD

After reading the stories in CUPID'S WILD ARROWS, you may begin to wonder what would have happened to Romeo and Juliet if they had lived. So do I.

My first fascination for intercultural romance started when I was at a tender age and was attending my very first Broadway musical in New York. I'll never forget listening then to Tony and Maria in WEST SIDE STORY singing "There's a place for us." Why did such a beautiful loving relationship of two people tolerating and accepting their differences have to end in such pain? Why does the media and 'entertainment'(!) world mostly only dramatize the pain and failures in intercultural love affairs?

As an American living in Switzerland, who had also lived in Canada and Finland with friends of many nationalities, cultures, religions and races, I have met many intercultural couples who seem to be tackling their challenges successfully and bringing up children who take their dual-cultural identities in their stride. Are they only exceptions?

When my first marriage to a Swiss ended in divorce, I felt the consequences of the decision that had made me live in Switzerland and bring up my children here. I had an open ear for stories about intercultural relationships then but I never wanted anything to do with a Swiss man again. But one should never say never. I met a Swiss who had even a worse opinion of American women than I had of Swiss men. Fortunately we were able to overcome our prejudices and learn that when you really want to understand someone from another culture, you'll find a way. And we did. And we're still working at it.

My determination to publish a collection of tales on intercultural relationships was born the moment I finished reading Susan Tiberghien's 'Ode to a Potato' included in this book. I thought it would be a light-hearted and entertaining project to ask a number of writers, translators, journalists, teachers and other 'word-workers' I knew to send me stories about their intercultural marriages that explain how they deal with their daily challenges and conflicting value systems. I was given names of people around the world who might submit a story. A writers' magazine with a broad international circulation announced my project. The word got around to a number of international organizations and writers' groups in Europe. But the first few weeks I received only warnings about the horribly depressing divorce stories I was bound to receive.

Within months, however, I was snowed under with stories. Hundreds were sent to me from all over the world. The biggest surprise was that, with very few exceptions which are all included in this book, almost all the stories were happy ones! I could not put a book together that seemed to imply that if you want to be sure your marriage works, just marry a foreigner! But then again, why not? For years we've only heard about the dramatic failures.

Those stories I considered to be the best 100 were sent to a number of other 'interculturally experienced' people (see acknowledgements). They have been a tremendous help, but as experts always seem to do, they disagreed. As a consequence, it was not easy to make a final selection from the many good and relevant stories submitted. Nevertheless, I hope we selected those stories that best show the real-life challenges intercultural couples may face.

Although this started out as a light-hearted project, I am aware that the collection would have profited from the inclusion of a story, for example, from a Croat married to a Serb. I wish I had received more stories from Muslims married to Christians. Where are the stories from all the Americans and British who used to live happily wed in Iraq? With all its inevitable shortcomings, it remains for the readers of this anthology to judge how close or relevant these stories are to their own experiences.

Information on intercultural marriage, dual-cultural families with research on negotiating cultural conflicts is not likely to be found at your neighborhood bookstore. Some 'proper' research in the field of interculturalism showed that it is difficult to set down specific rules for successful intercultural relationships. Trying to establish such rules may only help accentuate differences and draw up battle lines. There seems to be no rhyme or reason why some couples who come from different cultures have a vibrant and mutually enriching partnership while others with a more common heritage often seem to stumble over the smallest differences.

Many intercultural couples who were asked to write a story were not even aware of having cultural differences. They would explain to me how simple it was. I heard comments like: Some people are frightened by anything new or different, others seem to be drawn to anything exotic. Sometimes we marry people who share our views, sometimes we feel attracted to those who challenge our attitudes. Sometimes we only realize later what the explanation for the magic was. We can worry endlessly about whose rules to follow in making dinner, making love and making families get along. Can you succeed more easily if you don't think about it too much? The magic may disappear once you find out how it works, wherever you are.

Many people told me, all marriages are intercultural anyway. And today's marriages, even the mono-cultural ones, aren't known to be easy. But are the intercultural ones really more difficult? Don't they have some advantages? Doesn't the extra tolerance they demand help form a better relationship? Can't we profit from finding new ways of looking at the world? And besides, don't we all have some home-culture traditions that the world could easily do without?

'Adventurers' who fall in love with someone from another culture end up with much more than an exotic holiday. Once you marry into another culture, you cannot just cancel the trip and go home. If you succeed, you're on that trip for a lifetime. If you fail, going home will never be the same.

I intend to keep encouraging people who succeed in crossing cultural barriers to write about their experiences. The world deserves to hear from those who have tolerant and accepting relationships and not only from those who are mostly only letting off steam about cultures they do not want to understand.

As much as the stories in this book talk about differences, in the end I have learned from this project a lot about our cultures' similarities. It is comforting to know that all over the world there is an ever-increasing number of couples being struck by Cupid's wild arrows, for better or worse.

February 1993   Dianne Dicks

Acknowledgements

The editor wishes to thank all the hundreds of people around the world who submitted stories to this project, to all those who answered questions about their intercultural marriages and in particular to the following people who helped evaluate many of the manuscripts submitted and select the most appropriate stories for publication:

Anne-Louise Bornstein, Swiss
Anke Gloor, German
Leslie Guggiari, American,
    Cultural Connections, Gravesano
Steve Gregoris, Canadian
Annette Keller, Swiss
Carla Kohli, American
Betty Nauta, British
Maureen Oberli, British
Jackie and Gianni Primiano, British
Stuart Robinson, British,
    The Institute for Cross-Cultural
    Communication AG, Zug
Gillian Uster, South African

Appreciation is also expressed to the editors at Intercultural Press, Yarmouth, Maine, for their helpful recommendations. Many thanks to Dennis O'Connor of WRITERS' DIGEST in Cincinnati, Ohio, to Hannelore Hahn of the International Women's Writing Guild, New York, and to Nancy Kapstein, FAWCO, Brussels, for announcing this project.

Mrs. Uta Angerer, Frankfurt, is thanked for her help in arranging for a German edition of this collection by C.H. Beck Verlag in Munich and for her introducing the editor to the Office for Multicultural Affairs of the City of Frankfurt (Rosi Wolf-Almanasreh) and the IAF (Association of Women Married to Foreigners - Association of bi-national families and partnerships), Heidemarie Pandey.

Sincerest appreciation is due to Annette Keller for her extensive support throughout the years this book has been in preparation. And special thanks to Walter Kiefer, Martin Strauch and Loretta Strauch for all their encouragement and for whom I hope this project will always have special meaning.

List of Authors

Verena Bakri was born in Zurich, Switzerland. She lived and traveled throughout three continents working as a translator, language tutor and free-lance travel writer before meeting her Ethiopian husband in Philadelphia, Pennsylvania. They have lived and worked in Ethiopia, Uganda, Kenya and Zambia and are presently on assignment in Lagos, Nigeria, as part of the United Nations system.

Lila Bartsch was born in Isfahan, Iran, was educated in Iran and subsequently studied sociology in England. Married to an American in the United Nations program, she has lived in Europe as well as the United States, Fiji Islands and Indonesia and is at present residing in California. She writes in English, her adopted language, and many of her articles as a film critic have been published in various journals around the world.

Kim Baumann has a Swiss father and a Vietnamese mother but spent her childhood and teenage years in Australia. She is presently living with her Swiss grandparents on a farm in Switzerland. She plans to study chemistry.

Agnes Bieri was born in Ghana as the eldest of twelve children. After college in Ghana she taught cookery and housekeeping. She spent six years with her Swiss husband on several assignments in East African countries. They now live in Lucerne, Switzerland.

Claire Bonney grew up in northern New York and came to Switzerland to study Carnival and maskmaking traditions, completing her studies in art history and ethnology at the University of Zurich. She lives in Basel with her Swiss husband where she teaches art history and photography. She has written articles for such diverse publications as the CATHAY PACIFIC AIRLINES MAGAZINE and the NEUE ZÜRCHER ZEITUNG.

John A. Brossard is from Cambridge, Massachusetts, has degrees in Social Relations, Industrial Sociology and Theoretical Sociology and taught many years at a college in Washington State. With his wife he founded an international correspondence club. Now living in Hawaii, he writes articles for national magazines and reviews books and films for the American Association for the Advancement of Science.

Latease Copeland was born in Tuskegee, Alabama, grew up in Detroit, Michigan, attended universities in Washington, D.C., Nashville, Tennessee, and Detroit to obtain a degree in Communications. After a decade of living in Manhattan, New York, and working both there and in Europe as a fashion model and actress, she married and moved to Copenhagen, Denmark, where she now lives with her Danish husband and their two sons.

Dyanne Fry Cortez comes from Burnet, Texas, and has written articles for TEXAS HOMES, HILL COUNTRY VIEW and THE AUSTIN CRONICLE on the art, culture and characters of central Texas. While working as a reporter for the New Braunfels HERALD-ZEITUNG, she won an Associated Press award for her feature story on Black Heritage Month, as celebrated by a tiny African-American community in a German-American town.

Elayne Clift is a writer and health communication specialist in Potomac, Maryland. Her fiction, poetry, essays and articles have appeared in over two dozen magazines and periodicals in North America and abroad. She has written a poetry chapbook, 'And Still the Women Weep', a collection of essays 'Telling it Like it is: Reflections of a Not So Radical Feminist'. She serves as Washington, D.C., reporter for WINGS, a globally syndicated radio news program by and for women.

Jane S. Christ and Jacob Christ are co-authors. She grew up in Philadelphia, Pennsylvania, and has degrees in psychology and in social work. She worked as a psychotherapist in a number of places in the U.S. before meeting Jacob Christ in Atlanta, Georgia, where they were both working. He was born and completed his medical degrees in Switzerland before emigrating to the

U.S.A. to work in psychiatry, psychoanalysis and community mental health. Now these co-authors are in his Swiss homeland where he practices psychiatry and psychotherapy in Basel and where they both provide counselling for intercultural couples.

Dianne Dicks grew up in Indianapolis, Indiana, and after attending college in Florida, she participated in an exchange program of the Experiment in International Living which brought her to Switzerland, where, after several decades, she is still experimenting and married to a Swiss. She worked as an English teacher, translator and editor in pharmaceutical, banking and insurance fields before turning her hobby of collecting intercultural stories into a publishing business.

Glenda Johnson Elam is an American freelance writer, translator and researcher writing for numerous business publications. She lives and works in Rome, Italy, with her Italian husband.

Judy Erkanat is a freelance writer in San Jose, California, where she lives with her husband, who is a Turk, and their two daughters. She specializes in travel, childcare and ethnic topics. With over 70 articles in print, her writing has appeared in such publications as ALASKA AIRLINES MAGAZINE, ARAMCO WORLD and AAA MOTOUR MAGAZINE. She has also been a regular contributor to BAY AREA PARENTS NEWSMAGAZINE. She is active member of the Turkish-American community and an avid international traveller.

Vasco Esteves was born in Lissabon, Portugal, where he also attended university and was active in students' movements against fascism. He received a degree in mathematics in Germany where he has worked as a translator and interpreter before specializing in computing. He lives in Frankfurt with his German wife and her two children and is active socially and politically in causes pertaining to the rights of 'foreigners' living in Germany. He was an editor for the publication *'Wir ausländischen Mitbürger'* and many of his articles and poems have appeared in German in various publications.

Frances Favre was born in Adelaide, South Australia, but soon moved with her family to New York when her father joined the United Nations. She has an arts degree, worked for a few years as an actress in the English provinces of

Canada and back in Australia. She has written scripts for television and the occasional magazine short story. She met her Swiss husband on a trip to visit her mother in Geneva, Switzerland, where she now lives.

Beatrice Feder is a retired kindergarten teacher who lives in New York with her husband.

Mildred Gaugau grew up in Oklahoma and always dreamed of finding the legendary Bali Hai of Rogers and Hammersteins' 'South Pacific'. After her divorce and with her two daughters almost grown, she went to Western Samoa where her dreams came true. She and her Samoan husband ran a thousand acre plantation in the middle of an ancient fortress. Shortly after writing 'Penny in Samoa', her beloved Tavita was killed in a hurricane in Samoa. She now lives and works in Hailua Kona, Hawaii.

Leslie S. Guggiari was born in San Francisco but grew up in Boston. She has a degree in Asian studies and in intercultural administration and is on the governing council of SIETAR (The Society for Intercultural Education Training and Research) and a founding member of SIETAR EUROPA. She lives in the Italian part of Switzerland with her Swiss husband and their two adoptive Indian daughters where, besides teaching English and translating, she has her own consulting business in cross-cultural orientation for relocation and for adoption.

Marian S. Hong is an American who met her Chinese husband while they were attending college and working together at a summer job. They live in Jackson, Michigan, where she works in the personnel department of the local school.

Ivy Humphreys was born in Singapore and educated in Malaysia, in the United States and in England. She has worked as a geography teacher and as a university teacher in educational communications and technology. She left the faculty of a university in Malaysia to live in Birmingham, Britain, with her Welsh husband where she also teaches at the local university and school.

Margaret Ellen Jones is an American residing at Sparkman, Arkansas, after having lived in Mexico, Venezuela, Alaska and Canada. She is a freelance writer and teaches English, Spanish, French, humanities, music, and elementary education at Southern Arkansas University Tech in Camden, Arkansas. Her stories, poems and articles have appeared in several American magazines like ON THE LINE, FRIEND, TRUE LOVE, and INSTRUCTOR and her monthly column on American slang appears in MINI-WORLD, a magazine published in Tokyo.

Floramor Hager Kjær is a first generation Filipino-American, born and raised in northern California where she also attended college. She is living in Denmark with her Danish husband and their son.

Marlies Knoke was born in Germany and lived in different parts of the country before settling near Frankfurt. After completing her training in marketing, advertising and public relations, she was editor of a magazine and is now a freelance journalist for several German publications. She was married to a Pakistani for seven years and still writes frequently about issues pertaining to the situation of foreigners living in Germany.

Terri Knudsen is originally from Stillwater, Oklahoma, and has been living in Denmark for many years with her Danish husband and two sons. She has lived most of her adult years abroad. After university in Oklahoma, she served for two years as a Peace Corps Volunteer in Paraguay where she met her husband who was employed there by a Danish firm. They lived several years in Venezuela and in Bolivia before 'putting down roots' in Denmark where she teaches English to children and adults and gives classes for American studies.

Bill Kirkpatrick-Tanner is a New Yorker, living and working in Zurich, Switzerland.

Stanley Mason was born in the Canadian Rockies, reared on a British coalfield, educated at Oxford and acquired a European background by marrying an Italian-speaking Swiss. They live in Effretikon, Switzerland. His writings and translations have appeared in many Swiss publications. Two books of his poetry have been published as well as his English verse translation of Albrecht von Haller's famous poem written in 1732, DIE ALPEN. He recently won a prize in Zurich from the 'Stiftung Kreatives Alter' for his German poetry translated into English.

Angela Conti Mølgaard is a native of New Jersey and studied economics in New York and London. After a decade as an international banker, she became a full-time writer. Besides short stories and poetry, she has written and directed her own plays in London. Based in Copenhagen, she reports regularly on the arts, business, politics and New Age for major publications throughout Scandinavia. She is currently writing a novel based on her experience as a debt collector in South America.

Kate Mühlethaler was born in Cheshire, England. On leaving secretarial college, she received training as a teacher, worked in a primary school before moved to the U.S. where she became head teacher in a day-care centre. She has lived now in Switzerland with her Swiss husband for many years and teaches English.

Christine Miyaguchi is an American, born and raised in New York. She met her Japanese husband while working as an accountant for a Japanese firm on Long Island. After their marriage in New York, they lived several years in Japan before he was transferred back to Long Island where they are still living.

Sigrid K. Orlet was born in Arnsberg, Germany. She received her formal education in economics in Hamburg and in the U.S.A. in Toldeo, Ohio. She has moved with her German husband to Agoura, California, where she works as an instructor for English as a second language, as an interior designer, an art editor for LITERARY OLYMPICS and as a freelance writer. She has written a collection of humorous short stories in German about life in America and a travel guide for Southern California.

Nicole Oundjian is an Armenian writer who grew up in the United States but is now living in Denmark with her Danish husband.

Christa Pandey was born and raised in Germany where she met and married her Indian husband. More than twenty years ago they moved to the United States. In recent years she honed her English writing skills on two graduate degrees from a Texas University and writes articles for newspapers and newsletters. She is author of the German language ARAL AUTO-REISEBUCH USA, a travel guide to the United States.

Indu Prakash Pandey was born in a small village in Northern India. After receiving a number of degrees at universities in India and Holland, he taught Hindi and Hindi literature at the University of Bombay. In 1963 he was appointed to the South Asia Institute in Heidelberg (Germany) and later to the University of California in Berkeley and to the University of Bucharest (Rumania). In Frankfurt he founded the Indian Cultural Institute which he is running together with his German wife. He is the author of many books on modern Indian literature and other subjects.

Sarah Paris was born and grew up in Switzerland. She travelled extensively in France, Italy and Spain and wrote poems, short stories and articles. She worked as an executive assistant, translator, bartender and briefly for the Foreign Office in Switzerland before moving to Los Angeles in 1981 where she has worked in the film industry in a creative affairs department while writing a number of screenplays in English. Her film credits include: 'Call From Space' and 'The Magic Balloon'. She has written two novels in German and is working on a new filmscript in English.

Susan K. Perry was born in New York and spent much of her seventeenth year travelling in Israel and Europe. She earned a degree in Middle Eastern Studies from U.C.L.A. and married her Lebanese first husband. She later received another degree in Human Development Administration. She has written nearly 500 articles for such publications as PARENTING, PARENTS' CHOICE, USA TODAY, SEVENTEEN, THE LOS ANGELES TIMES, CURRENT HEALTH, and VALLEY MAGAZINE and writes regular parenting advice columns for SMART KIDS, L.A. PARENT, and WORKING WORLD. She is the author of PLAYING SMART and co-author of THE 12-MONTH PREGNANCY. She lives in Los Angeles with her second husband who is American.

Polly Platt grew up on a farm outside Philadelphia. After graduating from Wellesley College, she was a feature writer for the PHILADELPHIA EVENING BULLETIN, and then a reporter and feature writer for the NEW YORK POST. She has been living in Europe and free-lancing since then and has written the cross-culture column for INTERNATIONAL MANAGEMENT. Trained in cross-cultural communication in Washington, D.C., she founded her own company in Paris to give cultural adaptation seminars to corporate executives in Paris, Brussels and Vienna.

Jo Ann Hansen Rasch was born in New Zealand, but emigrated with her parents to the U.S. when she was eleven before undertaking extensive voyages with her family in the Pacific Islands, North America and Great Britain which motivated her to move alone to Europe when she was seventeen. She and her Swiss husband live by Lake Geneva. She has written two English text books, one about aeronautical radio communication, (she holds an international aeronatical radiotelephony licence) and another for the Swiss railways where she teaches English. She co-founded and co-edits a magazine for non-professional writers in French.

Janet Rüsch was born and grew up in the north of England. She has been living in Switzerland with her Swiss husband for over twenty years. She teaches English in Schaffhausen.

Susanne Sablan is native of Long Island, New York, but she has lived in Orlando, Florida, for many years where she is a part-time writer and full-time high school English teacher for gifted students. Her poems have been published in anthologies. She is currently the news liaison to the WEST ORANGE TIMES, the SOUTHWEST ORLANDO BULLETIN and the ORLANDO SEN-TINEL for her high school's 4000 student campus.

Donna Schaper is an American minister in the United Church of Christ and a writer with a long list of publishing credentials. Her books include: SUPERWOMAN TURNS FORTY, Narratives Against the Current; COM-MON SENSE FOR MEN AND WOMEN IN THE MINISTRY; STRIPPING DOWN, The Art of Spiritual Restoration, a collection of essays. She has a feature on News 12 Cablevision, Long Island, and does a regular column for THE OTHER SIDE, REGENERATION NEWS, GREENPRINTS and UPRIVER. Her articles appear in THE CHRISTIAN SCIENCE MONITOR, NEWSDAY, THE NEW YORK TIMES, THE L.A. TIMES, HOUSTON CHRONICLE, THE JEWISH MONTHLY and other periodicals interested in her interfaith and humorous approach to life. She lives with her Jewish Ameri-can husband and three children in Riverhead, New York.

Kristina Schellinski was born in Germany, is married to an Italian, has adopted English as a second mother tongue, works with the United Nations Children's Fund, first in New York, now in Geneva, Switzerland and lives in France. She covered the African famine for UNICEF and is working on a novel about a young man who lost his life while helping to beat the famine. She has published many articles while she worked as a journalist prior to and with UNICEF.

Gay Scott O'Connor is a multinational. She is Jamaican by birth and upbringing, British through her Father and Swiss my marriage. She lives with her three teenage children in the Canton of Schwyz in Switzerland where she is a painter and sculptor. She works under the professional name 'Gay' and uses the intense colours inspired by her Jamaican childhood.

Michael H. Sedge moved from the United States to Italy at the age of 19 and has been there ever since. He is regional president of the International Food, Wine & Travel Writers Association. In addition to authoring books such as THE ADVENTURE GUIDE TO ITALY and COMMERCIALIZATION OF THE OCEANS, he is a foreign correspondent for American publications like CARDI-OLOGY WORLD NEWS and FAMILY. He also reports from Italy for Japan's MINI-WORLD MAGAZINE. Beyond writing, he publishes the 'Markets Abroad' newsletter for writers and markets photographs.

Germaine W. Shames is an American with a well-worn passport from living and working on five continents. She has a degree in hotel and restaurant management and a master's in intercultural management. She is co-author of WORLD-CLASS SERVICE and writes articles on topics like Aboriginal land rights to international dining customs, the Middle East crisis and intercultural romance which have appeared in THE OAKLAND TRIBUNE, PALM BEACH ILLUSTRATED, THE FORT LAUDERDALE SUN, RESTAURANT HOSPI-TALITY, THE CORNELL QUARTERLY and others. She resides in New Jersey.

Moo-Lan Siew Silver was born in Malaysia and completed her schooling in Malaysia and New Zealand. She taught English in Malaysia before moving to the U.S. in 1972 and marrying an American. In the U.S. she worked in a library and taught English as a Second Language. Her husband's work takes the family to a different country every few years and they currently live in Denmark.

Linda Singh was born in a small town in northern Alabama and moved to a large city in northern Illinois when she was ten. After college she worked as an elementary school teacher. She has also lived in California and Singapore. She and her Indian husband now live in Illinois.

Susan Stafford was born in Britain but now lives and works in Switzerland with her Irish husband.

Nancy Steinbach grew up in Colorado, and after completing university there, she moved to California where she met her future German husband. She spent six years in Germany, and while her husband finished his studies there, she completed a degree in English Literature at a German university. They have since returned to California where Nancy teaches college English and is finishing a mystery novel.

Monica B. Suroosh is an American, married to an Iranian. They live in the foothills of the Rocky Mountains, near Denver, Colorado.

Susan Tiberghien spent the first twenty-five years of her life in New York, the second twenty-five years in Europe, and she's spending the third, balancing the two worlds through her writing. She leads a writers' workshop in Geneva, edits their literary review OFFSHOOTS and gives writing workshops in Geneva and New York. Many of her short stories and personal essays have been published in periodicals in America and Europe, including THE CHRISTIAN SCIENCE MONITOR and THE INTERNATIONAL HERALD TRIBUNE. She has had stories broadcast on the BBC World Service and the Monitor Radio. She is an active member of the Swiss Centre of International P.E.N.

Susan Tuttle-Laube was born and grew up in the State of New Jersey where her Swiss father had emigrated and married her German mother. After getting a degree in English Literature and Art she came to Switzerland to discover her Swiss roots and fell in love and married an American who had, coincidentally, been brought up in Switzerland. Today they live with their two sons in the Swiss town of Wettingen where she works as a translator and editor. Her stories appear regularly in a newsletter for newcomers to Switzerland and she won first prize in an English short-story contest sponsored by a Swiss bookseller.

Deborah L. Thomas grew up in Michigan and after her training as a dental hygienist, she spent several years working in central Switzerland in mouths of many different nationalities. She is currently back in Michigan studying for a degree in sports journalism

Masako S. Uzawa grew up in Hokkaido, the northern island of Japan. An English major at a college in Tokyo paved her way to winning a Fullbright scholarship to study social work at a university in North Carolina in the USA where she met a Swiss who later became her husband. They live near Basel in Switzerland where she works as a free-lance interpreter and translator.

Heidrun West grew up in central Europe in difficult times. Her stories have appeared in the NEW YORK TIMES as well as in several Swiss, American and German publications. She has given poetry readings both in the U.S.A. and in Switzerland in German and in English. She lives in the Canton of Schwyz with her British husband and two sons where she teaches English.

Rosi Wolf-Almanasreh grew up in Germany and first received schooling that qualified her to work in commerce and in marketing. But her realization of the social and legal discrimination experienced by her Palestinian husband and other intercultural couples motivated her to study law. She founded the IAF, an association of bi-national families and partnerships which today has centers all over Germany and has played a significant role in improving the legal situation of immigrants in private and public sectors in Germany. Since 1989 she is head of the Office for Multicultural Affairs in Frankfurt. She has been author and editor of many publications regarding the integration of immigrants and other minorities and has won a number of prestigious awards for her achievements in Germany.

En Vogue

by Janet Rüsch

I had been in Switzerland only a few months when my husband promised to introduce me to the thrills and delights of skiing. This topic was not particularly foremost in my mind when I was making my marriage vows — a thought definitely worth considering for future brides-to-be of Swiss men!

If you have ever practised any sport in Switzerland, you may have noticed that it does not really matter how well you do it, but how good you look doing it. Visit the local tennis club, for example, and you will probably see almost everybody sporting the latest fashions and colours produced by the leading names in sportswear design and brandishing the most modern and expensive rackets.

Fresh from England, I was not prepared for this fashion culture shock. I had played tennis during my high school years — quite well I should add — clad in a blouse I had made myself in the needlework class, and a pair of not very short shorts given to my mother by a friend of hers. Since the said friend was about five times my size, my mother altered them to fit me. In later years, I was still playing with the same racket, restrung a couple of times. Its obscure trademark was by then hardly legible. Skiing? Well, I had never even dreamt about it!

My husband eventually informed me that he had booked a week's holiday in a very up-market ski resort. "But," he said, "I am not buying you the equipment because you might not like this sport. We will hire the skis and poles when we get there. In the meantime, see what you can do about borrowing the rest of the outfit from a friend or someone."

Fair enough. But when you are as 'petite' as I am, it is a bit difficult to borrow clothing that fits. A friend lent me her boots. They were a size too big but I was assured that with two pairs of socks they would be just fine. Leather boots that had to be laced up were rapidly going out of fashion at that time, but that didn't matter, I thought.